THE SKILLS OF SKIING

Also by Walter Snellman

MASTERING THE MOUNTAIN

THE SKILLS OF SKIING

Walter Snellman

COLLIER BOOKS
Macmillan Publishing Company
New York

Macmillan Publishing Company
866 Third Avenue, New York, N.Y. 10022
Collier Macmillan Canada, Inc.

Library of Congress Cataloging in Publication Data
Snellman, Walt.
The skills of skiing.
1. Skis and skiing. I. Title.
GV854.S596   1985   796.93   85-11676
ISBN 0-02-029070-5 (pbk.)

Macmillan books are available at special discounts for bulk purchases for sales promotions, premiums, fund-raising, or educational use. For details, contact:

Special Sales Director
Macmillan Publishing Company
866 Third Avenue
New York, N.Y. 10022

10 9 8 7 6 5 4 3 2 1

Printed in the United States of America

Contents

Acknowledgments

My thanks to all those people who made this book possible, especially to:

Kim Jackson Snellman for her tireless typing, drawing, darkroom work, and moral support.

Pandora Jones, for her excellent Nordic demonstrations.

Lange USA, Raichle Molitor USA, and Volvo of America (Dynamic), who supplied technical advice and equipment.

White Stag, Roffe, and Demetre, who supplied clothing for the photos.

The instructors of Mammoth Mountain Ski Area, who demonstrated their skills for the photos.

And, of course, to all my students, who always manage to teach me so much about skiing.

Introduction

Skiing challenges your body, mind, and spirit. The diversity of terrain, weather, equipment, and individual style is unmatched by any other sport. Skiing doesn't have confined boundaries, artificial turf, rigid rules, or a perfect score, and every run on skis is unique. Mastering these variables requires many physical and mental skills. I've written this book to help you develop those skills so that you may enjoy each run, and skiing as a whole, to its fullest.

In Section I, The Winter World, you'll discover the clothes and preparation needed to combat the intensity of the winter environment. How to choose a ski area, what to look for in a ski school, and exercises for better skiing before you get to the snow are also included. You'll also learn that injury-free skiing is more than a matter of luck.

In Section II, Nordic Skiing, we'll discuss what equipment is suitable for what skiing environment, physical ability, and temperament. Then the technique section will take you from the first slide on cross-country skis right through the Telemark, so you'll have all the skills needed for skiing both in track and out of track.

In Section III, Alpine Skiing, the incredible variety in equipment will be covered; what the terms mean, how to choose the gear best for you, and how to maintain it for top performance. Special chapters explain lift riding and what to do in those confusing first days on skis. The heart of this Alpine section explains the skills of technique. Learning to ski today is much easier, thanks to a motor skills approach, where all maneuvers on skis require only three physical controlling actions. I've included many on-the-hill exercises to help you apply and refine these three actions as you progress rapidly from beginner to expert terrain.

Whether you're new to the sport or a seasoned veteran, you'll find ideas and skills here to improve your skiing. See you on the slopes!

I

THE WINTER WORLD

1
The Elements

Nonskiers are convinced that you have to be somewhat odd to enjoy a day out in the howling wind, with ice crystals freezing to your face, just so you can fall down in deep snow. But to a skier, being physically immersed in the elements is one of the joys of skiing. Few days are sunny and warm, but any day on skis can be fun and safe if you have the skills to surmount Mother Nature's inconveniences. The major elements you'll encounter are cold, altitude, snow, storms, and sun.

COLD

Cold is the most obvious winter element. Without it we'd have no snow, so it's integral to skiing. But when you're used to sitting in a seventy-degree room, exposure to zero degrees on the slopes can take the fun out and reduce a ski day to one of survival. You have several ways to combat the cold, but first you should know how cold affects you.

Your body strives to maintain a constant internal temperature. When heat is lost to the cold, your body begins to shiver involuntarily generating extra heat to make up for the loss. Goose bumps form, a throwback to the day when our bodies had more hair, to fluff up the hair for better insulation. If heat loss continues, the body conserves heat for the vital internal organs. Surface blood vessels constrict, reducing blood flow to the extremities. Your fingers and toes become cold and may even sting. This is a sure warning that it's time to warm up before they or any exposed flesh freeze.

Frostbite appears as a white, numb patch. It is the result of water freezing in the skin and can happen rapidly to uncovered cheeks and noses. On very cold or windy days have your companions look at you and you at them frequently, to check for frostbite. If you get it, immediately warm the frozen area back to body temperature. For the nose or cheeks, cover the area with your bare palm. If the fingertips are affected, place your hands inside your clothes next to your body. For toes, get inside and warm them with your hands. Do not rub the area with snow or place in hot water! Frostbite is not serious if it's treated right away, but once you have gotten it that area will be more susceptible to freezing.

If the body's temperature continues to drop, hypothermia ensues. It's not as common as frostbite, but hypothermia is more serious. This condition can kill even when the air temperature is above freezing. When the body's core temperature drops it begins to shiver uncontrollably. Speech is slurred and fuzzy, and the person may seem rather aimless. Coordination is poor and memory is unclear. If these symptoms are different from the normal condition of one of your party, immediately get him or her warm. On Alpine slopes go into the lodge. On Nordic trails far from a lodge, remove any wet clothing from the person and replace it with layers of warm, dry clothing. Give him or her quick-energy food and hot nonalcoholic liquids. Seek shelter for him or her and send out a party member for help.

I hope I didn't convince you to move south for the winter. These things need never happen to you if you employ a minimum of common sense.

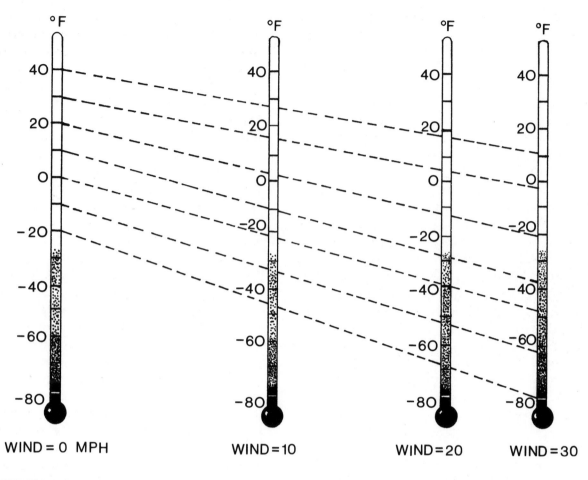

WIND = 0 MPH WIND = 10 WIND = 20 WIND = 30

AIR TEMPERATURE EQUIVALENT TEMPERATURE

On this windchill chart, find the equivalent temperature by following a dotted line from the air temperature thermometer to a thermometer with the wind speed. The shading indicates relative danger to exposed skin.

Cold is more than just a temperature reading, but there are simple ways to combat it.

First check is the thermometer, which will give you the current temperature, assuming it's not fooling you by hanging in the sun. The higher you go, the colder the air temperature will be, so dressing just warmly enough for the valley temperature won't provide adequate protection on the mountain. As a rule of thumb, figure on a five-degree F. temperature drop for every thousand feet of elevation gained. (For you metric buffs, that's three degrees C. for every 350 meters.) Also, extra sunshine near the base lodge could make you feel warmth that you won't have up on those shady north-facing slopes.

Wind is your worst enemy, and it will be stronger higher up the mountain, or even above the ground in a chair lift. Moving air is extremely effective at taking away heat. Weather reports call it the *windchill factor*. With a twenty-degree F. air temperature and a twenty-mile-per-hour wind you should dress as though it were minus ten degrees F., because that's how cold it will feel. At a windchill of minus twenty-five degrees F. exposed flesh can freeze in *one minute*. Even on a calm day just riding a chair lift subjects you to an eight-mile-per-hour wind, reducing twenty degrees F. to an effective two degrees. Skiing downhill also creates warmth-robbing wind equal to the speed at which you're traveling. You can estimate the windchill factor by adding ten to the actual wind speed and subtracting that total from the air temperature. Thus, for a ten-mile-per-hour wind subtract twenty degrees; for a twenty-mile-per-hour wind subtract thirty degrees, etc.

Moisture is another enemy. Wet clothes or skin conduct heat rapidly away from the body, especially when combined with a wind, to evaporate them faster. Even air humidity changes the effective temperature. A damp, foggy day feels much colder than it is. Conversely, dry air on a cold, clear day moderates the effective temperature.

So to stay warm you must protect yourself against temperature, wind, and moisture. Your first defense is the right clothing, designed for warmth before style. It should conserve the heat that your body produces, much like insulation in a house. Make sure you wear a wool hat. Without one you can lose half your body heat. Clothes work by trapping air, which is an insulator. Dressing in layers creates dead air traps to save your body warmth. Avoid exposing skin at the wrist, neck, or waist (when you bend over). Wear a tightly woven outer layer for wind protection.

Your clothing should also provide moisture resistance since anything that soaks up water is dangerous. Save your blue jeans for après ski. Never wear them on even the warmest days! As you're likely to get wet, wear clothes that insulate even when damp. Wool is the traditional natural fiber, but some synthetics imitate the properties of wool.

Adjust clothing so you're comfortable without being too warm. Since you're likely to perspire while skiing, an inner layer should both wick away moisture and insulate when damp. Polypropylene and dual-layer wool underwear are excellent. Panty hose are a poor choice, as they restrict circulation and don't wick away moisture. Don't put on all these layers until you're ready to go outside, and when you come in for a break, remove a few layers.

Three cold-sensitive areas are the face, feet, and hands. Your face will take the brunt of the weather, so you should use a weatherproofer lotion to insulate and moisturize your skin. Ignore vanity and save your skin with a face mask on bitter days.

For foot warmth, make sure your boots fit properly, as too tight a boot can restrict circulation and hence warmth. Too loose a boot, besides sacrificing control, could have pressure points which,

upon flexing, also cut off blood flow. Start off the day with warm, dry boots. Check for water leakage into your boots. Pull the snow cuffs on your ski pants over the boot tops or wear gaiters so snow won't sift in. Some boots leak in the overlapping plastic seams near the toe. See your boot dealer for a cure or make a temporary seal with duct tape. Moisture from foot perspiration soaks away heat, so wear insulating socks and change them at lunch or at least take your boots off to permit some drying. After skiing, thoroughly dry your boots by placing them in a warm place (not on a radiator), removing the liners, or by air-drying them with a hair dryer on a cool setting.

Mittens are warmer than gloves. Like boots, they must be kept dry. Use a waterproofer on the leather to prevent water soaking in, and air-dry the insides to remove perspiration. Glove liners greatly increase warmth, and you can easily carry a spare pair to change into during the day.

When your clothes alone can't conserve enough heat, you must turn on your furnace to generate more. Active skiing produces six times more body heat than just sitting. Before starting a run, jump around, stretch, and bend up and down to get the muscles limber. Your legs contain the largest muscles in your body, so use them to make a lot of small turns down the hill. Turn frequently where you normally would cruise. If you're still chilly, a sure warmer-upper is to climb uphill on skis.

While riding a chair lift stay warm by alternately clenching and relaxing your fists and your toes. Try to hold your legs straight out from the chair to work your thighs. Any sort of isometric muscle tension will warm you, even making faces, or wiggling your ears.

Food provides fuel for your body furnace, so you'll need a lot of calories to keep going. Don't try to diet and ski. For quick warmth and energy during the day eat some carbohydrates, perhaps a candy bar, fruit juice, or sugar drink. Be sure to drink water. You're losing a lot just by breathing in cold air, and a body low on water cuts down its blood flow. Even if you're not concerned about the long-term dangers of tobacco, nicotine constricts your capillaries, making you colder, as does caffeine. Also, forget about the myth of the brandy keg around the Saint Bernard's neck. Alcohol dilates blood vessels, producing a flush of temporary warmth, but at the expense of internal heat, and after a while you'll be colder than ever.

You can fight cold with adequate clothing, activity, and food, but even if you're well prepared for a twenty-below-zero day, cold leads to fatigue quickly, so take frequent breaks. A hot chocolate and camaraderie is one of the joys of skiing.

ALTITUDE

One ski area's ad proclaims, "The higher you go, the better the snow." True perhaps, but also the less air there is to breathe. Although the proportion of oxygen remains constant, the total amount of air decreases roughly 10 percent for every three thousand feet of elevation gained. Increasing altitude has interesting side effects too, such as reducing the boiling point of water. (Don't rush your pasta.)

The main concern is how higher elevation affects you personally. Upon rising more than a mile from your home elevation, you'll definitely feel a difference in body performance. You may think someone stuck rocks in your luggage, and every step may feel as though it's uphill. As a rough guideline, subtract 15 percent from your normal physical performance for each three thousand feet you've come up. Because the heart and lungs must initially work harder at a higher altitude, anyone with cardiovascular or respiratory problems should check with their doctor before going to extreme altitudes.

Some people are subject to altitude sickness, a short-term inconvenience, upon going to a higher altitude. This "mountain sickness" is characterized by a headache, fatigue, mild nausea, and sometimes sleeplessness. Being in good physical condition may help prevent this, but not necessarily. Surprisingly, young children are often most susceptible to altitude sickness.

Your body will adapt to the altitude rapidly, and after a couple days you won't notice much difference. Here are a few things you can do to adjust faster and to alleviate mountain sickness. Avoid overexerting the first few days by stopping frequently to look around. Drink lots of water, and cut back on salt. Stick to easily digestible foods. Emphasize carbohydrates. Go easy on alcohol and smoking, as their influence will hit harder those first days (talk about a Rocky Mountain high)!

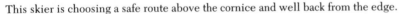

This skier is choosing a safe route above the cornice and well back from the edge.

SNOW

Not all snow is ideal. Even snow that falls as light powder changes due to the effects of wind, sun, and moisture. You'll stay on better snow if you learn to read the slopes to your advantage. North-facing runs, the most common ones at ski areas, have less exposure to direct sunshine and retain a better snow cover. But these slopes are colder and during icy conditions will be the last ones to soften. Follow the sun around the mountain. When you need warmth and light, ski the east-facing slopes in the morning, and the west-facing in the afternoon. Avoid exposed slopes when you're looking for the lightest powder or for the firmest snow in spring slush. If you enjoy spring "corn" snow, follow the morning sun. Ski a slope just as the sun warms it, and go to a more westerly facing pitch for the next run.

For handling the extremes of ice, powder, and heavy snow, you'll need to modify your skiing skills for each situation. The technique chapters will show you how.

Although many instructors, myself included, can tell you scare stories about avalanches, they are rare on runs within ski area boundaries. The ski patrol will deliberately cause slides before the slopes are opened to the public, and they will close certain slopes during the day if a slide danger develops.

As a Nordic skier or Alpine skier in the hills outside patrolled areas however, you should have a good knowledge of avalanche danger. Slides occur most frequently during or right after a snowstorm, before the snow has settled. They also can occur during very warm spring weather, as melting snow lubricates the layered snow. Avalanches are more likely on steeper slopes, particularly ones that are convex (bowed outward). Slides will funnel down through chutes and gullies, and onto the flats at their outlets. Be extra careful in these areas. Go around or cross them one person at a time. If a member of your party is caught in a slide, begin searching where you last saw the person and work downhill from there. Avalanches are frequent in Western areas, so if you're going into slide-prone areas, study books on the subject or attend special courses.

When the wind blows snow across a ridge top it can build out from the ridge into a dangerous cornice. This cornice can collapse when you ski on it because it has no support underneath. You'll see the snow hanging out in a sculptured line along a cornice, so stay well back from the edge and don't traverse beneath it.

STORMS

Skiing in stormy weather can be fun. Fewer people are on the slopes, the snow is generally better, and there's a feeling of oneness with nature. There are ways to enjoy the nasty weather.

The first requirement is to dress adequately. This means attire like that used for cold, but with special thought to water protection as well. One major clothing problem in stormy weather is soaking through on the seat and legs while riding chair lifts. You might wear waterproof nylon wind pants, or else ride surface lifts and enclosed aerial lifts.

The most common complaint in storms is "I can't see!" To relieve the gloomy scene, put on yellow goggles. Everything appears brighter and cheerier, but best of all, you can immediately see better. Yellow increases the contrast like a fog light, highlighting features and intensifying shadows. This reduces the "flat light" and improves your depth perception so you can see that unexpected bump before you hit it. Keep your goggles fog-free by eliminating moisture on the inside. The vent system should be wiped free of accumulating snow. Polish the inside lens (eyeglasses also) with a treated antifog cloth, and most importantly, keep them over your eyes. Once the goggles are pushed onto a wet hat they will certainly fog.

Carefully choose the slopes you will ski. Exploring is for sunny days. Stick to familiar trails so you'll know what's coming and ski confidently. Avoid wide-open areas. Although they contain fewer objects to hit, your vision is poorer on them. You'll probably also get a touch of vertigo on wide-open slopes, losing your balance and wondering which direction is down. It happens to everyone in a "white-out," that uncomfortable snow-fog situation in which your whole world turns into the inside of an icy cotton ball. Ski near trees, perhaps along a trail edge or in a glade. Trees provide an up-and-down reference point for balance. They also give you perspective, an idea of the relative size of things, allowing proper judgment of speed and terrain. Trees offer some contrast to the whiteness and provide a subtle shading to the snow, improving your vision. If you run out of trees, try skiing near people, lift towers, or trail markers.

Learn to rely on senses other than vision. For best use of your built-in balance sensors, stay loose and especially flexible in your ankles and knees. That way you'll compensate for a bump or gully you may not see. Occasionally touching your ski pole baskets to the snow gives sensory information regarding which way is up. Your feet are your contact with the snow. Let them become sensitive to subtle changes in grade or snow conditions. Adopt a positive mental attitude, in which you feel aggressive without being reckless. Skiing slower is a good idea, but do it by staying forward over your feet, rather than shying away from going downhill and reverting to poor technique.

Mountains intensify storms. The higher you go, the more severe the storm will be. If it's bad at the lodge, it will be worse on top. (One exception is a calm weather valley fog, with possible sunshine above.) During storms, clouds will hang in around upper slopes causing fog, although lower slopes may be clear. Ski the lower, sheltered runs where the wind and snow are more tolerable. Always check doubtful weather with the ski area information desk. They will tell you temperature and wind velocities on the hill.

Storms bring fresh snow. If you're looking for the best powder, the wind is going to be a big factor in where you can ski. The wind whips away loose snow, exposing an icy base on unsheltered runs. Fluffy powder snow is deposited in sheltered areas, such as tree glades, the lee (out of the wind) side of ridges, and the edges of trails next to a tree windbreak. If you're avoiding fresh powder, ask what trails are being groomed so you can ski the best-packed powder.

Away from civilization, the familiar becomes the unfamiliar in a storm. On Nordic trails the tracks can drift in quickly. Make sure you can follow trail markers placed in trees, rather than having to rely on tracks to guide you back. On Alpine trails also verify you're on the right trails and watch out for closed signs, which will be harder to see in fog.

With all the fun you're having skiing in the storms, don't forget to recognize your limitations.

You'll tire and get colder faster, so head in now and then for a hot drink by a warm fire.

SUN

Besides seeking out and enjoying the warm sun on a winter day, you must also protect against it. It's hard to think about sunburn in the winter, but it happens often in the mountains. Sunburn doesn't depend on temperature. In March the sun is especially dangerous, because it's as high as it was back in September on the beach. Also, the burning rays are much more intense at ski areas than at your home, due to thin, clean air and snow reflection. Even on cloudy days burning ultraviolet rays are present.

Apply sun protection liberally. You'll still tan, but you'll reduce the chance of burning. Lotions are labeled with sun-protection factors (S.P.F.) from two to fifteen. An "eight" label, for instance, means you can stay safely in the sun eight times as long as without any protection. Sunblocks have an S.P.F. of around fifteen; sunscreens, around eight; and suntan lotions, around four. Many ski professionals, having seen the wrinkles and skin cancer caused by too much sun, regularly use lotions of ten factor or higher.

Sun lotions have either a cream or alcohol base. The former helps moisturize your skin and provides some cold-weather protection. Alcohol-based lotions penetrate the skin better and do not rub off as easily from noseblowing and face plants. Either type is colorless and invisible on your skin. Remember to reapply during the day.

Your eyes can sunburn too, so always wear dark sunglasses or goggles. Sunburned retinas (snow blindness) are very painful and will incapacitate you for a day, or, even worse, could cause long-term damage. Also, wearing glasses cuts down on headaches caused by eye fatigue and squinting.

Your lips can also burn. Prevent them from cracking and swelling by applying a stick-type sunscreen and moisturizer. Carry it in a parka pocket along with your suntan lotion.

With the warm sun you may be tempted to shed some clothes. Skiing in shorts or sleeveless tops is fine until you take a spill. The snow will abrade your skin as you slide. You might want to consider the protection of a lightweight nylon shirt and thin gloves on those warm days.

2
The Ideal Ski Area

Somewhere there's an ideal ski area. It has luxurious inexpensive lodging right at the base of a huge mountain, chair lifts everywhere, miles of cross-country runs throughout the valley, plenty of daytime sun and nighttime snow, a diversity of tasty foods, a selection of entertainment and shops, and no crowds. Needless to say, I haven't found this area yet. But if you are like almost every other skier, you can't resist picking up those free colorful brochures promoting the ski areas, each one of which claims to be the perfect resort. Choosing which area to ski thus turns into another skillful aspect of the sport.

Your choice of weekend areas will be limited by the distance you're willing to travel, although most major population centers have more than one nearby. For a week-long vacation your options expand to the more than six hundred thirty areas in the United States and two hundred fifty in Canada, not to mention overseas.

Joining a local ski club is a good way to explore ski areas. They take frequent trips using the inexpensive transportation of charter buses or carpooling. Sometimes they own cabins at nearby areas where you can bring your own sleeping bag. Clubs sponsor long trips for extended weekends or for week with discounted group rates on fares and lodging. Don't overlook the club option even if you live in a nonsnow climate—some of the largest and most active ones are located in the heart of Texas and elsewhere in the South.

You can also discover ski areas by talking with skiing friends, attending the annual ski shows every fall in major cities, buying annual guides to North American ski areas, reading ads in the ski magazines, and visiting travel agents. However, the favorite source of information is the area brochure. It will give you an idea of the rates, lodging, and facilities available in town. The glossy photos of endless powder fields and smiling tanned skiers enjoying a bottle of wine over a leisurely lunch on the sundeck weren't necessarily all taken at the area in question, so you may need to dig a little deeper for all the facts.

Remember, too, skiing consumes only a part of the day. Plan ahead what you prefer at après ski time or what to do on a very stormy day. Some lodges have swimming pools (heated, of course). Art buffs should ask if there any galleries in town. For inveterate shoppers, inquire about unusual boutiques. Resorts also offer sleigh rides, ice skating, dog sled rides, hot-air ballooning, or soaring. Inquire about the existence of an accessible choice of restaurants and nightclubs. If you just require a crackling fire and a book, write ahead to verify that your lodge, room, or condo has a fireplace. If you are bringing young children with you, make sure the resort has a day-care center and perhaps an evening sitting service to amuse them.

When writing for a brochure, always request a trail map providing more details about the ski terrain. Take the drawing of the area on the map with a pinch of salt. Ski areas hire artists for one talent —their ability to make the Matterhorn look pale when compared with a drawing of their own ski hill.

Nordic skiers will want to know the total dis-

11,100 FT.

VERTICAL DROP OF 3,100 FEET

8,000 FT.

Vertical drop.

(Photo courtesy Aspen Skiing Corp.)

tance of the trails. This is traditionally given in kilometers, which sounds more impressive than miles. To calculate miles, multiply kilometers by six-tenths to come up with the equivalent distance. Check for additional Nordic trails in the vicinity of the area resort. Many areas are near national forests, which often maintain free trails, and nearby private areas may also offer many trails for a small daily fee.

Alpine skiers should evaluate the area's vertical drop, which is the difference in elevation between the top and bottom of the ski area. (The figure is usually given in feet, so if you think in metric divide by three to arrive at the distance in meters.) Generally, one area with twice the vertical of another can offer three or four times the skiable area of its smaller rival. However, some areas make up for a lack of vertical by spreading out sideways along a ridge, or by having slopes on several sides of the same mountain. So you should check the number of lifts and trails as well.

The total number of lifts may include counting one lift that unloads at midway as two. Also, lifts side by side may relieve congestion, but they don't open up as much terrain as widely separated lifts. Look at the length of each lift and the vertical drop it covers. "Lift capacity" refers to the total number of skiers that can be transported uphill in each hour. It's an indication of the number of lifts and how efficient they are. Check for rope tows listed in the lifts. Riding them is quickly tiring.

The number of trails is also a variable, as some areas count every diversion around a tree as a separate trail, while others count a hundred acres in a glade of trees as only one trail. All areas rate trails as easier, more difficult, or most difficult. There is no standard for this rating, so sometimes one area's intermediate may be another's advanced, but it's a good general guide. If you're a beginner, don't choose an area with mostly expert or most difficult runs. Areas may also rate their terrain suitability by percentages; for example, 25 percent of the area consists of easiest trails, 50 percent more difficult, and 25 percent most difficult. This will give you a good indication of what the mountain is like.

If you're a beginner, look for a separate beginner's area or even your own hill and lifts. Some areas funnel advanced skiers through the beginner runs, and a beginner at these areas will wish he or she had doubled his life insurance. At any level, if you intend to take lessons, you may wish to consider the quality of the ski school.

Frequently a resort states their "skiable area." This is the total acreage within their area boundary where you can ski. The figure is generally a good indication of an area's total size.

Another frequently stated figure is the longest run. This is the longest single combination of trails from top to bottom, and may be stated as a figure like "10,560 feet." It's the easiest way down and of interest only to beginners, who will be both impressed and exhausted, whether it's nine thousand or nineteen thousand feet.

A main requirement should be adequate transportation. Your own car or a rental gives maximum mobility at any area, but I especially enjoy resorts where you don't have to worry about a car. Either everything is compact and within walking distance, or the town or lodge provides courtesy bus services. If you do rent a car, specify a "skierized" one, which should have snow tires and a lockable ski rack. Speaking of transportation, if you fly, don't forget to arrange ahead for transportation (public bus or lodge limousine) from the airport to the ski area.

As the time for your trip approaches, check the area's ski conditions. Snow depth gives a rough indication of snow coverage. It's always measured as unpacked depth in a sheltered area high on the mountain. What really counts is the trail condition. Some areas require three feet of snow just to cover stumps and rocks, while half a foot of snow makes other trails golf-course smooth. Sometimes areas experiment with cloud seeding to increase their overall snowfall, but this is still of questionable value. Manmade snow however, can greatly supplement nature's variety. This is a rather dense snow created by shooting air and water into the freezing atmosphere. Some resorts cover many trails from top to bottom with man-made snow. Major areas also groom the snow to condition and reposition what snow is available. Large over-the-snow machines called snow cats break up the hard surface to recondition it to a softer texture, and push the snow around to cover thin spots.

Ski conditions are also defined by the type of snow cover. *Packed powder* is the ideal condition, but the term is used too frequently by area operators to describe anything vaguely white on the ground. Ski areas are competitive, and a report of "frozen granular" (very firm packed snow) or "spring conditions" (ice to slush with bare spots), could turn away customers. Conditions change rapidly anyway, so unless you're calling a morning report for the same-day skiing at your local area, don't count on the surface condition report. Pay attention to how much of the existing area is open for skiing. It's an excellent indicator of the true snow coverage, which is expressed either by a percentage of terrain open or by listing which lifts and trails are open.

Send for those brochures early, but don't worry too much about choosing the perfect area. There are many great ones around, and with a positive attitude toward the sport any hill can be the ideal one for you.

3
Mental and Physical Conditioning

Skiing is a sport of dynamic balance. You must constantly readjust your body position as your speed varies and as you ski over terrain changes. There are ways to improve this balancing ability, and many of them take place before ski season.

Your sense of balance is useful only if you have the physical strength to respond. Consequently, you should have some type of physical conditioning program. Before you start groaning, this doesn't necessarily mean a 5:00 A.M. calisthenics routine, but instead taking the time to engage in some physical activities that you enjoy that encompass the three essential conditioning aspects for skiing—endurance, strength, and agility. (Consult your doctor before engaging in any new, strenuous exercise program.)

Endurance enables you to ski for miles on a Nordic trail or top to bottom on an Alpine run without having to stop every few minutes to catch your breath. This endurance factor is aerobic. The heart and lungs must work harder to supply oxygen to demanding muscles. To increase your endurance try swimming, jogging, rapid walking, rowing, jumping rope, hiking, or bicycling. These activities will elevate your heart rate and breathing for longer than five minutes at a time, since that is the muscles' normal limit of stored oxygen.

Rapid direction changes and quick balancing movements in skiing require sudden bursts of strength. This explosive effort requires muscular strength. You can build muscles with weight training or with isometric exercises. Concentrate on strengthening the thighs, buttocks, abdomen, lower back, and shoulders. You can also vary your

rhythm in an endurance sport to build strength. For instance, while jogging suddenly sprint a few yards and then drop back to your original pace. The same burst of speed during other endurance sports will increase strength too. Field and court games such as tennis, handball, soccer, volleyball, racquetball, and basketball require sudden spurts of muscular effort. You don't need to become totally musclebound to ski. The best skiers have a firm musculature without excessive bulges.

The third conditioning factor is agility, the ability to move your body joints nimbly through the wide range of motions required in skiing. Yoga, modern dance, and all stretching routines are especially useful to promote flexibility. Sports requiring quick footwork such as soccer increase agility while also improving the eye-foot coordination leading to better balance. Women who wear high heels regularly should pay special attention to improving the flexibility of the Achilles tendon, which tends to shorten. Walk directly uphill in low heels, or do toe raises on a book to stretch the tendon. Before any exercise and especially before the first ski run of the day, stretch as many muscles as possible, not only in the legs but throughout your entire body. Limber up again after a rest period, or when you're chilled from a cold chair lift ride.

Luckily, most sports will improve all three conditioning factors. It is easy to incorporate endurance, strength, and agility in a training routine. For instance, if you jog, instead of just plodding around the track, jump over imaginary obstacles, hop on one or two feet, sprint full speed briefly, change direction rapidly, and skip and click your heels together in midair. Always stretch to relax your muscles as you cool down after exertion.

An excellent all-around conditioner is aerobic dance (also known as jazz exercise or jazzercize.) This can be a very tough workout. The first time I tried to match the instructor I was left in an exhausted heap on the floor. Many local groups are available, and some TV stations air good early-morning shows.

Make your exercise enjoyable so you'll stick with it. Sweating is more fun when in company, so get a group of friends to join you. Many local park department programs offer indoor court games, conditioning sessions, or weight training. Join a gym, health spa, or "Y." Instead of taking an elevator, walk up the stairs. With imagination, exercise can be incorporated into any part of your life.

One nonphysical factor that affects your balancing ability is your mental outlook. Worry about falling and you probably will. Don't be overly concerned about taking a spill. Falls are a normal and sometimes enjoyable part of the sport. A day without one good nose plant can be a dull one, and it happens to everyone. Falls are good opportunities to analyze what didn't work the way you thought it would. Instead of getting angry, examine what really caused the loss of balance and how to correct the problem.

If you feel hesitant on skis, you're probably worried about gaining too much speed. Perhaps you have found yourself traversing a steep slope, reluctant to make the turn that will plunge you into the fall line. Good technique and confident knowledge of your ability to control your skis in any situation will improve your outlook. Practice various means of speed control discussed in the technique chapters. Once you have confidence that you can always stop or slow down you'll be able to ski faster in total balance.

If you are having a rough day, try to avoid too harsh a judgment of yourself and your abilities.

Once you get "up tight" mentally your muscles also tense up, reducing their sensitivity to signal imbalances, which in turn degrades your skiing. Trying too hard can make you ski worse. Relax, take a few deep breaths, and stretch. Then take an easy run with an open mind. Do every type of turn you do well, from wedges on up. Vary your rhythm and your speed. Feel what works right and enjoy it. As soon as your balance has been reestablished, you'll ski better for the rest of the day.

Prior to ski season you can help your mental attitude by participating in sports involving speed. Sailing, sailboarding, kayaking, ice- or roller-skating, and bicycling are good choices. Besides improving your reactions, you'll condition yourself to thinking of rapid motion and balance recovery as normal activities.

After all those active improvements, you may be pleased to hear about one you can do without breaking a sweat. It's simply detailed daydreaming; you can improve your skiing by thinking positively about it. Just sit and imagine yourself on a slope, making smooth turn after turn. See everything as you would through your eyes when skiing. Take the same time for each turn as you'd need in turns out on the slopes. Concentrate on everything you'd see, feel, hear, or smell on the hill. Listen to the snow squeaking under your skis, feel the cold wind on your face, see the village at the base of the hill, and smell the pine trees. One hopes you'll almost feel your leg muscles contracting, and maybe your hand will twitch toward the pole plant. Go ahead and try a mogul or two. Steepen the slope. Increase your speed. You can handle it!

When you do get on the slopes, use the same creative daydreaming technique now and then. At the top of a run take a few seconds to imagine yourself making the greatest run ever down there —then immediately push off and ski just as you saw yourself in your imagination. It's amazing what a positive mental attitude can do to improve your balance and technique!

4
School Days

Taking lessons is a widely accepted form of learning, especially in sports. They are not always necessary; some great skiers develop as a result of trial and error, imitating others, and studying books. (This book will give you many ideas to become as good a skier as you wish.) However, lessons can prove a breakthrough to accelerate your progress when you are stymied. The learning chapters and terminology of this book are organized in a sequence similar to what you'll encounter in ski schools.

Ski instruction has improved immensely recently. Forget the stereotype of the blond Teutonic ski god shouting, "Bend ze knees!" Modern instructors tailor a lesson around the individuals they are teaching. They are often familiar with learning theories such as the "inner game," and have dropped the old demands for mechanical precision of movements in favor of the new outlook of functional skiing. Some will say very little technically, instead guiding you through various exercises to quickly improve your skills. You won't always have a good lesson, though, so here are several things you should know to improve your chances.

TYPES OF LESSONS

Lessons are either "private" or "group." A private lesson is best if you have some specific problem you wish to surmount; if you have a particular learning or physical impediment; if you're intense and want a maximum of instruction in a minimum time; or if you're shy enough and you simply don't want to learn with a group. A private lesson at major resorts costs thirty-five to forty-five dollars per hour for one person. If you can find other people at your level of ability who will share the lesson, your cost decreases. Usually a private lesson is limited to four people. Your lift riding time is still included in your lesson time, but private lessons always "cut" the lift lines to maximize your skiing time.

Beginners or typical skiers wanting to improve in all areas should try a group lesson. It can be an entertaining experience; you'll meet all sorts of people, you'll benefit from watching the other members' skiing performance in relation to the instructor's, and you'll get a chance to stop and rest or to pull things together mentally now and then. Group lessons cost from twenty-five to thirty-five dollars per day, which is usually four hours. Sometimes they run for five hours with a break for lunch. At most areas you can take a one-and-a-half- or two-hour lesson, but the more lesson time the better. At your weekend area you might sign up for a series of one- or two-hour weekly lessons with the same students and instructor for each session.

Many destination resorts offer three- or five-day packages starting on Monday in which you'll stay with the same group every day. This way the instructor gets to know you well, and can plan ahead for each day's lesson. Frequently these multiday packages offer extras, including parties and races. An ideal class has six or seven students, but this is seldom economical for a ski school. During busy periods expect as many as a dozen students. If there are more than twelve, you won't get enough attention in the class to make the lesson worthwhile.

Some areas also offer a closed group lesson, in which you can hire an instructor for your own group on a daily basis.

For advanced skiers, a few progressive areas offer "master" classes or "ski the whole mountain" classes. These tackle special concerns of the more experienced skier, such as bumps, powder, or the steeps. Racing classes may also be available. These concentrate on running gates. Some areas have special "mountain discovery" classes that guide groups to the best snow and hidden runs. Sometimes they offer out-of-bounds skiing for a superb powder experience.

THE SKI SCHOOL

At certain weekend areas private ski schools contract with the area to bring in students to teach on the mountain. Joining one of these schools provides the option of skiing several areas, as the school travels to different areas each weekend with the same students on a seasonal basis.

Most major resorts have excellent ski schools. To evaluate the lesson quality at a given ski school, first find out if the school is affiliated with the PSIA (Professional Ski Instructors of America), and in Canada, the CSIA (Canadian Ski Instructors Alliance). If so, they conform to a uniform tried-and-proven teaching method. The American Teaching Method (ATM) is a standard, and you will fit into any ski school using it. Beware of schools with fantastic claims of instant parallel skiing, or some new international technique.

Ask what percentage of the school's instructors are professionally certified. Before hiring instructors, schools generally test to determine a candidate's skiing ability, knowledge of technique, and ability to relate to others. After a year or two of teaching the instructor is eligible to take a rigorous test in one of the regional divisions of PSIA. Passing this test gives "associate certified" status. The final test, when passed, awards "full certified" status. A ski school with a large percentage of certified instructors will have an experienced, dedicated staff.

A good ski school places you into your first class by watching you ski. This "ski off" can be an unnerving experience. Up to a dozen instructors watch you ski on a test hill to evaluate your skill level for placement in the class best suited for you. If you have an exceptionally good or bad run don't worry, because you can transfer to another class if necessary. Some ski schools will ask you to watch a videotape to fit yourself into the classes shown on it. Others simply ask you how you ski. In the latter two cases, make sure you can transfer if needed, as this grouping is not as reliable as a "ski off." For beginner classes everyone starts out the same.

Ski schools sometimes offer extra services, such as a videotape so you can see yourself ski, or classroom time to learn ski care or to see films. They are rare, but some progressive areas are realizing there is more to instruction than drills on the hill. Sometimes these services are called other names, such as "ski education center."

You will be given a certain class designation (for instance, "C") to identify your class and its meeting place. Do not place too much importance on your letter level. There has been too much emphasis in the past on trying to grade categories of skiers. All classes are working on the same skills, the only difference being skill refinement, slope experience, and the speed of skiing. Many areas use a PSIA rating of "A" through "F" for convenience in organizing classes. Very roughly, these classes include:

A—Introduction to skiing (first-time beginners). Straight runs and speed control.
B—Turning (higher beginner). Linking wedge turns.
C—Improving turns (intermediate). Finishing turns in a skid (christie) on easier terrain.
D—Wide-track turning (advanced intermediate). Starting turns with simultaneous leg motions (parallel) and varying turn radius on easier and more difficult terrain.
E—Dynamic turning (advanced). Using skis efficiently by rebounding and carving and skiing bumps in more difficult and some most difficult terrain.
F—All snow and terrain (expert). Work on the steeps, big bumps, powder, and speed.

Some schools avoid this rigid classification system

by forming classes in the "ski off" designated green, blue, and black, while others give an arbitrary number.

THE INSTRUCTOR AND YOU

If you are taking a private lesson, you'll have your choice of instructors. Do speak up if you have a preference. If you don't specify, you'll receive whoever is next on the list to work. Perhaps some friends raved about a lesson with a particular instructor, and you'd like that person. Or maybe you have a specific request for someone very patient, or someone who speaks a preferred language, or someone familiar with a technique you learned twenty years ago.

If you get along well with your instructor, you may want to arrange for another session at the end of your lesson. You can also book another lesson through the ski school office. Try to schedule as much in advance as possible, as popular instructors often have full schedules. If you must cancel a lesson, let the instructor know as early as possible, as he or she has reserved time for you and won't get paid if you don't take the lesson.

In private or class lessons be honest with the instructor about why you're taking them; from the specific, such as speed control, bumps, or steeper slopes, to seeing more of the mountain, cutting lines, or having companions to ski with. They are all equally valid reasons for taking lessons, and the instructor will tailor your lesson to your needs. It's your time and money, and you should get as much as you can.

During the lesson, keep an open mind and a positive attitude. Don't be upset if the instructor makes you do something you already think you know how to do. If you're trying to improve parallel turns and the instructor asks you to do a wedge turn, he or she is doing it to improve one of your skills. For best results, observe and mimic the instructor.

If you had a particularly good (or bad) lesson, let your instructor know, along with the ski school director or supervisor [in person or by letter]. They appreciate hearing how their staff is doing.

Remember that the instructor is a human being. He or she may appear to lead an ideal, carefree life, but they have the same problems and bills you do. They are trying to satisfy everyone's goals, adjust to their personalities, look out constantly for the students' safety, and push for improvement while still providing a fun and ego-satisfying time. If you enjoyed your lesson, a tip (either individually or as a group) is certainly in order.

Finally, realize your own limitations. Classes are not magic that instantly transform you into Olympic material. Anything good takes time, especially ski improvement.

5
Slope Safety

Don't skip this chapter! No one wants to read about safety, as it's usually on a par with studying a driver's manual. However, your freedom from accidents on the slopes depends on knowing and following a few commonsense rules of the road.

A lift ticket allows you to share the slopes with others. You are not alone, so always ski in control for your own safety, and for that of other skiers. Some of the worst injuries occur from collisions between skiers, so be alert and ready to stop at any time. Some counties and states have passed laws punishing reckless skiers who cause accidents. At the very least, reckless skiers generally have their lift privileges taken away by the ski patrol.

The ski patrols are not only law enforcers. If you have any problems on the slopes, turn to the patrol. They will answer your questions on the latest trail conditions, give directions, and tend to your first-aid needs. (Their uniforms usually have crosses on them.)

When you're stopping for a breather on the trail, rest at the edge so other skiers have room to ski by. Before you resume, look uphill first to avoid cutting someone off, and while skiing, look behind you before making any sudden, unpredictable moves. Learn to sense the presence of nearby skiers by the sounds of their skis and by using your peripheral vision. Be especially alert where trails merge and where catwalks diagonally cross ski slopes.

Everyone skis at different speeds, so overtaking and passing happens all the time. It is rude to run over someone's ski tips at forty miles per hour,

Ski on slopes within your ability.

shouting, "On your right!" in the other ear. The downhill skier always has the right of way, and when you pass leave as much room as possible. Slow down in confined areas, and, if necessary, tell the downhill skier you're passing.

Plan your route down the mountain ahead of time so you'll stay on trails within your ability. When you buy your lift ticket always ask for a trail map and carry it with you. It will show you all the ways around the mountain and will also rate each trail's difficulty. Areas use the uniform trail desig-

A green circle indicates easiest trails, a blue square more difficult, a black diamond most difficult.

nation system, marking their easiest trails with a green circle, their more difficult trails with a blue square, and their most difficult trails with a black diamond. Again, one area's "easier" trails may be more challenging than another's, and daily changing snow conditions affect the trail difficulty as well.

Obey all closed signs. They are there for a good reason. If you're lost or injured while venturing into a closed area, you could be liable for the expense of search and rescue. Various warning signs alert you to areas requiring extra caution, where there may be congestion, obstacles, or equipment working. Solitary bamboo poles are not for slalom turns, but instead mark the upper side of an exposed rock, stump, or bare patch.

Properly functioning equipment reduces the risk of injury in falls. Have a ski shop verify the release settings on your bindings periodically. Inspect the bindings frequently for settings that may have changed due to vibration and keep them properly lubricated and free of dirt. Make sure your ski brakes work to prevent the unpleasant possibility of a runaway ski. For a complete maintenance inspection see the chapter "The Care and Feeding of Your Equipment."

In the event of an accident, place skis in the shape of an *X* uphill of the injured skier with the tails securely in the snow. Notify the ski patrol by skiing to the nearest lift operator station or by phoning in from a patrol phone on the slopes. Their locations are shown on your trail map. Know the name of the slope where the injury occurred so you can give accurate directions to the patrol.

Don't pit yourself against the toughest slope on every run. Take some relaxing runs and rest when you're tired. Most accidents occur before lunch and near the end of the day; these are good times to ski a little easier.

ESPECIALLY FOR NORDIC SKIING

Where there are tracks, a large number of people will be skiing the same course in opposite directions. Stay to the right if there are parallel sets of tracks. When you overtake another skier in your track you should leave that track to pass him.

On a grade, the skier going downhill has the right of way over the one going uphill. When stop-

ping for a breather, step out of the track. Leave your four-footed friends at home since dogs ruin tracks by punching holes in them in their enthusiasm to keep up with you.

Recognize your limitations. Stay on trails within your skill ability or choose a tour suited to your physical condition. Plan your longer trips with special care and be prepared for weather changes. Let others know where you are going and your expected return time.

Now that you've read all these cautionary words, let me reassure you that skiing is a safe sport. Your chance for injury on any one ski day is around one in one thousand. By using the commonsense advice in this chapter you'll considerably reduce even that slender chance.

These signs mean what they say!

II

NORDIC SKIING

The Nordic World

Welcome to a new fad that's really an old fad. The population of active cross-country skiers has exploded in recent years, although the sport has been around for a long time. People are touring on skis now just as the Scandinavians did over four thousand years ago. The sport could rightly be called just plain *skiing*, but the recently popular Alpine style of downhill skiing has adopted that term, so it's commonly known as cross-country or Nordic skiing.

This is a sport for anyone who likes the outdoors and fresh, cool winter air. Nordic skiers are not limited by age or physical condition, as anyone can ski at his or her own pace. It's possible wherever there's snow, and the equipment is relatively inexpensive. Cross-country skiing offers the opportunities to exercise your whole body as much as you want, to socialize or to be alone, to see areas formerly isolated by winter snow, or to compete in races. Generally, anyone who likes to run or walk likes to cross-country ski. The motions are similar, but skiing has the added benefit of a floatinglike glide between steps, coupled with the delights of speed changes on varying terrain.

The majority of cross-country skiing takes place in tracks. Skiing on a track gives you the optimum conditions for efficient gliding and speed. The snow is packed, and your skis won't stray from their forward course. These tracks are found at hundreds of commercial areas, which use special equipment to set and maintain tracked trails. They often offer such amenities as warming huts, refreshments, rentals, instruction, and lodging.

These commercial areas may be associated with Alpine resorts, or they may be independent, and they charge a nominal fee for trail use. Maintained tracks are also available in many federal and state forests, national parks, and even in some city and county parks.

Out-of-track skiing also attracts many. It opens up large expanses of terrain. You can go anywhere, be by yourself. However, untracked snow can be difficult and exhausting, especially when it's soft and deep. You'll find off-track skiing easier once the snow has settled or after somone else has blazed his or her own track. After a new snowfall tracks magically appear on golf courses, in the woods, and even on snowbound city streets.

A few souls prefer to use Nordic equipment on packed runs at Alpine ski resorts. This certainly perfects one's high-speed downhill technique, while making an ordinary descent on Alpine gear into a challenging one on Nordic gear. Others like to go Nordic mountaineering, a winter equivalent of summer climbing. This requires specialized equipment combining Alpine and Nordic features as well as an extensive knowledge of avalanches, camping, and survival. Some enthusiasts even ski all year, using wheeled skis on the pavement once the snow has melted. They are also taking advantage of the excellent all-around physical conditioning that Nordic skiing provides.

We'll discuss all the aspects of this exciting Nordic world, examining the typical equipment you'll need and the skills you'll use to ski safely both up and down any hill.

6
Equipment—Light Is Right

Choosing equipment can be an exciting but bewildering experience. Due to the recent popularity of Nordic skiing hundreds of models of skis and boots are now available. Before you get bogged down in buying gear, rent or borrow some and get out on the snow for experience with some equipment. You will then have a better idea of your preferences and what to look for.

When you are ready to buy, go to a specialized cross-country shop or to an Alpine store with a large Nordic department. Make sure the salespeople are themselves Nordic skiers. You'll want equipment suitable for where you like to ski, which may be in track, out of track, or a combination of these. You'll need the proper gear for your desired activity level, the number of times you go per season, the snow conditions, and your price range.

Most importantly, buy skis, boots, bindings, and poles as a matched system. There is no uniform classification of equipment types. The traditional system recognizes four groups:

1. racing—ultralightweight gear for use by experienced skiers in tracks;
2. light touring—lightweight gear for use mainly in tracks;
3. touring—heavier, more durable gear for out-of-track skiing; and
4. mountaineering—heaviest gear for Alpine backcountry and deep, untracked snow.

Manufacturers use different categories to describe their products. The racing and mountaineering classifications are fairly standard, but the most popular range of touring and light touring are often combined into the categories of "recreational" and "performance." The recreational line is aimed at beginners while the performance line is for more advanced skiers. Some manufacturers confuse the issue by labeling these two categories "touring" and "performance" respectively. Here are some variables to consider for each piece of equipment you'll need.

SKIS

Nowadays most Nordic skis (otherwise known as "skinny skis") are fiberglass, with a plastic-type base. If you're new to the sport and are looking at used skis to buy, you may come across a pair with a wood base. Put them back; you're asking for extra work. Your first decision when buying is where you'll be using the skis. If you ski primarily in tracks, the skis should be light and narrow, but they won't turn well outside the tracks. The off-track skis are slightly wider for support and heavier for durability but consequently offer more drag in a track. A combination ski is a good compromise if you plan to ski on and off track.

Your next decision concerns your ability. The whole idea behind a cross-country ski is that when you press and weight the ski it will grip the snow, allowing you to push forward. But when weight is relieved from the ski, it can slide forward without gripping. If you're inclined to ski at a leisurely pace or aren't particularly athletic, you'll want an easier-flexing recreational ski for proper grip and slide. A more advanced or athletic skier who

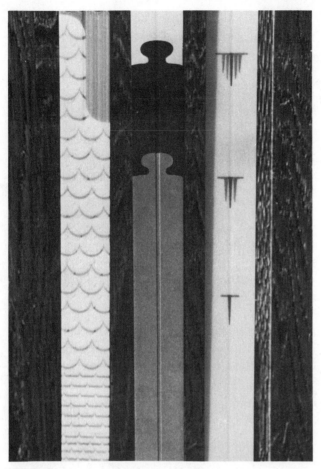

The three major types of bases (l. to r.): waxless patterned, waxless composite, and waxable.

places greater force on a ski will want a stiffer performance type.

Now you come to the big controversy—waxable or waxless? The traditional way to make a ski grip has been to apply a wax that matches the snow's temperature and crystalline structure. A more modern way is to have a textured pattern or a special material built into the base, which grips the snow. Both waxable and waxless skis have their strong and weak points.

A waxable base is a versatile ski for all snow, with proper preparation. It allows you to match your ski exactly to the prevailing conditions for best performance. This traditionally means planning ahead, perhaps cleaning off old wax and applying new before each trip. Also, you must carry waxes with you for a possible change in temperature or snow surface conditions. A complete wax outfit for all conditions could include as many as

eight hard waxes for all temperatures of snow in its original condition and three klisters, which are sticky liquids used on snow that has melted to an altered form.

Some tourers delight in matching their wits and waxes to the snow conditions. If you don't, new simplified wax systems require just two waxes. One is for above-freezing temperatures and one for below-freezing temperatures. You don't even need a thermometer. If the snow will ball up in your hand, use the above-freezing (wet snow) type. If the snow fluffs away in your hand use the below-freezing (dry snow) type. As a beginner, try this system until you want to fine-tune your waxing skills, but choose only one brand of wax to apply since each manufacturer has its own color-coded system and temperature blends, and different brands are not necessarily compatible.

Waxing is relatively easy. For best results, do it indoors on a warm, dry ski. Start by scraping off old waxes with a plastic scraper. Finish that job with a liquid wax remover. Select your wax for the day. If in doubt regarding the temperature, put on the colder wax, as a softer, warmer wax can be applied over it on the trail. Crayon the wax onto the base. The critical area is the kicker, that third of the ski under the boot that grips the snow. However, some manufacturers recommend waxing along the whole ski. For warmer temperatures, apply a thicker layer. Then smooth the wax out with a "cork," a rectangular block that was once made from cork but nowadays will probably be made of hard foam. For colder temperatures, make the wax smoother than for warmer temperatures.

The purists will never forgive me for admitting this, but I like waxless skis. You may too, if you don't want to hassle with waxes and want to just pop out the door for a quick tour on the spur of the moment. Waxless skis are especially good for rapidly changing snow conditions around freezing temperature, in which you may encounter anything from hard to wet snow in a short distance. Waxless skis do have the disadvantage of generally not gripping as well as a properly waxed ski in certain extremes, namely ice. Also, they can produce some drag in the glide. Consequently, they may not be as fast or as effortless as properly prepared waxable skis.

The waxless bases frequently have a texture pattern on the plastic material in the kick zone under the foot. If you imagine fish scales on a ski bottom, you'll have a rough idea of how the patterned bases work. The pattern offers resistance to sliding backward, but is relatively smooth to a forward glide. The individual designs on the base vary with intended use, as some grip better in soft snow, some turn easier off track, and so forth. Certain designs will "hum" as they slide along the snow. If you demand absolute quiet on a trail, they may annoy you.

The newest waxless bases don't have a three-dimensional pattern. Instead, these heterogeneous or composite bases depend upon the properties of special materials to grip the snow. One type incorporates microscopic fibers imbedded into the plastic base. These fibers grip in one direction but lie flat in the glide. Another type adds a polymer material in the kick area. The polymer chemically changes its grip as the temperature changes. These composite bases work over a wide range of snow conditions, and are quiet and moderately fast.

Once you've chosen your base, it's time to select the length. An old rule of thumb is to choose a ski that comes to the palm of your upstretched hand. Another way is the paper test. If you stand on a pair of skis with your weight equal on each foot, a strip of paper placed under the skis should pull out with only slight resistance. With your weight entirely on one ski, the paper should be held

The traditional test for proper ski length.

Choosing skis by their flex. Weight on one ski grips the paper, but weight on two skis doesn't.

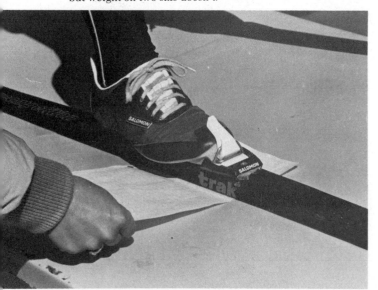

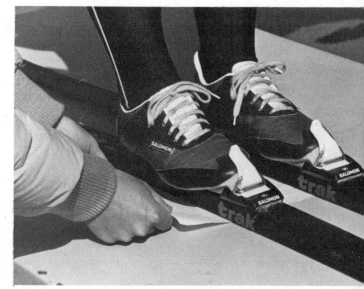

firmly in place. Another traditional test for ski length is to place the skis bottom to bottom and hold them in the middle. Squeeze with two hands and you should be able to flatten them, but you shouldn't be able to squeeze them together with just one hand. You can also follow the manufacturer's recommendations on length for your weight and ability.

Finally, if you still have a choice left, buy skis in your favorite color!

BOOTS AND BINDINGS

Boots and bindings must match one another and also be suitable to the type of Nordic skiing you do. Mountaineering boots are stiff and heavy. Touring boots for off-track use are cut above the ankle to give extra support. Light touring boots are cut at the ankle, and racing boots resemble jogging shoes with a low cut and minimum weight.

Boots (otherwise known as "shoes") should fit comfortably with a little toe clearance in front, but snug at the heels and instep. It's important to flex them and be certain that a single large crease doesn't form, which will cut into your toes. Most good boots are made of leather, allowing your feet to breathe while also preventing water penetration. A few of the more expensive lightweight models feature synthetic uppers of breathable and waterproof materials such as Gore-Tex®.

The most common boot/binding system is the 75mm Nordic norm, sometimes called *three-pin bindings,* as three metal pins stick upward to fit into three holes in the boot toe bottom. A wire

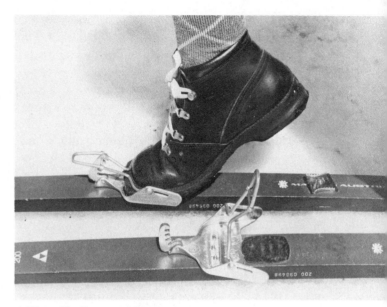

A 75mm Nordic norm system.

Three common boots are (l. to r.): heavy touring, light touring, and racing.

An extremely flexible and lightweight racing system.

bail-and-latch mechanism holds the sole pressed down over the pins. All 75mm Nordic norm boots fit all 75mm bindings, and they are interchangeable. In case you wonder about the bare foot often engraved on each binding, it is because the system is not symmetrical. The left or right boot must go into the corresponding left or right binding.

More recently developed systems using a narrower symmetrical binding and a boot toe extension for better flex are becoming quite common. The 50mm norm is one very popular model. In the 50mm touring norm the binding is made to accommodate a 12mm-thick sole, one thick enough to insulate the foot well. Correspondingly, the system is sometimes called *50/12*. The 50 mm racing norm has a thinner plastic sole 7mm thick and is known as a 50/7. These narrower norms often give better ski control with relatively less foot twisting than the 75mm norm.

Several other systems have been promoted by particular manufacturers, for example, the Salomon Nordic System. The SNS uses a metal-to-metal mounting design, and flex takes place in a binding insert, rather than in the boot sole. The Norm 38 from Adidas is another widely used system.

One problem with having the boot attachment point only at the front is that the foot must twist sideways to turn. With a lot of torque the boot heel can slide off the skis. Some boots combat this with built-in steel shanks in the soles or with plastic stabilizing ridges molded along the boot sole. A variety of heel plates are sold, which attach to the skis to prevent heel slippage. The plates grip the heel when it's pressed onto the ski. The most common type has serrated edges that bite into the heel sole. Another type has wedges that mate with a matching groove in the heel. Your ski shop can advise you on the safety of each type, as any heel fastening tends to increase injuries in falls.

POLES

At last, a relatively simple piece of equipment to choose. But don't grab the first pair you see! You'll want a lightweight, strong model, so ask your dealer about the merits of the fiberglass-and-metal-shaft types he or she carries. To get the correct length, stand with an arm outstretched hori-

Correct pole length.

A basket for off-track skiing (l.) and one for tracked skiing (r.)

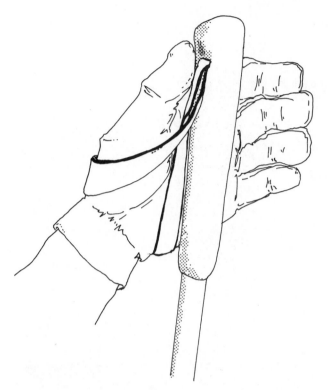

Wearing the pole strap correctly.

zontally. The pole should just fit under your armpit.

Choose a basket compatible with your type of skiing. The traditional round basket gives support in softer, off-track snow. Small, nonsymmetrical baskets are designed for track use, where the snow is firmer. They are aerodynamically designed to "fly" through the air, reducing wind resistance and effort expended. Finally, the strap should be adjustable to fit any gloves you plan to wear. To wear the strap correctly place your hand upward through the loop and clasp the pole grip, trapping the strap between your thumb and other fingers.

CLOTHING

To quote an old Cole Porter song, "anything goes." Like the individualism of skiing, outfits can be quite varied. The key point is function. Choose your clothes for maximum freedom of movement while retaining warmth.

You'll be quite active while Nordic skiing, so you won't need the heavy insulating garments common to Alpine skiing, in which much inactive time is spent on lifts or in lines. All your activity generates heat, which you'll retain through trapped layers of air. Dress in several layers of lightweight articles and adjust them as needed on the trail. On anything longer than a brief jaunt you'll need a small pack with extra clothing for when you stop and to hold surplus clothing when you get too warm skiing.

You'll probably want thermal underwear as an inner layer. A wool layer absorbs perspiration, and a polypropylene one wicks moisture away from the skin. The latter is generally better for extended, strenuous trips, but either provides warmth even when it's wet. Lightweight sweaters, wool shirts, or nylon windbreakers are good removable top layers. The traditional lower garment is the knee-length knicker worn with high socks. A wind-and-water-repellent noninsulated outer layer will protect you on blustery days. Manufacturers have emulated the success of fashionable Alpine gear, and now sell comfortable stretchy one- or two-piece racer-look suits in all colors.

Keep the extremities warm. A wool or wool-blend sock retains heat when it's wet. To prevent wetness, waterproof your boots as recommended by their manufacturer. Wear gaiters in conditions where snow will drift in over the boot top. For extra-cold days, you can buy an insulated over-boot. (If you're not style-conscious, you can even make one from a large old sock with the toe area removed.) Wear wool mittens or gloves. For comfort and durability choose a pair with extra reinforcements where the pole strap rubs between the thumb and fingers. In warmer weather you may prefer a glove with an open weave on the back. During extreme cold consider a windproof mitten shell over your mittens. You'll also lose a lot of heat through your head, so a wool hat is best. You can take it off to cool down and cover it with the hood of your parka when you need extra wind protection.

7
Nordic Technique

Nordic and Alpine skiing are members of the same family. Nordic is the original, all-purpose skiing method in which you ski downhill, uphill, and on the level. Alpine skiing is a specialized version of just the downhill part of Nordic skiing. Nordic skiers sometimes refer to Alpine skiing as "yo-yo" skiing, since you ski down, ride up, and ski down again.

Nordic equipment differs from Alpine primarily in three areas: (1) the boot is attached only at the toe, allowing a natural walking motion by lifting the heel with each step; (2) the ski can grip into the snow when pressured, enabling the skier to climb grades; and (3) the equipment is designed to cause the skier minimum fatigue. If you're an Alpine skier, you'll be surprised at the lightness of the gear and your apparent lack of control, as you've been dependent on a rigidly held heel for strictly downhill cruising. But you'll find that

much of the technique is the same, with the addition of a walking-type movement to propel you on the level and up hills. Because Nordic is very basic, we'll describe the maneuvers without detailed exercises. The best way to learn cross-country is to go out and practice these maneuvers. If you have problems, they will probably occur while you're making downhill turns at speed. You can apply the exercises from the Alpine technique chapters for control.

ON THE FLATS

The Diagonal Stride

The diagonal stride is a simple yet elegant maneuver. It is the most basic cross-country skill and also the most outstanding. The diagonal stride is unlike any action in Alpine skiing, but you'll use it

Start by walking naturally on skis.

Increase your stride by leaning forward, almost like leaning into a hurricane wind. Your strides become more efficient. Now add the poles to your natural arm swing. Plant them angling slightly backward and push to add thrust. You're doing the diagonal stride!

This vital maneuver has some secrets for efficient diagonal strides. When you are gliding, your body weight should be only on the forward foot. The ankle and knee of this leg are slightly flexed for balance, and the rear leg and arm are fully extended. Keep your body angled forward, up to as much as forty-five degrees if you are out for maximum speed.

Let your arms swing directly forward and back for efficient poling, without any sideways movement. This may be tough at first as you learn balance, but don't put your arms out to the side like outriggers. Extra motions of the arms or body to the side are wasted. They reduce your forward push, and tire you over a long distance. During the pole plant, the pole is angled, with the pole handle slightly ahead of the basket. The elbow and wrist should be comfortably flexed. Aid your forward motion by pulling downward and backward along the shaft. As your arm continues past your body, the push is relieved and your hand relaxes its grip on the handle. The strap will keep your pole from going anywhere, and the relaxation of your open hand saves muscular effort and adds smoothness to your stride. It's not always necessary to pole with each arm swing. You can vary your pole plant frequency by resting an arm every other stride.

more than any other maneuver while Nordic skiing.

The stride is called diagonal because the diagonally opposite arm and leg move simultaneously. The way to appreciate this is simply to walk and swing your arms naturally. Now put on the skis—but not the poles—walk, and swing your arms. You'll find your skis glide when you bring a foot forward. Resist the temptation to lift a ski when gliding it forward. It's less work to slide it on the snow. Let your weight flow onto that gliding ski. Just as in walking, either one foot or the other is weighted, never both at the same time. When you're used to this slide you'll find you go farther and faster on each step than you would in walking.

The diagonal stride is basic to Nordic skiing.

A long glide is one of the great thrills of the sport. The pushoff phase is crucial to a good stride. Just as the rear leg starts to pass your weighted forward ski, push off that weighted ski and transfer all your weight to the new forward ski. This push is your main propulsion. By pressuring a ski into the snow, you cause its wax or patterned base to grip the snow momentarily. Angling this pressure backward pushes you forward. To increase the pressure of the push, flex into it. Bend your ankle and knee, just as you would while walking or jogging. Now you can forcefully extend your ankle and knee. Your forward lean and forward motion automatically convert this upward motion into a backward push for propulsion.

These phases of a diagonal stride may sound difficult at first. When you're having problems, go back to the walk or jog without skis and then apply the same motions. Strive for rhythm and fluid movement. Lean forward and keep your weight on only one foot at a time, flexing as you go from one to the other. It's easy once you relax and let your body do it, but if you're getting stuck, follow a good skier and match his or her rhythm or else take a lesson from an instructor.

The diagonal stride is your main means of forward movement on skis. Once you master this basic motion you should be able to maintain a ten-

Double-pole plants use the whole upper body to push forward.

mile-per-hour pace on level terrain. Of course you can also vary the stride rhythm to suit your mood —rapid and vigorous or slower and relaxed.

Double Poling

Double poling is used for variety while skiing on the level or as an easy way to speed up on slight downhills. The basic double pole starts while you are in motion by extending both arms forward with a swinging motion and planting the poles at a slight backward angle. You should feel that your shoulders and upper body have come forward also, so that the poles are supporting you. Now bend at the waist and let the weight of your upper body push onto the poles, rather than using arm

Complete an arm swing by releasing your grip on the pole.

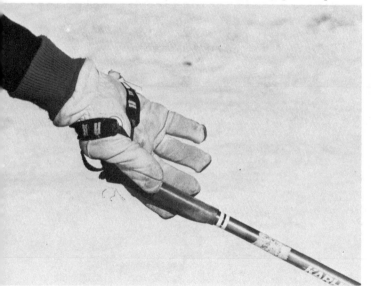

The one-step double pole adds a push from a ski.

strength exclusively to push. As you follow through, your back should end up nearly parallel to the ground while your eyes still look ahead. Your hands release their grips on the poles just as in diagonal striding. Then rise up from the waist, swing your arms forward, grip the poles, and push again. It is important with double poling to remember to bend at the waist. A good bend will give you follow-through for maximum thrust. Keep your seat over your feet.

You can combine a stride with the double pole. A common way is the one-step double pole. You'll push off as in a diagonal stride, but bring both hands forward. As you're gliding on the forward foot, plant both poles and bend into the double pole. The rear leg comes alongside as you finish

the push, and you glide on two skis, ready for another kick from either leg. You can easily imagine other variations on this, such as two kick steps followed by a double pole.

Skating

Just as its name implies, skating resembles ice skating, with the advantage of very long blades. Skating is a speedy way to get across flats. From a flexed position put your weight onto the inside edge of one ski. Extend powerfully from your coiled position, pivoting the unweighted ski outward at an angle. When the pushing leg is extended stride onto the diverged ski, taking all your weight off the pushing ski. Keep the ski flat to

Skating across the flats.

After striding onto that ski, match the pushing ski by picking it up and bringing it parallel. Repeat by pushing off the same ski again until the direction change is completed. Use a double-pole plant for additional push. A skate turn is also useful to move from one track to another.

GOING UPHILL

Unless you ski on a frozen lake or a Kansas wheat field, you will encounter uphill stretches. These can be more demanding than skiing across the flats, but with good technique they won't be exhausting. You can vary the pace on these stretches from relaxing to strenuous. Remember that when you're going uphill in a track there may be someone coming downhill in that same track. They have the right of way and may not be able to stop anyway, so step aside while they zoom by. When we talk about uphill and downhill we'll use the term *fall line*, which is the route directly downhill from where you're standing.

glide, then flex when you're ready to push again, angle the ski onto its inside edge, and repeat the sequence. Strive for rhythm and smooth-flowing movements. Aid the push with either a single- or a double-pole plant.

Skate Turn

By combining the skate with a step you can maintain speed on the flat and change direction at the same time. With a skate motion, simply point the unweighted ski in the direction you wish to go.

Uphill Diagonal Stride

Your basic diagonal stride is used on gentle and moderate uphill grades. Because of the slope you won't have a free glide phase, and you'll feel more as though you're jogging. The stride becomes shorter and the poles must be planted farther behind and from a lower position. You'll need a definite weight transfer to make each ski grip. Push vigorously off the poles. Any problems will arise from planting the pole too far up the hill and from dropping your seat, which tends to pull you back-

The kick turn.

ward. Keep the pole plants angled backward, and your body angled forward, and your chin up!

Uphill Traverse

A *traverse* is a path across a hill, rather than a course straight up or straight down. In order to traverse, you must balance on the two uphill edges of your skis. The pressured edges dig in to keep you from sliding sideways down the hill, as would happen if you stood on flat skis.

As the hill becomes steeper, you can still use the uphill diagonal stride, but now you will also zigzag, traversing at angles to the fall line. This makes your angle of ascent less so that the skis can still bite and hold, and you won't slide backward.

Kick Turn

It's often necessary to change direction on a hillside so you can face the opposite way. We'll use a kick turn to manage this task with style. Although it's most useful on a slope or in confined trees, it's most easily learned on the flat. Place your skis across the fall line, poles uphill, and kick the lower ski out. Let the tip fall around to where the tail was, and in one smooth motion step the other ski around to match. The trick is to make a good kick with the lower leg. If you're on a hillside, you will edge the uphill sides of the skis to prevent your sliding down sideways.

Herringbone

This technique will enable you to go straight up the fall line of a hill that is too steep for the skis to

A herringbone takes you directly uphill.

grip in the diagonal stride. Just angle your skis outward at the tips, and step upward from the inside edge of one ski to the inside edge of the other. Planting the pole opposite the weighted ski will help keep you from sliding backward. The herringbone can be tiring and somewhat awkward, but it is fast.

Sidestep

On the steepest hills you'll need to sidestep. With the skis across the hill drive your knees and ankles upward to stand on the uphill edges. Pick up the higher ski and move it laterally uphill, replacing it onto its uphill edge. Standing on that uphill ski, pick up the lower ski and place it next to the uphill ski. Repeat, using the poles to each side for balance. You can sidestep down intimidating slopes with this maneuver, too. The sidestep is also useful to gain or lose elevation while traversing forward on an open hillside.

GOING DOWNHILL

After all that uphill effort you're ready to relax and go downhill. Of course, if you're really after speed, you'll continue to stride or double pole downhill, but most of us like a breather now and then and enjoy letting gravity do some of the work for us.

Straight Runs

This is your primary downhill running position. Stand upright with feet comfortably apart (or in each track). Keep weight equal and also centered on each foot. Your hands are by your sides, with poles pointed backward. Flex at the ankles and knees. You're in an athletic stance, ready to balance for any changes of terrain or speed.

Let your legs act as shock absorbers as you ski over the dips and rises during your run. Flex at the knees on the bumps and extend at the knees in the hollows.

At times you'll want to go faster, either for greater thrills or to coast farther on a run out. To do this, reduce wind resistance by assuming a tuck position. Bring your body down toward your thighs. Maximum speed comes with the lowest egg-shaped position but is also most tiring on your thighs. A high tuck with straighter legs gives good speed, is less tiring, and allows you to absorb terrain changes better.

Slowing Down

No matter how daring you are, you'll need to slow down now and then. The primary way is in a *wedge*, a position with tips together and tails apart that forms an *A* as you look down at the skis. Stand flexed with ankles and knees bent and equal weight on both feet. The skis cross your direction of travel to slow you down. This wider stance adds stability. Press the knees and ankles toward each other to increase the skis' edging. This puts more resistance against the snow to brake your speed even more. Pushing the tails farther apart slows you down as well. A wide wedge is often called a *snowplow*.

If you're skiing down tracks, you can use this variation of the wedge to slow down. Simply pick one ski out of the track and pivot it out into a half wedge. Keep most of your weight on the tracking ski, controlling pressure and edging on the wedged ski as needed for slowing.

The wedge controls speed.

A tuck increases speed.

Using the poles in a side drag to slow down.

Sometimes the downhill is so steep you'll wish you also had an anchor to throw out. Well, you can use the poles much like an anchor in the pole drag. Remove the pole straps and hold the poles together on one side. Pull with one hand on the grips, pushing with the other hand in the middle of the poles to dig the points and baskets into the snow. To increase leverage rest the poles across the front of one knee. (I don't advise sitting on the poles to increase leverage, as some old-timers do —it can be hard on the anatomy.) For another variation of the pole drag place one pole grip behind each shoulder and each hand midway down the pole shaft.

TURNS

Turns are a vital part of skiing, both to avoid trees directly in your path and to slow down. Alpine turns were developed from these earlier Nordic turns. We'll use the terms *inside* and *outside* while talking about turns. An inside ski is the one that takes the inner path of the two skis in a turn. The outside ski takes the longer, outer path. When we use the term *parallel* we mean both skis are pointing in the same direction.

Step Turn

An easy way to change direction is simply to step or skate as you would on the flat. Pick up one ski, point it in the direction you want to go, and match it with the other ski. Take small steps to preserve your balance and remember to edge the sides of your skis in the direction of your turn. At higher speeds you'll lean your body in the direction of the turn. The step turn is especially handy for getting out of a fast downhill track or turning when you're in nasty, heavy snow, where other methods won't work.

Wedge Turns

Wedge turns are just like their Alpine counterpart. They are a primary way to turn on all slopes and in snow conditions other than deep, unpacked snow. In a wedge each ski points in a different direction. Just let the one pointing in your desired turn direction take over. You can do this by increasing ankle and knee flex on the dominant ski and pressuring it harder. You can aid the turn by increasing the edge of the dominant ski and by

A wedge turn.

A parallel turn.

pivoting your feet in the direction you're going.

Anytime your skis go steeper into the fall line they speed up. A big clue in the wedge (or any other) turn is to get forward as you start into the turn. This way your skis won't run out ahead of you.

Stem Turns

Stem turns are simply wedge turns that start from a traverse. Just push out the tail of the upper ski to start pointing it in the direction of the desired turn. Pressure the ski and place it on the inside edge and you'll enter into the turn.

In the stem christie you finish a turn in a parallel position. While completing a stem turn your inside ski is only lightly weighted. This ski can be slid in parallel. You'll skid sideways somewhat as you match the skis, and you've made a christie! This skid helps to slow you down.

When you're comfortable with the christie you

can add a pole plant. The inside (downhill) pole is planted at the same time you push off the lower ski to weight the stemmed upper ski. The pole plant will help your balance and also your skid.

Parallel Turns

Parallel turns are made when both skis are started into the new turn direction simultaneously. Flex downward at the ankles and knees and then extend upward, planting the inside pole at the same time. While the skis are lightened you pivot your feet in the direction of the new turn. Apply weight to the outside ski of the turn and flex downward to finish.

The big clue is to flex and extend with smoothness and rhythm, rather than with jerky motions. As the snow becomes deeper or your turns become shorter, you will want to increase the amount of your flexion and extension. It's not necessary to make parallel turns in Nordic skiing, but

they are fun and useful both on steeper slopes and in powder. Study the Alpine technique for additional ways to do them.

The Telemark

Now we come to the premier turn and the goal of many Nordic skiers—the Telemark. This is one turn that can't be done on Alpine equipment. It's both functional and graceful. It's primarily useful in heavy, deep, or cut-up snow, but is fun to do on packed surfaces also. You'll need a little speed to make it work. The Telemark is initiated like a small stem turn. However, you sink and drop the inside foot back, so that the inside ski tip is back toward the leading boot. The tip should be at least as far back as midway between the tip and boot of the leading ski. This is the Telemark position, which is held throughout the turn. Pressure is increased on the leading ski as in a diagonal stride, keeping just enough weight on the rear one for balance. Pivot the outside ski and lean into the turn to put both skis on their inside edges. At the end of this essentially carved turn bring the trailing ski forward for a stride or for another turn. I guarantee you'll never forget the feeling of accomplishment accompanying your first successful Telemark.

The Telemark.

8
Nordic Racing

If you are competitive or like to socialize, you might enjoy citizens' races. These are equivalent to the fun (or sometimes serious) jogging races and they are open to everyone. Find out about these races from your local ski shop or through race listings in Nordic periodicals. The other type of race is a sanctioned race. It's equivalent to a track-and-field competition, and the entrants must be classified by a national ski association.

In citizens' races you pay a small entry fee, take off in a mass start, and go. Awards are given by categories, so that you don't have to be the first person over the finish line to win, just the first in your class by age or sex. These races can be an entertaining way to improve your skiing and to meet other skiers.

There is no special technique involved in racing. As you would expect, efficient skiing with no

wasted motions promotes the fastest skiers. Weaving and bobbing, or even throwing your arms out too much on pole plants, will waste precious energy and time. Races are also great opportunities to watch "good" skiers to see how efficiently they can ski.

Here are a few hints to improve your race time. (1) First of all, you should have some conditioning under your belt, so don't enter a fifty-kilometer race if all you've ever done is fifteen kilometers. These are supposed to be enjoyable races, so enter the one that will be fun for you. (2) Besides conditioning ahead of time you can improve your performance on race day by getting adequate sleep and good meals the day before. Drink plenty of liquids both before and during the race. (3) Try to go over the course beforehand, so you know what to expect for terrain and when you'll need to conserve or expend extra energy. (4) Carry alternate waxes and clothing to the race site for race day weather changes. (5) Arrive early enough at the starting point to sign in, get your bib, prepare your skis, and warm up. (6) Enjoy the race and the party afterward. Even if you don't win, you will find pleasure in working your body and in exceeding your best time in previous races.

A mass start in a major competition. (Photo courtesy John King)

9
Nordic Glossary

BACKSLIP—A backward slide resulting from poor ski grip.

BAIL—A metal piece that clamps over the boot toe to fasten it to the ski.

BASE WAX—A wax applied prior to the day's wax to make the latter wear longer.

CHRISTIE—Finishing a turn in a parallel stance.

CITIZENS' RACE—A cross-country race for recreational skiers.

CORK—A block of cork or foam used to polish wax on ski bases.

DIAGONAL STRIDE—The basic Nordic form of propulsion, equivalent to walking, in which the opposite leg and arm move forward at the same time.

DOUBLE POLE—Using both poles at the same time to push forward.

GAITER—A water-repellent fabric cuff that is worn over the boot top to keep snow out of the boot.

GLIDE—Sliding forward.

GLIDER—A nongripping wax used at the ski tip and tail to improve the glide.

GRIP—Traction against the snow resulting from pressure on a ski, making a push forward possible.

HARD WAX—A solid wax in a can for new snow that has not melted and changed to another form.

HEEL PLATE—A device on the ski to keep the boot heel from twisting off sideways.

HERRINGBONE—A method of going directly up a hill, duckwalking with tips apart and tails close together.

KICK—A thrust on a gripping snow to propel a skier forward.

KICKER—The base area under the foot, which provides the main grip; also the wax applied to this area.

KLISTER—A sticky wax in tubes for old snow that has changed form from its original state by melting.

NORDIC NORM—A standard that defines boot and binding compatibility; often refers to the 75mm-wide system.

PARALLEL TURN—A turn in which both skis are rotated at the same time.

PIN BINDING—A binding with short cylindrical pins projecting upward to mate with matching holes in the sole at the boot toe.

POLING—Thrusting from the arms onto the poles for forward motion.

RACING NORM—A 50mm width standard for racing boots and bindings.

SKATE TURN—A turn in which one ski tip at a time is picked up and moved in the new direction.

SNOWPLOW—A wide wedge.

STEM—Spreading one ski tail out to make a wedge position.

STRIDE—The arm and leg movements, coordinated as in walking, that push a skier forward.

TELEMARK—A downhill turn characterized by flexed knees and the outside ski radically ahead of the inside ski.

TRAVERSE—To go across a hill rather than directly up or down the fall line.

TWO-WAX SYSTEM—Two waxes to cover all

conditions, one used for below freezing and one for above.

WAXABLE SKIS—Skis that require a special wax applied to the base for gripping the snow.

WAXLESS SKIS—Skis that grip the snow by some means other than wax.

WAX ZONE—An area marked on the ski base showing where to place kicker and glide waxes.

WEDGE—A stance with ski tips close together and tails spread apart, used for slowing and turning.

WIDE-RANGE WAX SYSTEM—A simplified two- or three-wax system for all snow conditions.

III

ALPINE SKIING

The Alpine World

What a crazy sport! Who in their right mind would leave a warm house, drive long distances, and pay money so they could ride an open, swaying chair in a blizzard, cartwheel down a mountain, eagerly repeat the process, and then reminisce fondly about it later?

There is a fascination to Alpine skiing. It's a world of glamorous resorts, high-tech equipment, big business, and intense racing. It's also a world where often there's just you, a mountain, a few trees, and ten billion snowflakes. You leave your problems back in stressful society and return to a challenge of a more elemental type.

The Alpine world is one of speed, but also one where time seems suspended. You discover something about your body and inner self as you fly down a mountain harmonizing with gravity and nature. You experience serenity, your body is strengthened and your spirit renewed.

Welcome to the world of Alpine skiing!

10
Gearing Up

Get ready to spend some money! Ski gear is expensive. We'll examine what equipment will suit you best so you can purchase the proper gear at the right price.

If you're new to the sport, rent your gear for the first few times. Don't buy anything until you're sure you like the sport and you are ready for gear more sophisticated than the specialized learning type.

A reputable ski shop is the best place to buy ski equipment. They have experienced personnel, a wide selection to match your needs, and the expertise to solve any problems that might occur after you purchase this equipment. If you're on a budget, consider buying last season's gear at special ski shop sales in the spring and early fall. Equipment does improve each year, but not so drastically as to make last year's gear obsolete.

Ski swaps and newspaper ads are another way to find inexpensive gear. However, when buying used equipment, if you find articles over five years old you may be handicapping yourself as to performance and safety. Also, you should ascertain if the equipment is suitable for your ability level and if it functions correctly.

BOOTS

Boots determine how well you ski. They shouldn't be an afterthought, chosen to match your ski cosmetics. They are your most important piece of equipment. Some skiers who ski only occasionally buy just boots, knowing that they can always rent skis, but renting properly fitted boots is difficult.

Boots perform many functions. They transmit all your turning forces directly to the skis; whether pivoting forces where your foot rotates, edging forces where your ankle moves laterally to angle a ski on edge, or pressure forces where your foot pulls up or pushes down on a ski. At the same time the boots have to keep your feet warm, absorb shocks of varying terrain, and feel comfortable enough to be worn all day.

You'll want a ski boot appropriate for your skiing level. The three general categories are recreational, sport, and racing. Recreational boots are designed for the casual, learning skier. They are forgiving, meaning they allow a newer skier to use exaggerated movements and get away with it. They are comfortable and soft-flexing enough that terrain changes such as bumps or choppy snow won't throw the skier all over. At the other end of the spectrum, racing boots are designed for a high-speed skier who has subtle skill control. They are stiff, close-fitting, and give instant response to any turning force. In between are the sport boots, sometimes called high-performance boots. They are stiffer and more responsive than recreational boots but slightly slower and less precise than racing boots. They are also less tiring and more forgiving than racing boots. An intermediate skier, particularly an athletic one, should be looking at this type of boot, which is also suited to advanced skiers.

Physically, boots come in two different styles, rear entry and front entry; and manufacturers and skiers argue over which is better. These styles are just approaches to the same problem of performance and fit. The traditional front-entry boot, sometimes called a *conventional* boot, has several buckles down the front that pull the overlapping pieces of outer shell closer together to make a tighter fit. Some front-entry boots have an external hinged tongue, which flips out of the way for easier entry and which "floats" to reduce skin abrasion. Buckle adjustment is crucial to fit so there are usually fine graduations in the buckle tightening system, known as a micro-adjustment.

The rear-entry boots are sometimes called *convenience* boots, as they are easy to slip into and only have one or two buckles. An internal cable in the boot pulls a strap over the instep to tighten the fit, rather than changing the size of the shell as conventional boots do. This internal fit is controlled by a lever separate from the shell-closing buckle, and it does not have to be adjusted each time the boot is put on. Other ways to fine tune the fit include additional internal straps on the forefoot or air bladders over the instep and around the ankle. The latter are inflated with a built-in pump.

Inside the outer shell all boots have an inner boot, which is removable for drying and custom-fitting. Also called *liners* or *bladders*, they pad you

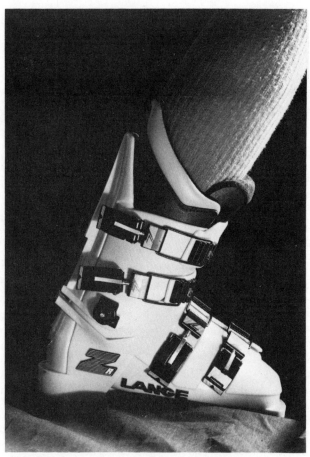

A conventional front-entry boot showing forward lean.

Rear-entry boots are easy to get into.

from the hard shell while remaining firm enough to transmit controlling forces to the skis. The liners conform to the shape of your particular foot. Some liners do this with a low-memory foam, which takes a set around foot protrusions. Higher-priced boots use "flow," a yielding plastic like a Silly Putty that flows slowly to mold around critical fit areas. Alternative custom-fit liners involve injecting a foam or electrically heating a pliable liner material, both of which then mold to your feet.

There are a few key terms to know when buying boots. Shells are hinged so they will pivot forward the same way your ankle does. *Flex* refers to the stiffness of this forward and backward movement of the shell. When the shell is moved beyond its neutral point it resists and tries to spring back. The flex both absorbs shocks and affects how pressure is transferred to the tips or tails of the skis with ankle flex. A stiffer flex is more responsive, but also more demanding and tiring than the soft flex of a recreational boot. Some boots have an adjustment to change flex to suit your particular type of skiing. For example, a day of high-speed turns on ice requires a stiffer flex than a day in moguls or deep snow.

Forward lean is the angle at which the boot pushes your lower leg forward. It's a combination

A cant adjustment and microadjusting buckles are useful features.

of a raised heel in the footbed plus the forward angle of the upper shaft. This makes you stand with flexed knees. Racing boots have a large forward lean, whereas recreational boots have less for a more upright, less fatiguing stance. Some boots let you change the forward lean angle by turning adjustment knobs or inserting a wedge-shaped plastic spacer.

Few lower legs form a perfect right angle with the feet. If your lower legs naturally flare outward, you will tend to ride your outside edges, causing wandering skis and inadequate edging. If your lower legs naturally flare inward, you will ride your inside edges constantly, leading to crossing tips or catching inside edges. A *cant adjustment* angles the upper boot shaft laterally to compensate for leg structure. Some boots have a built-in cant angle that fits the majority of skier legs. Others have a variable setting to adjust each boot over a wide range of cant angles.

All feet are not created equal. Try more than one brand in boots. Some manufacturers use lasts (shoe forms) that may be too wide or narrow for your foot. The most important consideration is proper fit. Pay no attention to the size stamped on the boot. Some manufacturers use an English sizing system, others the American, and some tell you to buy the boot two sizes below street shoe size. Some dispense with normal sizing and measure the volume of your foot. Many boots come in

A boot shaft set at a positive, or outward, cant. This boot also has a forward lean adjuster.

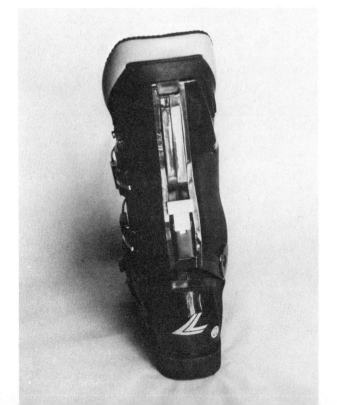

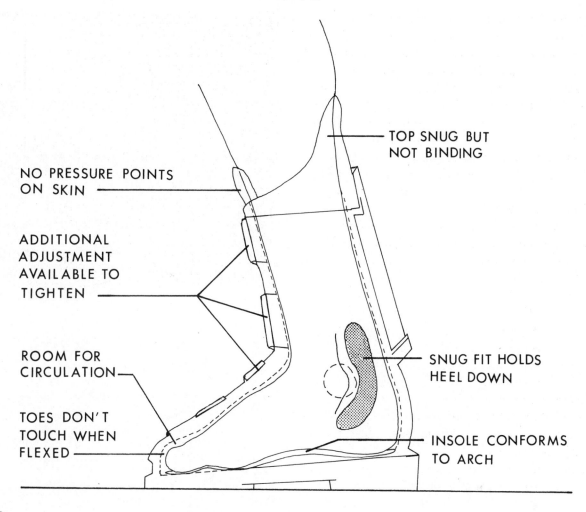

NO PRESSURE POINTS ON SKIN

ADDITIONAL ADJUSTMENT AVAILABLE TO TIGHTEN

ROOM FOR CIRCULATION

TOES DON'T TOUCH WHEN FLEXED

TOP SNUG BUT NOT BINDING

SNUG FIT HOLDS HEEL DOWN

INSOLE CONFORMS TO ARCH

Boot fit.

men's and women's models. Besides having more stylish colors, the women's models are scaled to fit the female's differing proportions in the heel, ankle, and calf. But many skiers find that a unisex model fits them just fine.

There are a lot of factors involved in selecting the best boot. Buy them in a ski shop that has a trained boot-fitting specialist. Tell your skill level, what slopes you ski, how often, how fast, and your ski length. The specialist will take into account your physical size and then have a good starting idea of what boots you might like. Here are some pointers for trying on boots:

1) Wear thin socks. Every liner will compress with wear, and you can switch to thicker socks when it does.

2) When you put your foot in there should be some solid support before you buckle up. If you need to tighten all the buckles radically, the shell is too big.

3) Leave a boot on for ten minutes to allow the liner to conform to your foot.

4) With no knee flex your toes should just touch the front. However, when you flex forward they will pull away. You should be able to wiggle your toes. If you can't, blood circulation may be restricted, causing cold toes.

5) The boot should grip snugly at the heel, instep, ankle, and ball of the foot. There should be no cramps, hot spots, or pressure points. Pain is magnified by at least a factor of ten on the slopes. Although the boot fitter can compensate for problems, it's best to start without any major ones.

6) When you flex forward the heel should not lift off the bottom by more than one-quarter of an inch. Also while flexing, pressure should be distributed along your shin and not concentrated in one spot.

Once you have selected them, have the boots custom-fitted to each foot. The ski shop can add or remove padding, modify the footbed, and expand the shell. After you've worn them for a few days you'll probably want to bring them back in for a fine-tuning of their fit.

Your ski boot specialist can also advise you about *orthotics*, which are firm custom-molded footbeds. Some skiers find them useful to increase their support and edging and reduce blistering and bruising. They are often recommended by podiatrists for severe pronation (weak ankles) in which a foot rolls inward with leg edging motions and spreads out when weight is placed on it.

BINDINGS

Don't skimp on your bindings. They cost only half as much as either your skis or boots and they are worth every penny. Knee injuries are the most common ski accidents, and many of them could have been prevented with proper binding protection. You should be especially wary if you pur-

The major release angles of bindings.

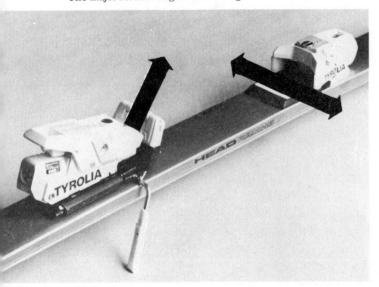

chase used bindings. They may be so worn or so outdated that they are unsafe.

Bindings are mechanical marvels that perform several tasks. They hold your boots firmly to the skis without any free play, but when you need to release in a fall, they release the boot before any strain can damage your leg. Bindings also distinguish between a fall and a momentary shock, such as when hitting a bump. They remain reliable despite extreme cold or immersion in water. On top of all this, they are expected to be easy to get into, lightweight, and attractive.

The most popular modern bindings have separate heel and toe pieces. They are all called *step-ins*. You cock the heel unit with a ski pole, insert your toe, and step down on your heel to latch. To release, you depress or lift the heel latch with your pole tip and step your heel out.

Bindings have two major release directions, laterally left and right at the toe, and vertically up at the heel. These directions cover the majority of falls. Most toe pieces also compensate for extreme pressure downward or upward at the toe in certain falls. A pressure-sensing mechanism and inclined pivot assure release in a backward twisting fall, or in a fall in which one ski is trapped under the other. Some heel units also release diagonally, as an additional safety factor. Other heel units engage the boot heel on a turntable, which rotates to aid twisting release.

Release depends upon compressing springs to a preset amount. This makes the release "elastic," in which the binding partially twists into the release position. If the necessary force is not reached, the binding snaps back to its normal position, a "return to center." This feature also gives shock absorption.

Ski brakes are integrated into the binding. These retract when your boot is inserted, but spring open the instant your boot leaves. They dig into the snow to keep your ski from running away. Outdated bindings will have a retention strap, erroneously called a *safety strap*, which clips around your leg. This keeps the ski from going anywhere in a fall, instead letting it swing around to bang you in the head. However, retention straps are often necessary in deep powder, when it's essential not to lose the ski.

An antifriction pad is incorporated in the toe

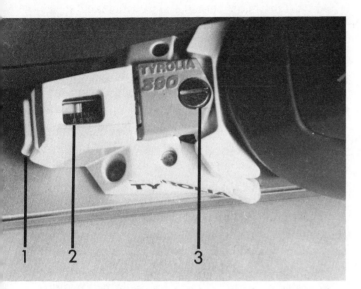

Toe features: (1) release adjustment; (2) release setting; (3) toe hold-down height adjuster.

unit. A flat area on your boot sole rests on it. When you take a twisting fall this slippery Teflon pad helps your boot to slide out of the toe unit.

Bindings should always be mounted by a ski shop. Although all binding adjustments should be done by a shop, it's helpful to have a working knowledge of your binding. The toe unit will have a screw to adjust the overall height of the toe hold-

Heel features: (1) heel hold-down height adjuster; (2) release lever; (3) release setting; (4) release adjuster; (5) forward pressure setting; (6) forward pressure adjustment (hidden under heel).

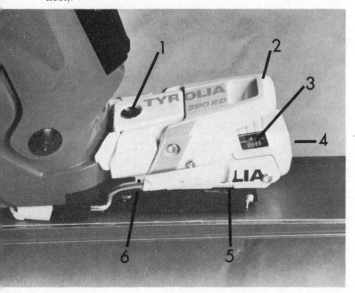

down, and also a slotted screw to adjust the release setting. There may be additional screws to change the position of pivoting pincers, which fit on either side of the boot toe. The heel unit will have a screw to adjust the release setting and also a mostly hidden screw or a tab to vary forward pressure. Sometimes there is a screw to adjust heel hold-down height.

The release setting is visually shown in a window with a pointer next to numbers from one to ten. All bindings conform to a set of standards known as DIN (Deutsche Industrie-Norm [German Industrial Standard]), which include forces required to release bindings. In theory all bindings set at the same DIN number should release at the same force. Your particular DIN setting depends upon your weight, strength, skiing speed, and age. Memorize the number the ski shop sets so you can check it to be sure it doesn't change accidentally.

To find your approximate DIN binding setting, divide your weight (in pounds) by thirty. The answer is your DIN setting for all-around intermediate skiing. If you're at the learning stage and under 150 pounds, subtract 0.5 from this setting; as a learner over 150 pounds, subtract 1.0 from this setting. If you're a more advanced, speedy skier and under 150 pounds, and 0.5 to this setting. Add 1.0 if you're over 150 pounds and aggressive.

You should also know about the visual indicator that shows forward pressure. The heel piece must push the boot forward to press firmly against the toe piece. Too little pressure and the boot is loose or falls out. Too much pressure and the toe won't release properly. Usually the indicator is a small arrow on the side of the heel unit. With proper pressure the arrow lines up within grooves inscribed on the binding base.

Each binding manufacturer offers several models. They are generally mechanically similar. High-performance bindings use heavier springs for higher release settings and alloy castings for extreme durability. Recreational bindings use lighter springs for lower release values and plastic housings for lower cost. If you're a 110-pound beginner, you can't use the highest-priced binding, which is made for heavy racers. Buy a binding that has a release range which includes your DIN value.

SKIS

Ski selection can be confusing. Thirty manufacturers offer five hundred models, each of which is advertised as the one to make you into a great skier. Years ago a skier selected a ski by flexing the tip, middle, and tail, and also by dropping the ski tail-first onto the floor to listen to it "twang." That's still fun to do in the ski shops, but with the new skis there are many other considerations to examine.

The primary rule in purchasing skis is to pick the type of ski suited to your particular skiing. Every ski manufacturer offers a wide range of selection within three general categories: recreational, sport, and racing. Each category is designed for a certain ability skier. There are also learning skis, designed for first-time skiers. They are short, about chest height, and are not skis you'll want to buy, as you'd very quickly outgrow them.

Recreational skis perform well at lower speeds on groomed terrain. They turn easily and are suited for relaxed, leisurely skiing. *Forgiving* is a common term used in describing this category, as they allow you to make errors in technique without disastrous results. If you are fairly new to the sport, if you're skidding your turn finishes, and if you go up to fifteen miles per hour, they are the type you'd want. Sport shops often offer them in a package with boots and bindings at a discounted price.

Sport skis are designed for use in varied snow conditions by the upper-intermediate to advanced skier. Sometimes called *performance skis*, they are somewhat forgiving, but respond faster than recreational skis. They work best in the fifteen-to-twenty-five-mile-per-hour range, in both skidded and carved turns on most all terrain.

Racing skis are the highest-performance models. Often this group is called *competition*. It includes both true racing models designed primarily for courses, and also high-performance skis for the advanced to expert skier. Racing skis are precise and quick responding, but don't allow much room for error. They are designed for higher speed, and various models cover all terrain or snow.

Some skiers ski mainly soft snow, others ice; some prefer bumps and others like high-speed cruising. Thus skis become more specialized as performance increases. In the racing and sport categories there are various subclasses. A slalom ski is made for quick, short turns on ice or hardpack. It starts and finishes turns aggressively. It's highly damped to prevent vibration and rather stiff. Slalom skis don't work too well in soft snow. They are a favorite choice among Eastern skiers. A giant slalom or "GS" ski is made for wider, higher-speed turns. It has a softer tip and tail than a slalom, so it starts and finishes turns more gently. The softer tip makes it better than a slalom in deeper or broken snow, and it's the favorite choice of many Western skiers. A very popular ski for good recreational skiers is the all-around high performance. It's a soft-flexing ski suitable for all snow from eastern hardpack to western powder. This detuned racing ski, sometimes called a *recreational racing ski,"* is not as high-strung as a full-blown racer. However, it is versatile enough to work on all terrain and even on racecourses.

Ski length.

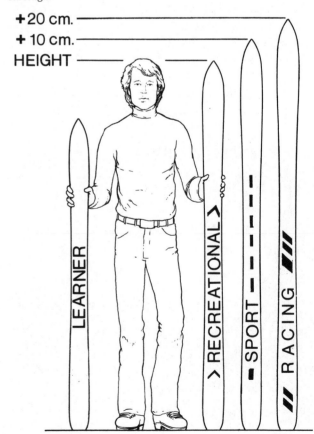

+20 cm.
+10 cm.
HEIGHT

LEARNER > RECREATIONAL > • SPORT • – • // RACING //

Powder skis are wide and soft-flexing, qualities needed for the deep and the cruddy snow. Mogul skis have a slalom design for quick turns, but also a softer tip to absorb shock. Cruisers are made for high-speed GS turns. They are soft-flexing, highly damped skis suitable for a smooth ride on any snow. Super G skis handle a combination of downhill speed and giant slalom turns. You'd better be a hot skier with a wide-open mountain to be on these!

Correct ski length differs for each person. A ski too short won't track well at speed, and a too-long ski is stable but hard work to turn. Some manufacturers offer sizing charts on which you crank in all your individual factors and come out with a correct length in centimeters. As a general guide to length, first figure out your height in centimeters. To do this multiply your height in inches by 2.54. The memorize the figure so you'll never have to multiply that out again. If you're buying a recreational ski, you'll want its length about equal to your height or up to five centimeters taller. In the sport group the correct length is about ten to fifteen centimeters greater than your height, and in the racing group twenty to twenty-five centimeters greater than your height. These are approximations and should be adjusted according to how heavy you are for your height, whether you cruise or ski bumps, and how fast you ski.

Space-age technology applied to ski construction.

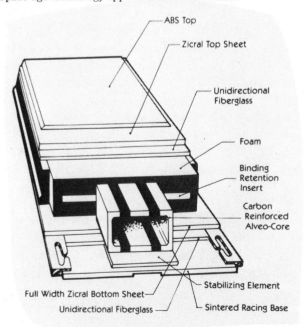

- ABS Top
- Zicral Top Sheet
- Unidirectional Fiberglass
- Foam
- Binding Retention Insert
- Carbon Reinforced Alveo-Core
- Stabilizing Element
- Full Width Zicral Bottom Sheet
- Unidirectional Fiberglass
- Sintered Racing Base

If you look at a cutaway of a ski, you'll discover one reason why they cost so much. Ski insides are fascinating glimpses into space-age technology. Each manufacturer combines various materials to achieve similar ski responses, so don't be too influenced by whether the ski has polycarbonated kryptonite fibers or compressed sagebrush. Do pay attention to the guarantee, however. It shows whether the manufacturer really believes that all those insides will hold together on the slopes.

One difference does exist among the ski base materials. More expensive skis use a "sintered base" made from an extra-hard polyethylene. Compared to a standard extruded base, the sintered bases are faster, hold wax better, and are more abrasion-resistant. In the finishing stage of manufacture they are "stone ground" rather than sanded. Although costing more initially, sintered bases reduce the number of times you'll need your skis tuned and waxed.

You'll run into several somewhat technical terms while reading brochures or tests in ski periodicals, and you may want to know how to interpret them. While looking at technical figures, don't be swayed by just one of them. How a ski reacts on the snow is a combination of all these figures. The weight of a ski is fairly obvious. A lighter ski is generally easier to maneuver and a heavy ski is more stable. Of course, the weight varies with the length. If the "waist width" is given, that figure refers to the dimension at the narrowest part of the ski. Wide skis are more stable, but not as quick moving from edge to edge as narrower skis.

The "turn index" is an interesting measure of the physical sidecut of a ski. Sidecut is simply the hourglass shape of a ski due to its wide tip and tail compared to the waist. Sometimes called the *sidecut radius* or *natural turning radius*, this figure indicates how wide a turn the ski carves. Higher numbers indicate skis made for long, high-speed turns, and lower numbers indicate skis made for short, quick turns.

Skis deform, or flex, from their natural bowed shape when you put weight on them. The "overall stiffness" refers to how easily the whole ski flexes when pressured in the middle. A high flex number means a stiff ski, one more suited to hard snow, to a heavier skier, and to high speed. A low flex number refers to a soft ski, one better for bumps, for slower speed, and for a lighter skier. When you weight a ski, the pressure is distributed unequally throughout the length of the ski. The shovel, middle, and heel all flex differently. A ski with low numbers for the shovel stiffness and tail stiffness is soft in these areas. It's generally a forgiving ski, good in powder, in moguls, and at high speed, as the tips float and absorb shock. Skis with stiff shovels and tails enter turns more quickly and hold better on hard snow.

If you can, try before you buy. Many ski shops rent demonstration skis and deduct the rental fee from your purchase if you decide to buy. Sometimes the manufacturer's local representative sponsors "demo days" at ski areas during which he or she pulls up to the slopes with a vanload of the latest skis. You can try them out for a few hours at no charge.

After all this information about choosing skis, I have some final advice. Choose skis whose color or graphics you like! Skiing is very psychological and ego-satisfying. If you prefer fire engine red, you'll ski much better on a pair that color than you will on forest green ones. Live it up!

POLES

Buying poles is relatively easy. Basically, get a pair that feels good, in your price range, with graphics you like. But consider these few fine points.

You want a well-balanced pole that responds quickly. If you take a different model pole in each hand and start whipping the tips back and forth in simulated plants, you can feel a difference. Technically, how fast a pole can swing into a plant is called its *swing weight*. More expensive poles have shafts made of a strong 7000-series aluminum alloy. They have an edge in feel over less expensive poles made from a thicker and heavier 6000-series alloy.

Grips are either a strapless or a strap type. The strapless are quick to put on and off. They are also quite safe if you catch the basket on anything, as the pole pulls away from the hand. However, if you are prone to releasing your poles in a fall, you'll be picking them up after each spill.

Unlike the strap grips of years ago, the new strap

Strap and strapless pole grips.

type provides a platform to rest the base of your hand against. Straps have the advantage of allowing the pole pivot point to move to the top of the grip, eliminating extra cocking of your wrist. Your hands stay attached to the poles when you release the grips, so you can easily place your hands on top for certain maneuvers, or can let the poles dangle while you adjust zippers and the like. Poles with straps also hang up easily for storage. Try to buy releasable or "break-away straps," so that if your basket snags something you won't dislocate a shoulder.

In either style, try the grips with the thickest mittens you'll be wearing. Some grips won't accommodate large hands. A few grips offer extra protection over the thumb; a valuable asset, as hurt thumbs are the second most common slope injury.

Avoid baskets with an open ring. Most modern baskets come in a snowflake design that has no large holes to snag obstacles. Some baskets have shaped slots where the other pole shaft clips to hold them together.

Only very low-quality poles have a drawn point made from the shaft. Better poles have an inserted tip. To avoid puncture wounds, this tip should not be pencil-shaped, but rather a rounded, or crater, shape with a sharp rim. Good tips can be sharpened or replaced when they become dull.

Length is somewhat a matter of preference.

Measuring for correct pole length.

layer wool or a polypropylene type is best. A cotton turtleneck goes on top. It has an elasticized knit neck and cuffs to keep out drafts, and the neck band can be turned up for extra protection. (If you purchase one with a zipper at the neck you can unzip the turtleneck on sunny spring days to turn it into a conventional collar.) A wool or wool-blend sweater goes over this.

Stretch wool ski pants are the traditional leg covering. Many skiers prefer insulated warm-up pants, especially the bib style, which provides extra snow protection and warmth. With either of these you'll want an insulated parka. One- or two-piece matching suits are popular, taking care of the leg and body outer covering at the same time. Many skiers like the powder suit, a loose-fitting noninsulated garment worn over your other clothing. Wear a wool hat, large enough to cover the ear tips and snug enough so that it won't blow off in a strong wind. It provides warmth even when wet.

Quality handcovering is a good investment. Mittens are warmer than gloves, although some skiers prefer the dexterity of individual fingers. In either case, preserve the leather with a special leather oil or saddle soap. If you prefer low-maintenance gloves or mittens, several manufacturers are making them of waterproof fabrics. They are lightweight, flexible, and surprisingly durable. For extra warmth, wear wool or silk glove liners.

When buying ski apparel, remember that the outer layers must protect you from wind and snow. The fabrics should be water-repellent, tear-, and abrasion-resistant. They should also be "nongliss" so when the snow snakes trip you on steeper terrain you won't slide great distances. Cuffs on the parka or windshirt bottom and on the sleeves keep out snow and cold air and are extremely important in the insulated pants to keep snow out of the boot tops. Quality skiwear has a flap either over or behind the zippers for extra wind protection. These zippers function more easily if they have large pulls you can grasp while wearing mittens.

Lots of pockets are handy. You'll find ways to fill them all. Remember to carry skin and lip sun protection, a trail map, and Kleenex. You might want a pocket camera, money, candy bar, and face mask in the pockets also.

You'll need goggles or sunglasses. In either case

While in the store turn the pole upside down, put the grip on the floor, and grasp the shaft just below the basket. Your forearm should be parallel to the ground for correct length. Longer poles can always be cut down in length, but shorter poles can only be given to shorter skiers.

APPAREL AND ACCESSORIES

Function before fashion is a good choice in apparel. However, a visit to a ski shop will convince you that you can easily have both. Styles and colors in ski clothes change seasonally as in the high-fashion world. If you're economizing, choose functional clothes in basic colors. You can get by without special ski apparel if you wear lots of wool. That includes pants. Blue jeans will soak up water and make you cold.

Dress in layers for maximum protection. Each layer traps insulating air. It's also easier to strip down when you're too warm, and by coordinating the layers you have the look of several outfits.

Start with long underwear for cold days. A two-

they should be distortion-free and filter out damaging ultraviolet rays. Lens color choice is a personal preference. The traditional favorite for snowy days is yellow, and for sunny days gray or brown. For all-around use, gold-green is a favorite. Some lenses darken with increased sunlight. Polarized lenses are best for maximum glare reduction.

Most goggles resist fogging with a chemical coating on the inside of the lens and also an airflow system to remove moisture. Some have a double insulated lens to reduce fogging and to keep snow from melting on the outside lens. Soft, flexible lenses are popular, as they don't crack as easily as rigid ones if you accidentally sit or step on them. When buying, look through the edges of the lens and reject them if you see distortion. Check the fit of the frame to your face. If you wear glasses, you'll need a deeper, larger model to accommodate them. Even "scratch-resistant" plastic will scratch, so store the goggles in a soft protective bag. When the inside lens gets wet blot it with a soft cloth, but don't rub. If you need to clean the outside lens, use mild soap and water, wiping gently.

11
The Care and Feeding of Your Equipment

You should routinely maintain your ski gear for top performance. This is just like checking the oil, water, and gas levels in your car. It takes only a minute and saves hours of problems.

BINDINGS

Bindings are rugged devices, but like any mechanical contraption with moving parts, they can go out of whack. They are your protection against injury, so routine attention to them is important.

Visually check your bindings before each day's use. They are full of screws, which can loosen from vibration. Make sure the screws that hold the binding to the skis are still there and tight.

After stepping into your bindings, wiggle each foot to see if there's any free play between the boot and binding. Up-and-down play indicates the toe or heel hold-downs need adjusting. Side-to-side play at the toe often means the forward pressure adjustment has slipped. It's a good idea to check this forward pressure visual indicator now and then to make sure you're still within the OK range. Also inspect the brakes. They should all be fully retracted.

Even if everything looks fine, perform an on-the-snow release check once in a while. Take a spill just to see if the bindings function! Check binding release on a level area. For the toes, place a ski on its inside edge, flex deeply in that leg, and twist inward to release. If this stresses your knee joint, your binding release may be set too high. Another toe check is to kick a boot toe outward with the heel of the other boot. The heel release

is easier if you can brace the ski tip against something solid. Flex a knee forward, pulling up your heel. Be sure to balance with your poles, as you'll catapult forward when the binding pops upward.

Dirt is a major binding enemy. Wipe off the boot contact surfaces frequently. Clean out the mud and pebbles that accumulate under the pad activating the brakes. If an antifriction pad is scratched, have it replaced. Certain bindings recommend an occasional lubricant spray such as silicone. If you're not sure about your particular bindings, stop at your ski shop for a quick lube job.

Whenever you take off your skis, it's a good idea to whisk loose wet snow off the binding areas. This snow can freeze up if you place your skis in the shade, or take them to a colder area on a gondola. The ice layer changes the way your boots fit the bindings, and you could pop out unexpectedly.

BOOTS

Boots are relatively maintenance-free. Your main job will be thoroughly drying the inner liners. Besides keeping your feet warm, this will preserve the liner materials. Remove the liners to dry them or place your hair dryer in them for a few minutes. Be sure it is on a "cool" setting. *Never* subject either the boots or liners to direct heat, such as near a fire or over a radiator, because they can melt or deform the liner material.

The shell is quite tough and abrasion-resistant. However, these boots are not made for walking

A replaceable heel insert.

and the sole wears quickly. This abrasion at the heel and toe can cause binding malfunction. Limit your pavement walking but if you must, consider wearing a pair of rubber slip-on sole protectors. They also grip into the snow to prevent falls. If your boots have a replaceable heel insert, change it when it starts to wear over. Anytime you step off the snow you're picking up dirt particles, which affect binding release. Carefully clean off the boot sole and the complete heel and toe areas where the binding latches before stepping into them. Rubbing your boots in fresh snow does this job quickly.

POLES

Poles are almost maintenance-free! Check your baskets now and then. If they are cracked near the shaft, replace them before they fall off on the slopes. You want the grips to stay attached to the poles also. Twist and pull upward on each one while holding the shaft in the other hand. If they come loose, have them glued on. Check your shafts for bends by rolling the shaft between the grip and basket on a tabletop. A ski shop can straighten slight bends before they become worse.

SKIS

I run across too many students having difficulty skiing when much of their problem is caused by nontuned skis. Skis may need maintenance after only a few days on the slope. Ski shops can wax

skis in a few minutes or do a complete tune-up overnight. However, you can do much of this maintenance yourself.

Turn your skis over and look at the bottoms. Ideal bases are flat, smoothly waxed, free of gouges, with shiny, sharp edges. Few skis meet all these criteria. The most frequent maintenance they'll require is waxing, but we'll go through a complete tune-up in sequence so you know all the steps. Arrange a work space, ideally a bench with a ski vise. Dry your skis, let them warm to room temperature, and wipe the bottoms clean.

Ski brakes are going to get in your way for all tuning operations. Prop them out of the way by wrapping a heavy rubber band around the prongs and over the binding, or by sliding a Popsicle stick under the prongs. Use your ingenuity if these items are not handy.

Base repair. Sintered bases are quite durable and seldom need repair. The softer extruded bases are subject to scrapes and gouges. These drag in the snow and also hinder easy turning. Large gouges that go down to the fiberglass base or expose a long section of steel edge should be repaired by your ski shop. Repair small gouges in extruded bases with a stick of polyethylene, commonly called a *P-tex candle*. Light it with a disposable butane lighter and hold the candle flame downward until it's burning steadily. Watch where the drips go, as they can start a fire where

Prop the brakes out of the way while tuning.

they land, and they really smart when they drop on your skin. If you are fastidious, catch the drips on a steel scraper. Hold the burning candle just above the ski base, allowing the melting P-tex to flow into the gouges. Overfill the area so it protrudes slightly above the base. Extinguish the candle in a glass of water and let the repaired areas harden. Now scrape the P-tex down to the base level using a steel scraper. You'll want to hold the scraper about forty-five degrees to the ski with the thin edge making contact with the ski base. Rub with a Scotch Brite pad or with extra-fine steel wool for a final buffing to hide the repairs.

Bottom filing (or flat filing). If you can see that your edges are rusty or rounded with major cuts across them, you may need a major tune-up at a shop. Bottom filing sharpens the edges and makes the bases flat (hence flat filing). Snow abrasion wears away the plastic bottom material faster than the steel edges, so the edges eventually stick up above the base. This is called *railing*, when indeed the skis seem to ride on rails and refuse to turn or slide sideways. A rough idea of the base condition can be obtained by holding the skis bottom to bottom, lightly pressing out some camber, and sliding the skis sideways across each other. Railed skis catch one edge against another. For an accurate base inspection, use a rigid straightedge such as a true bar or your steel scraper. Hold the straightedge across a base and sight down along the ski toward a light source. If you can see light under the straightedge, then you are holding a railed ski. Move the straightedge all along the ski, as some areas will be railed worse than others. Occasionally you may encounter an improperly tuned ski with a convex base that is higher than the steel edges. Use the steel scraper on this ski to scrape down the excess base.

You should know if your skis came with perfectly straight edges or with beveled edges, edges that are ground upward from the base by a degree or two. Many high-performance skis have beveled edges, and some skiers prefer to bevel their edges anyway, as it makes the skis less "catchy" and easier to turn. Beveled edges should not be filed flat to the base. See the special instructions in the last paragraph of this bottom-filing section for their care.

My favorite file for flat filing is the ten-inch mill

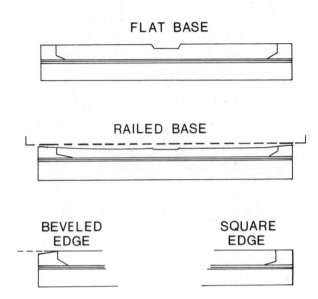

A flat base, a railed base, beveled edges, and square edges.

bastard. The file is designed to cut in only one direction. If you want to push the file away from you, hold the file tang (the pointed end or handle) in your right hand. If you feel more comfortable pulling the file toward you, hold the tang in your left hand. Either grip uses the cutting teeth properly. If you are using any other-style file, be sure you know the correct way to hold it.

Hold the file flat on the base, with the left side farther away than the right so that the file makes a forty-five-degree angle to the edges. File in overlapping strokes, working from tip to tail. Lift the file between strokes so it doesn't dig into the edges in its noncutting direction. Use light pressure, keeping it even on both edges. Keep your hands close to the skis, with thumbs on top over the edges to avoid distorting the flatness of the file.

Little metal filings are pared off with each stroke, so wipe the base frequently to avoid embedding them there. Also, clean the file frequently with a file card, a set of stiff metal wires on a handle. Brush in the direction of the file grooves. Particles of wax or other material clogging the grooves can also be removed with a solvent or with hot water. Your file may last for six to twelve filings; then it's time for a new one.

Check with your straightedge so you'll know when the base is flat again. You can also see the file begin to ride on the plastic instead of just on the metal edges.

Generally, beveled edges are filed one edge at a time by wrapping tape on the file where it rides on the far side of the base. This tape should be a maximum of half a millimeter thick—not much more than a business card. Another method, which requires practice, is to hold the file at the extreme ends and bend it while filing. Too much beveling can cause the ski to lose its edge hold and to chatter on hard snow. Check with your ski shop for their recommended tools and specific directions for your particular skis.

Side filing.   Side filing finishes the sharpening job by removing metal from the edge on the thin sidewall of the ski. The idea is to file that edge to a perfect ninety-degree angle, and slight variations in the angle of the file will change that angle. With practice you may be able to hold a file at a true right angle by running a finger or your knuckles on the base as a guide. However, for best results use a commercially made file holder with a guide block that runs along the base.

Clamp the ski with a side edge upward. As in bottom filing, use overlapping smooth strokes in the file's cutting direction. The edges do not protrude much from the side wall, so this is not a vigorous type of filing that can remove too much edge, but rather a smoothing, touch-up job.

Finishing touches to filing.   The edges are now sharpened all the way to the ends, where you don't need much edge. Sharp tips and tails cause the skis to "hook" and "grab." Take your file at a forty-five-degree angle to the edge and lightly dull the last three inches of the tails and six inches back from the tips. These amounts are variable depending on how you like your skis to react and the type of snow you're skiing. If you carry a pocket stone, you can dull your skis on the slopes, or even take out burrs that you acquire when you accidentally run over a hefty rock in the snow.

The remaining sharpened edges have microscopic burrs all along them, which make them feel too sharp. These burrs can cause an erratic grip on the snow and are removed with a fine-grade pocket whetstone. Hold the stone flat on the base and run it along the edge. Then hold it flat on the side edge and run the length of the ski. If you hit a rough area, rub a little with the stone. Now hold the stone at a forty-five-degree angle to the edge and run it very lightly along the whole length. You can substitute fine emery cloth wrapped around a wooden block or around the file for the whetstone. You now have an edge that will scrape a little white from a fingernail run across it and that will do an even better job on snow.

Major repairs.   Ski bases become too damaged for minor repairs after enough miles on abrasive snow and granite outcroppings. Your ski shop has special machines to grind down the bases to a new smooth surface, which then needs base preparation and hand filing. This sanding can only be done a few times before you're out of base, but each time it's like owning a new pair of skis.

Waxing.   All skis need frequent waxing! In fact, on abrasive snow, waxing can be a daily requirement, to reduce friction so that you can control them and turn more easily. Look at your bases. If the polyethylene is whitish, they are oxidized and are long overdue for a waxing job.

Some touch-up waxes spray or wipe on, and certain waxes for slush rub on, but for the most durability you'll need to "hot wax." Buy an old flatiron (the nonsteam variety) at your local thrift shop—once wax is on it you won't want to iron anything else with it. Choose a block of Alpine wax (different from cross-country wax) suitable for the temperature. Manufacturers color-code their waxes. For instance, one brand might be red for above thirty-two degrees F., blue for eighteen to thirty-two degrees, and green for below eighteen de-

The grip for pulling a file toward you.

Drip on the wax, iron it smooth at low heat, and scrape down to a thin layer.

grees. If you have new skis that haven't been "prepped," seal the bases first with a soft wax intended for warm weather, then apply the appropriate condition wax.

Turn your iron to the "wool" setting. It should melt the wax without making it smoke. Wipe your ski bases clean and dry. Hold the bar of wax against the iron and drip a stream down one side of the ski base and up the other. Then iron the wax smooth, *keeping the iron moving constantly.* Too much heat will damage the base. If there are any bare spots, add more wax. When it has hardened scrape down the excess with a plastic scraper, leaving only a thin layer on the base. If your skis have grooves, clean out wax that has settled in there. A teaspoon works well on rounded grooves. For square grooves try a blunt screwdriver of the correct width. And apply some auto wax to the top

surface. It hides scratches and makes snow slide off easily.

Transporting skis to the slopes can be rough on them. A ski bag prevents new scratches and gouges, particularly on public transportation. If you carry skis on a car roof rack, you're embedding them with road grime and salt, hard on the skis and murder on the bindings. If you don't have ski bags, at least buy the short binding covers, which offer some protection. Airlines will usually let you have some of their plastic ski travel bags, which you can put over the skis for roof rack rides.

Put a thick coat of wax on your skis before storing them for the summer. This keeps the edges from rusting. Scrape it off in the fall, and your boards are ready to go. Keep them clean, sharp, and waxed, and your skis will outperform any non-tuned thousand-dollar wonder ski.

12
Going Up

Thank goodness for lifts! Their invention spurred the popularity of Alpine skiing, which changed the whole spectrum of skiing from equipment to technique. As you've discovered after walking uphill for five minutes, they are indispensable.

A few areas have a special free lift just for beginners, but at most you'll need to buy a lift ticket. (An exception is for ski school beginners' classes, where the first ride is usually free.) You can save some money by checking various rates for the tickets. Certain areas have a reduced-cost "beginners' lifts only" ticket. If you're getting a late start in the day, most areas offer a half-day rate, generally starting between noon and 1:00 P.M. As a student, senior citizen, or member of the armed forces, you may get a reduced price. Multiday tickets discount the daily cost, but weigh the advantages of buying these against the fact that you might not use all the days because of storms. If you ski frequently at one area, a season pass or discount card offers the lowest rate per day.

Your daily ticket usually sticks to a metal loop, which is first attached to your clothing. Read the directions on how to apply the sticky side of the ticket to the loop so it stays on. Ticket checkers frown on placing the tickets on hats, gloves, or other apparel easily traded from one person to another. Attach the ticket to an item of clothing you'll wear all day and not to a parka you may want to discard in the hot afternoon sun.

Slopes magically become steeper when you're at the top staring down them. Plan which lifts you'll take by studying the area trail map or talk to the patrol about lifts for skiers of your ability.

Many aerial lifts are also access lifts to easier slopes and beginners' lifts. You may ride these downhill again to get back to the base lodge. Check your lift ticket privileges, as you may be able to ride certain lifts for a scenic nonski ride to the mountain summit and back again.

One final step before the lift ride is to tuck in loose clothing. Long scarves, gloves dangling from zippers, parkas tied around the waist, and braids have an affinity for attaching themselves to lift machinery and refusing to let go when you want to get off. I remember spending an hour one bitter cold day retrieving a rucksack entwined in a chair, while my friends were enjoying lunch by a fire.

Make sure you know how to ride the lift you're in line for. If in doubt, ask the operator and observe others loading ahead of you.

SURFACE LIFTS

Rope tows are the original uphill lifts and are still found at smaller, low-budget areas. Step over to the rope with your skis pointing straight up the track. Your pole straps should be around your wrists. With strapless grips you'll need to grip the rope with one hand, and the poles with the other. Gently grasp the rope, letting it slide through your gloves. Gradually increase pressure until you're moving the same speed as the rope. When you reach the top just let go of the rope and step away. Experienced rope tow riders wear thick leather mittens and grasp the rope with the outside arm behind the back to relieve arm strain.

A Mitey Mite is a slow-moving rope tow with

The T-bar pulls you along.

The Poma Lift, sometimes called a *platter pull*, is made for one person. Move to the loading area with your skis pointed up the track and both poles in the hand away from the attendant. When he or she hands you the bar, pull it down and place the platter between your legs and against your fanny. Don't sit, but just stand upright and the seat-shaped disk will pull you along. To unload, pull down on the bar, bring the disk out from between your legs, let go gently, and ski away.

Stand up as the poma pulls you uphill.

handles. Approach it as you would a rope tow. When a handle comes by just grasp it with one or both hands. At the top let go and step away.

The T-Bar is a common two-person surface lift. It is not intended to be sat upon, but rather to pull you along by the bar, which is shaped like an upside-down *T*. This rests behind your fanny. After the skiers ahead of you have loaded, move right in. Stand next to your partner with poles held midway in the outside hand (the hand away from your partner.) Point your skis straight up the hill. Look over your inside shoulder to grasp the bar as the attendant hands it to you. Place the *T* under your bottom, and it will pull you along. There may be a lurch as you start out, but your flexed knees will absorb the shock and any others you may encounter along the track. Keep your skis flat on the snow. If they tend to hit your partner's skis, lean toward your partner, and your feet will move away and back into their own track. While gliding along decide whether you or your partner will unload first. Whoever has the honor skis out of the way at the top and the remaining rider pulls the *T* down and out from under him or her, releases it gently, and skis away. If you take a spill while riding, just let go of the bar and move quickly out of the track. Reassemble yourself and ski back to the loading ramp for another try. If you must unload anywhere before the top, do it above a support tower, releasing the bar gently to avoid wrapping it around the cable.

The J-bar is a variation on the T-bar. As you guessed, the bar is shaped like a *J* and ridden singly but otherwise similarly.

AERIAL LIFTS

Trams and Gondolas are the premier aerial lifts and are especially great on stormy days. Riding them is pretty much self-evident; skis go on the outside of the gondolas, and you take your poles inside. On a tram you'll be standing all the way, so loosen your boots ahead of time. You won't have room to move once you're stuffed in a car with sixty-two people who ate garlic for breakfast.

Chair Lifts were invented by a company that unloaded banana boats using a conveyor-belt system equipped with hooks. Chairs are actually the easiest and most enjoyable lifts to ride. They generally hold two people cozily, although triple and quadruple lifts are increasingly popular. As you move into line, find a partner to ride with. Calling out "Single" will elicit response from a nonpaired person (a great way to meet people). Remove your

Loading: grasp the support bar, sit down, and enjoy the ride.

until you ski away from it. As you ski down the ramp *lean forward* to stay balanced over the skis. Without this forward lean from the ankles you'll fall backward as your skis accelerate down a short unloading ramp. Move wall away from the ramp, leaving room for others to unload. If for some reason you forget to get off the chair, don't jump. The operator will help you off. It may seem embarrassing, but it can happen to anyone.

Lift stoppage is perfectly normal. Automatic safety devices and operators controlling the lifts stop them the instant anyone has difficulty loading or unloading. If a surface lift stops while you are riding it, just stay in the track. If you are on an aerial lift and it stops, have patience and faith. Even in the rare event of a breakdown, auxiliary drive motors will get you to the top.

Don't be so enamored of skiing down that you miss the pleasures of riding uphill. Lift rides are great times to talk to your partner or to listen to nature's sounds. Look around to see the whole length of a trail you'll soon be skiing down. Observe other skiers below you and their technique to see why it's good or bad. Watch the clouds drift by, identify trees, see the snow sparkle, find animal tracks in the snow, or turn your eyes to the magnificence of the hills around you. It's a time to relax your muscles, catch your breath, and refresh your soul.

Unloading: stand up and lean forward.

pole straps from your wrist. After a chair has swung past to load the skiers ahead of you, move in quickly and stand next to your partner on the indicated spot, a recessed board that has been cleared of snow. Point your skis straight ahead the way the chairs go. Use your ski poles to move in, but once in position hold them by the middle and out of the way in the hand away from the support bar. Some chairs have one support bar rising from the middle of the seat, in which case look for it over your inside shoulder, toward your partner. If the chair has two support bars, one rising from each side of the seat, look for it over your outside shoulder. As the chair comes, pretend someone is handing you a kitchen chair. Grasp the support bar with your free hand and sit down when the chair touches the back of your legs. Let the skis run straight ahead on the ramp, and you are soon airborne. If your chair has a footrest, pull it down, relax, and enjoy the ride.

Push the footrest back up before you get off. When you reach the unloading ramp stand straight up from the knees so that you are no longer in the chair. Hold the poles out of the way in one hand and keep the other hand on the edge of the chair

13
Your First Time

Your first time on skis can be an enthralling and mystifying experience as you enter a whole new world. You'll experience terror, exhilaration, and a sense of accomplishment as you streak along at two or three miles per hour, fighting to stay upright and wondering if you'll ever slow down. You'll remember that first run fondly throughout your skiing career.

This chapter will help you through your first few days of skiing so that your experience will be enjoyable and safe. We'll keep technical jargon to a minimum. This is a time to go out and discover the joys of skiing without trying to think about technical details. The technique chapters that follow will help you improve upon the basic skills you'll develop in these first days.

EQUIPPING YOURSELF

For your first couple of times on skis I'd suggest renting all the gear. Beginner skis are shorter than the recreational skis you may want to purchase eventually. Borrowing equipment from a friend might be okay, but don't hinder yourself by taking skis more than chin height, boots that don't fit, or skis with gouged bases and rusty edges. Also, if you do borrow equipment, have the bindings professionally adjusted.

If you're planning a one-day trip to a ski area, you might want to rent from a local store. This way you can try on and become familiar with the gear in the privacy of your living room the evening before your adventure. (I'd especially advise putting the boots and skis on to get the feeling of standing on them and also to practice getting up from the floor.) By renting locally you'll also avoid the hassle of having to fight lines of people at the ski area rental shop at nine o'clock Saturday morning. However, if you're going for several days, you may prefer to rent your equipment at the ski area. That way you can easily exchange boots that don't fit well, or you can have any other necessary adjustments made.

Whenever you rent your gear, take time at the rental shop to make sure you know how the boots fasten and how the bindings latch and release.

Once you have the gear take a minute to study the skis and poles so you can recognize them. There will be 4,999 other pairs of skis and poles propped against the ski racks when you come out after lunch at the ski area. They will all look vaguely the same. It's a good idea to write down the serial numbers of your skis. For fastest identification place a piece of masking tape on each ski and pole and write your name on it. Even if you can find where you left your skis, this prevents some other confused first-timer from mistakenly taking them because they look just like his.

GETTING TO THE SLOPES

Before you can ski, you have to get to the snow from wherever your transportation leaves you. As you stand there in awkward boots with heavy skis and dagger-sharp poles, you may look around for the ski caddy. However, walking with the gear is really simple.

First, unfasten all your upper boot buckles. If

you have a single buckle in the rear, loosen it. You want to be able to flex your ankle, which then gives you the freedom to walk normally or even to climb stairs easily.

Next, fasten your skis together bottom to bottom. The safety brakes will clip them to one another if you place one tail first on the snow, hold the other one slightly higher, press them together, and slide the top ski down until the brakes lock. Now pick them up and place them flat on your shoulder within the area where the binding is attached. The skis will balance there. Grip them with one hand near the tails to keep them effortlessly in place. Both poles go in the other hand. Some models clip together if you place the tip of one within a notch in the other's basket.

Ski brakes clip the skis together.

Before you move, think what happens if you twist around now. The tips of the skis will swing around to hit your former friends. Use care, and if necessary, tilt the skis' angle so the tips are higher in the air. In very confined, crowded areas, take the skis off your shoulder and carry them upright in front of you, resting the tails on the snow as you walk.

While you're walking, use the pole tips as you would a cane to provide support on the slick area.

SADDLING UP

When you arrive at the ski area you'll find a base facility with food, day storage lockers, and rest rooms. Visit whichever facilities you need, bypass the lift ticket window, and head to the absolute beginner's area.

Find a level spot to practice and to put on your skis. Pull the skis apart and place them down on the snow side by side. Stick your poles into the snow, one on the outside of each ski. Fasten your boot buckles snugly but not overly tight. Now straddle the skis and open the bindings. Lean on a pole for balance and check your boot sole for sticking snow, which would prevent it from fitting into the binding. Knock off loose snow by tapping your boot with the other pole shaft. If ice is caked on the sole, dislodge if with the point of the pole. Once all the snow is off the boot sole, don't step it onto the snow again, or you will have to repeat the performance. Use both poles for balance and step toe first into the binding. Press your heel down to latch the binding. You're now attached to one very slippery ski, so be sure to use a pole to balance and to prevent sliding as you repeat the procedure putting on the other ski.

Attaching your poles comes next. If you have a strapless style, make sure each hand is holding the correct poles. They are often marked "L" and "R," which saves trial and error. You might try a piece of tape or a dab of paint on your poles for quick recognition. If you have a strap style, insert your hand upward through the loop. Spread the thumb from the fingers so that the strap rests in your palm as you grasp the grip. This will give you support without having to clench the grip to death.

Now you have everything fastened on, from skis to head, and you are ready to slide!

To put on your skis, knock loose snow off the boot and step in toe first.

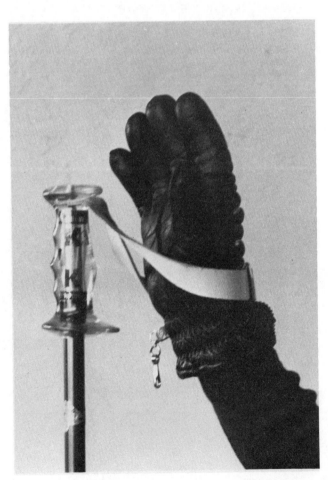

Putting on a pole strap.

SLIDING

Once you're standing you'll be glad you're on a level area. Those skis are slippery little devils and they want to go. They're really big feet adapted to the snow by improvements, including smooth bottoms and steel edges. The exercises that follow are suggestions for ways to become familiar with the skis.

Discovering the skis. Hold one pole on each side for balance. Pick up one ski and twist it, then repeat with the other foot. Pick up both feet by hopping, using the poles for balance. Lift one tip in the air, keeping the tail on the snow. Then lift the tail, keeping the tip on the snow. Put your ski bottoms flat on the snow, then stand on the big toe sides of your feet so the ski bottoms are no longer flat on the snow.

The skis aren't all that intimidating. They respond to what your feet do, so try some sliding on flat terrain.

First motions on skis. Step sideways by lifting one foot, moving it straight sideways (tip and tail equal amounts) and putting it down. Match the second ski by lifting and moving it toward the first. Use your poles for balance. Repeat for several yards to the left and right.

Ski straight ahead by sliding first one ski ahead, then the other. Let your arms swing as in walking, and push on the poles slightly, with the baskets alternately touching the snow. Glide the skis across the snow, without lifting them.

Put both poles in the snow just behind your boots and push so that both skis slide ahead. Repeat several times before you coast to a stop. See how fast you can go. To change direction while standing, lift one ski tip and move the toe outward so that the tip spreads apart from the other one. Put the first one down and lift the second ski tip, matching it to the first ski. Repeat until you have stepped around in a circle. Try it in the other direction. Next, slide forward and step around at the same time. Combine your steps and sliding to make a big figure eight on the snow.

Again, to change direction, lift a ski tail and move the heel outward so that the tail spreads apart from the other one. Move the second foot to match the first ski. Step around in a circle in both directions.

Now you're loosened up and finding that motion is harmonious with skiing. Once you're on good terms with your skis on the flats you're ready to slide downhill. Choose a gentle slope with a good flat run out, or even a slight uphill run out at its base. That way you will coast to a stop rather than ending up at sea level. Climb a few feet up the hill. Walking straight up the grade won't work, as your skis slide backward almost as well as forward, so you'll need a new technique.

Sidestepping. Turn sideways to a gentle hill. Step up the hill one foot at a time, keeping weight on the side of each foot that is closest to uphill. Push your hips and knees uphill to stay on the uphill edges of the skis. Move the tip and tail an equal amount and keep the skis directly across the hill so they don't slide forward or backward. Take small steps, balancing with your poles.

Sidestepping resembles walking sideways up a set of stairs. You must keep the ski bottoms at an angle to the slope. Your most common mistake

Sidestepping.

Sidestepping resembles walking sideways up a set of stairs.

Fall lines.

will be to flatten the skis on the snow, letting them slide sideways back down to where you started. Also you'll find that it's a little tricky to read the slope at first. If your tips are even slightly pointed downhill, you'll slide that way. Or, more disconcertingly, if the tips are pointed uphill you'll slide backward. The way directly downhill is called the *fall line*. It may not sound very encouraging, but it is simply the path down which a snowball would roll if it were released at your feet. Frequently, the fall line may not be the same direction the trail will be taking, and it changes

depending upon variations in the slope contours. Anytime your skis start to slide forward they are starting to point down the fall line.

Once you're a few feet up the hill you'll be ready to face down the fall line for your run. A simple maneuver lets you do this without sliding before you are ready.

Standing change of direction. While standing sideways to the fall line, place both pole baskets shoulder width apart in the snow, directly downhill from your boots and as far downhill as you can reach. With elbows straight and hands on top of the poles, lean heavily on

A standing change of direction.

the poles to keep from sliding as you face downhill. Alternately step each ski around, using small steps. You'll end up facing the fall line with the ski tips between your pole baskets.

Remember to keep your elbows locked straight with your hands on top of the poles. This eliminates strain on your arms. You can see why this is often called a *bullfighter turn*. If you continued stepping your skis around you could face the opposite way from where you started. This will often be useful to change direction on a hillside.

Once you're facing in the fall line you're ready to ski. Relax, take some deep breaths, and uncramp those curled up toes. Check to see that people or other obstacles are not in your path and you're set to go.

Your first straight runs. Stand in a balanced, upright position, with your feet comfortably apart. Pull the ski pole baskets from the snow and point them behind you. Let your skis run down the hill to a stop on a level run out. Keep your body over your feet as your skis accelerate down the fall line. Repeat this a number of times. On one run, flex up and down while moving. See if you can touch your ankles. On another, push with the poles to increase speed as you go downhill. On a third, briefly pick up one ski, put it down, and pick up the other. Try stepping sideways while moving straight ahead to avoid imaginary (or real) obstacles in your path. Finally, hop your skis slightly off the snow while skiing.

That's the first thrill of Alpine skiing. One hopes you're now hooked for life, with no cure.

It is difficult to maintain balance as your skis try to speed away from the rest of you. The best way to adjust to speed changes is to start with a good balanced stance.

An athletic stance. Imagine you're playing some sport you already know how to do on a court or field. You're waiting for some action to happen, as, for instance, receiving a tennis serve. Your body will be loose but poised to move in any direction. Feet are apart, ankles and knees flexed, hands slightly in front, and eyes looking ahead.

This position is called an athletic stance because it is basic to most sports. You are balanced over your feet, ready to respond in any direction, but you are not strained. Feet are comfortably apart for greater stability. Also notice that your ankles and knees are flexed in a good stance. Stiff legs inhibit motion, so bend your knees. Hands are out for balance, and the chin is up so your eyes are looking ahead. Keeping your vision ahead improves your balance and enables you to see and avoid obstacles.

A common complaint of beginners is tired muscles. This is often from trying to use muscles rather than the skeletal structure to support the body's weight. If you stick your fanny out and then bend forward at the waist to compensate, you're in a very tiring, not to mention awkward, position. Instead tuck your seat in by thrusting your pelvis upward and forward, eliminating the strain of an arched lower back. Your weight should be centered over your feet.

Seesaw. Stand on your skis in an athletic stance with feet apart under your hips. Slowly rock backward and forward. Feel the strain when you're too far back or too far forward. Find a neutral stance in which you can stand comfortably.

Often skiers mistakenly sit back, pressuring only the heels. It's not a good position. If you do this, you'll feel pressure against the upper back of the boot. When you're "on your toes" in sports you're pressuring the balls of the feet and are ready to

In your first straight runs lift a ski, push for speed, touch your ankles, and jump.

respond. You should feel a slight pressure against the padded boot tongue in this ready position.

Get used to holding your hands in front with the pole tips pointed backward. This is a safe, non-strenuous position. Poles are never used to stop. If a point digs into the snow in front of you, the grip could jam into your stomach, a painful experience.

A good stance is a balanced starting point for dynamic action, but remember that it's not a static position to be held rigidly all the way down the slope.

For effortless balance, stay centered over your feet rather than too far forward or back.

SPILLS

Once or twice in your ski career you may take a spill. (Most of the time falls are caused by "snow snakes," sneaky sadistic creatures that hide under the snow and reach out to snatch your ankle to flip you over as you ski by.) If you feel yourself falling, and are unable to recover your balance, don't fight it. We're all endowed with plenty of natural padding. Simply crouch and let the posterior contact the ground first, to the side of the skis. This action will skid you to a stop. Avoid falling forward between your skis, as it's hard on the knees, head, and nose.

So there you are, literally on the hill. After you've finished inspecting the snowflakes, untangle yourself. Arrange your feet on your downhill side so gravity will help you stand up. Take great care to get both skis pointing in the same direction *across* the fall line, so that when you stand up they won't slide forward or backward. Pull your feet close to your body and put the uphill hand next to the fanny. Place your poles vertically, baskets down, in the snow next to your uphill hand, and place your downhill hand on the top of the poles. Now give a good, sharp shove off the snow by pushing yourself up with the uphill hand (in the snow) and pulling yourself up with the downhill hand (on the poles). This throws your weight onto the downhill foot. At the same time, move the uphill ski farther uphill, getting it underneath your body. Stand up using the leg muscles. It should be one smooth continuous motion. The secret is to get your "nose over your toes" as you rise. This puts your weight directly over the feet and you stand up by using the strongest muscles in the body, the thighs.

Don't be psyched out by all the words required to describe standing up, because it's really no dif-

Getting up from a spill.

ferent from standing up in your living room (a good place to try it with skis on). If you push straight upward and outward, get the fanny over the feet, and use the leg muscles, it should be easy. Your problems, if any, will come from pushing your feet out ahead of your body. If you do have difficulty, try getting up in two stages, by first rising onto the uphill knee, with the fanny clear of the snow, and then pushing straight up, moving the uphill foot under your body to stand up. Some skiers prefer to put their hands on top of each pole

and lever themselves up. With a little practice you can find your own favorite way. If all else fails, you can always release one foot from its heel binding and then stand up.

It's possible that one or both of your bindings will release during a spill. In this event, just stand up and place your skis across the fall line so they won't slide either forward or backward as you attach them. If the heel units need resetting, cock them for entry. Knock the snow off your downhill boot first and step in. Then do the same for your

Alternate ways to get up.

uphill boot. Putting the downhill ski on first makes balancing much easier and keeps you from sliding sideways down the hill.

Falls are a learning experience and a normal occurrence in skiing. A day without a good head plant is a dull day indeed. You can definitely reduce your number of spills by following two famous words of advice—"don't panic!" Your feet accelerate quickly on a hill, so keep the rest of your body up with them. Remember your natural athletic stance and return to it for best balance.

SLOWING

Not all hills are gentle ones with flat run outs, so you'll need to know how to slow down before you reach the parking lot. One way to control speed is by applying the brakes. Although skis are slippery, they can also slow down by digging into the snow. You may have heard of the term *snowplow*. We'll use its modern counterpart. The wedge is a position in which your skis make the letter *A* as

you look down at them. If you watch someone coming toward you in a wedge, it looks as though the skis are forming the letter *V*. In either case, the ski tips are close together and the tails are apart. Just as in your straight runs, you should be flexed in the ankles and knees, and balanced over your feet.

The wedge. Use a bullfighter change of direction to face down the fall line of a gentle slope. Make a wedge, with tips close together and tails apart. Remove the poles and see how much slower you go in a wedge as opposed to straight parallel running. Feel the pressure in each foot as the skis push against the snow. Increase the size of the wedge to go slower, and decrease the size to go faster.

The wedge is a very stable position, as it gives you a wider base of support. It's also an excellent learning position, as all the skills you'll learn in a wedge apply to more advanced skiing. If you get out of control, you probably lost the wedge. Get back into it for stability and slowing.

Your main problems in the wedge will come

Increase wedge size to slow down.

A gliding wedge.

A braking wedge to slow down.

from not pushing both skis out across your direction of travel. Look at your wedge tracks. They should be symmetrical. If only one ski is pushed out, the other ski will head straight down the fall line and not help at all to slow you down. Develop a sensitivity in each foot as to whether you are sliding or slowing on that ski.

The larger wedge slows you more than the smaller one because each ski is positioned more across the fall line. However, too large a wedge is awkward. You can make a smaller wedge work more effectively by increasing the amount your skis push against the snow on their edges.

Gliding and braking wedges. While skiing in a wedge keep your feet (and skis) flat on the snow. In the "gliding wedge" you'll go relatively fast. Now, in the same size wedge, stand on the big toe side of each foot, by rolling your ankles and knees toward each other slightly. You'll slow down immediately in this "braking wedge." Press against each foot to keep the skis apart while you slow or stop.

You may find that your skis have a tendency to cross in the wedges, especially in a braking wedge. You've just discovered one way of turning that you'll soon be using. In the meantime just pick up the top crossed ski and lift it back to where you want it. Should you happen to make a turn, don't worry about how you did it. Just do a few

more. We'll discuss turns in the skills chapters.

The wedges are not static body positions, but simply modifications of your basic athletic stance. Retain some motion in your skiing.

Body flexibility. As you climb up the slope, mark each side of your intended downward path with gloves or snowballs. While skiing down in a wedge, pick up each of these objects by flexing deeply in the waist, knees, and ankles and then straightening to a normal upright position.

Any problems you encounter in this exercise will probably be from not staying centered over your feet or from losing your wedge.

If you are learning with a friend, there are games that improve ability. One favorite is a snowball fight, with the rules being that you can only throw while sliding. Another game is to have a race. This can be modified to make the winner the last one to get to the finish line, meaning the person who can slow down better wins. If you're really ambitious, try tag or Frisbee throwing while skiing.

You've now survived your first ski experience. These are your hardest times on skis, when you exert a lot of energy climbing uphill and getting up after spills. Skiing really becomes easier now; from here on it's all downhill.

14
Technique Skills

A neophyte struggling down the beginners' slope skis just like the Olympic racer running the gates. They may not look the same, but each skier uses the very same physical skills to control his or her descent. After all, the whole object of the sport is to slide downhill, perhaps to change direction on the way, and to remain standing up in the process. The only thing that separates a beginner's struggles from the fluid runs of the world champion is the efficiency with which the expert physically controls the skis. These technique chapters will help you discover and refine the essential basic skills so you can become as proficient as you'd like.

Modern ski instructors and coaches have discovered that "good" skiers stand out not because of *what* they do on skis, but rather by *how* they do it. Years ago ski schools taught a rigid program of "what" to do. They started students in snowplows, and progressed them to a stem turn only after they made perfect snowplow turns. This demand for excellence at each stage continued until finally the pupil achieved the goal of skiing "parallel." The emphasis was on standing in accepted stylish positions and learning totally new maneuvers for each situation. Needless to say, not everyone progressed in this situation. Many students stayed at certain levels so long they picked up ingrained habits that hindered them in more advanced skiing.

Several factors changed this instructional emphasis on form. One was the fact that although students in each country were learning with different progressions, the technique of the top skiers of each country was similar. In other words, the end product was the same, despite the various methods used to get there. Another factor affecting learning was the demise of parallel skiing as the ultimate form. Racers began stepping and stemming their turns, maneuvers previously taught and deemed suitable only at the beginner level. At the same time modern ski technology produced easier-turning skis in shorter lengths. Skiers now needed less violent controlling actions to take advantage of the ski design. Finally, the top skiers and freestylers were innovating techniques that were never taught in classes, but that worked successfully on the hill.

Thus a modern learning system evolved that recognizes that there is no one "right" way to ski. There is only efficient and inefficient skiing, with room for individual style. This system is based on the common denominator that efficient skiers use similar motions to control their skis.

To improve, skiers now follow a loosely structured progression of maneuvers. These refine the same basic skills at all levels, eliminating the need to memorize dozens of totally different turns. Under this skills concept skiers apply just three distinct physical motions, known as motor skills, to perform any maneuver.

The first skill is *pivoting*, used to rotate one or both skis to the left or right of the original path. There is no general agreement on nomenclature for this skill. It's often called *steering*, which is a good term but lacks a concrete image to visualize. Some instructors refer to it as "turning," but this confuses students with the whole concept of mak-

Pivoting.

the ski flatter to the snow decreases edging. This controls how much the steel edge bites into the surface. Snow resistance against the edge makes a ski slow down or turn.

The third skill is *pressuring*, used to control how much weight is placed on or taken off each ski. Sometimes we'll refer to increasing the pressure as "weighting" or as "positive pressure." It helps flex a ski's edge into the snow for turning. When decreasing the pressure we may refer to

ing a turn as opposed to twisting a ski. We'll use pivoting and realize that it means rotating the tip and tail in different directions. This has the obvious benefit of directing the skis into a new path.

The second skill is *edging*, used to adjust the angle of the ski base to the snow. In fact, when a ski is tipped up off the snow it rides on a steel edge. To tip a ski more increases edging. To make

Edging (Photo courtesy Lange, USA).

Pressure control.

"unweighting" or to "negative pressure." This helps you to jump playfully or lighten the skis for starting new turns easily.

You can remember these motor skills by taking the first letters of each and putting some PEP into your skiing. Often these three skills are associated with the planes in which you can move a ski. A rotary motion applied along the length of your lower leg results in a pivot. A lateral, or left-and-right, motion of the lower leg controls edging. Up-

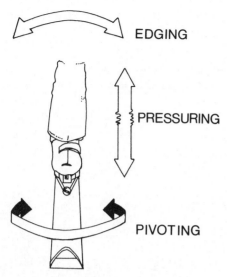

EDGING

PRESSURING

PIVOTING

How the motor skills affect a ski.

and-down leg motions are a primary means of controlling the pressure on a ski.

At the beginning, practicing these skills will be tricky, as you strive to maintain upright stability despite changes in speed, direction, and terrain. We'll call that *balancing*. It's not a separate motor skill, but almost an art. You're born with the sense of balance, a complex interaction among nerve endings, muscle and tendon sense terminals, the inner ear, and vision. Whenever your body approaches an unbalanced position, the balance sensors signal appropriate muscles to make a corrective action. As you don't consciously think the motions, it is known as a reflex action. Thus it's not a new skill that you have to learn for skiing, but rather a sense that you can improve. In the chapter on mental and physical conditioning you'll find many general ideas on how to improve balance.

The following technique chapters present a series of exercises similar to those taught in ski schools. Each exercise will have an immediate goal, such as controlling speed or making a turn. But more importantly, each one will be refining your skills, which can then be applied to other terrain or snow situations. For instance, imagine that all you've ever skied on is hardpack and you encounter deep Western powder for the first time. You don't have to learn a new turn to master the powder. All you do is revise the emphasis on certain skills. (In this case you'd apply more pivoting force and more unweighting force than you have been using on packed snow.)

The technique is divided into sections for beginners, intermediates, and advanced skiers. This is strictly for convenience. If you have been on skis only a few days, you'll naturally start with the beginner section. But if you're a seasoned veteran, you may still want to glance through the "easier" sections. You may get a few surprises as you find a skill application you didn't know.

I've tried to use standard terminology in the skill improvement exercises. This eliminates the confusion where one ski school's "ostrich turn" may be another's "giraffe turn." I've also taken many approaches to get the same results. Everyone's personality and physical makeup differ, so what works for one skier may not work well for another. However, the more ways you can turn, slow down, or speed up, the more versatile a skier you'll be.

Visualize each exercise before you try it. While doing the exercise, don't worry about how you look. Instead, obtain a sensory feedback from every part of your body so you can understand what the skill does. Form will follow function. If you learn how to pivot, edge, and pressure your skis effectively, you'll automatically ski smoothly and gracefully. Everything good takes time, so don't rush yourself or get frustrated. Relax and have fun skiing—that's the most important skill of all!

15
Beginner Technique

This chapter will acquaint you with how the skills function to create turns and to control speed. Although it's primarily aimed at skiers who are ready to ski on the "easiest way down" trails marked by green circles, others may benefit. It's also for those skiers who already ski some easier runs but don't have their skills perfected to move up comfortably onto more difficult trails.

If you've never been on skis, you will quickly progress to this chapter. But read the chapter "Your First Time." Then you'll be familiar with the skis, with straight running, and with a wedge to slow. All skiers venturing onto trails should also be aware of the rules of the road, presented in the chapter "Slope Safety."

You'll be using a wedge most of the time while learning the skills. Don't think of it as strictly a lower-level stance. The wedge principles are basic to all advanced turns. In fact, many coaches have their racers go back to the wedge to perfect their skills, and you'll do the same in the advanced technique chapter.

WEDGE TURNS

Turns are useful things for avoiding obstacles such as people and trees, which keep popping into your path. They also slow you down. Anytime your skis are pointed directly downhill (the fall line) they want to accelerate toward light speed. When your skis are across the fall line they decelerate. Turns continuously put your skis in and out of the fall line, thus controlling speed. Finally, turns are a dance on the snow, with a tempo varying from rapid to slow.

I always enjoy asking a beginner class how they make turns, because the answers are so different. Some students say they push from one foot to the other, others say they turn their feet, and others say they stand on the sides of their feet. All of those answers are correct, because there are many ways to make a turn, depending upon which motor skill is emphasized.

If you decide to change your direction while walking, you pivot and then step on each foot. You can also do this with your skis on to make a stepping turn for slowing down.

Stepped change of direction. Ski in a straight run. To move out of the fall line pick up the tip of the right ski and move it outward. Match the left ski to it by picking up the tip and pivoting it in. Continue to step around until your skis are across the fall line and you come to a stop. Repeat from the fall line, this time stepping outward to the left side.

In this outward step you twist one toe at a time in a new direction. Move your leg outward as you pick up the ski so that your long skis don't cross in back. This makes the ski pivot about its tail. You're also pressuring first one foot and then the other as you step out of the fall line. It's a fast way to get out of the fall line and is often used by racers to gain height on a gate prior to starting a turn around it.

Picking up skis is extra work, so most of your turns will be made with skis on the snow. The chapter "Your First Time" describes a wedge as a stance with tips close and tails apart. It's especially useful for extra stability, for additional slowing, and for learning the elements of turning. You are skiing in both straight runs and in a wedge, so it's important to be able to change from one to the other.

Wedge from a straight run. Ski straight down a gentle hill with feet comfortably apart. Pivot both feet by pointing the toes in and pushing the heels out. Let your feet slide apart slightly for a wider base as you pivot them. Go back to a straight run from a wedge by gradually pivoting both toes straight ahead and letting the feet come closer together. Use a bouncing, or hopping, motion if you feel it helps you go from one position to the other.

While twisting the toes inward move your feet apart slightly so the tips don't cross. You're now pivoting the skis around the tip area. Sometimes the obstinate skis do have a mind of their own and decide to cross. If so, just pick up the top one and put it back where it belongs.

Once you're skiing in a small wedge you'll want to pivot your feet to turn. This can be practiced first without skis.

Pivoting the feet. Stand in your boots on a smooth, hard-packed level area. Use both poles for support and twist your feet left and right, so that your toes and heels move equal amounts.

For your turns you'll need to be centered over your feet. If you're too far back or forward you'll be fighting for balance and pivoting only the heels or toes.

For these first turns keep your skis flat on the snow and the wedge small. You'll recall that a wedge with flat, quick-sliding skis is called a *gliding wedge.* This eliminates friction and lets you concentrate on the first type of turn, a rotary one.

Foot-pivoted turns. Glide down a gentle slope in a small wedge, keeping skis flat on the snow and weight equal on each foot. Turn by rotating your feet simultaneously. Feel your toes press against the front side of each boot in the direction you wish to go and your heels press on the opposite rear side of each boot. Make a

series of small connected turns without skiing far out of the fall line.

This pivoting movement will be present to some degree to guide every turn you make. It can be an extremely powerful force.

The power of pivoting. Sit on a chair with feet apart on the floor. Have a partner hold your right foot in place while you try to rotate it counterclockwise, pushing your toes to the left. Now increase the force by also rotating your knee to the left. Have your partner tell you how hard he or she must resist to keep your foot from rotating.

You're finding that you have a tremendous power to rotate your feet. Your hips, shoulders, and hands do not have to move to create this turning force. We'll use them in the future to aid the rotary force, but for now realize that the lower body supplies the power.

You also felt a greater force when you pivoted the knee into the turn. Along with rotating the lower leg you're rotating the upper leg about the axis of the femur from the pelvis to the knee. This greatly increases the torque (a technical term for a rotational force). Try some turns using all the pivoting force you can apply.

Foot- and knee-pivoted turns. Glide down a gentle slope with your feet comfortably apart in a small wedge. Link a series of short turns by rotating your feet and knees in the direction you wish to go.

You'll find that these pivoted turns, sometimes called *steered turns,* are so easy they are awesome.

If you're having trouble, it's probably from not staying centered over your feet. The greatest rotary force can be applied when your hips are over your feet and when you're flexed at the ankles and knees.

Stance affects pivoting force. Hold on to a chair back or ski pole for balance. Stand rigidly upright, without knee flex. Move your hips out away from your right foot, then twist that foot inward as far as you can. Now move your hips back over your feet, and you'll find you can increase the degree of twist. Finally, flex the knees and ankles for the greatest amount of twisting power available.

A lowered stance from deep flexing in the knee and ankle joints will come in handy later on in

Turn the feet in the direction you want to go.

The skier turns to his left by sharply edging a ski.

carved a long, gentle turn in the snow. Anytime you edge a ski and pressure it into the snow it wants to turn. Before we try linking shorter turns we'll go to the basic wedge and review how to edge.

Edge control in a wedge. Slide down a gentle hill in a small wedge. Keep weight equal on each foot. Flatten your skis by rolling your ankles and knees outward an equal amount (gliding wedge) and feel your speed pick up. Increase edging by rolling your ankles and knees inward an equal amount (braking wedge). You'll feel immediate resistance and will slow down.

At this slower speed most of your edging is done by knee movements left and right. Ideally it would be ankle movements, but with the rigid boots this becomes a lateral knee movement. (Upon reading this everyone in the medical field is immediately saying that there is very limited lateral movement in that joint, and it's really a complicated combination of leg bones pivoting in their sockets. True, but for simplicity let's think of it as just a knee movement inward or outward.)

You should become sensitive to the snow brushing against the edges as feedback on how much edge you have applied. If you had any problem edging the skis, check to see that you had some bend in your knees. You'll need flex to control edging for turns.

Edging to turn. Ski down the fall line of a gentle hill in a gliding wedge, keeping weight equal on each foot. Now increase the edging of your right ski by angling the right knee inward (to the left). Immediately you begin to turn left. Flatten the right ski and increase edging on the left ski, and you'll turn to the right. Make a series of turns one after the other letting the edges carry you around.

When using pivoting you turned flat skis by rotating them. Now you're letting the skis turn by themselves, simply by edging one ski more than the other. The edged ski bites more deeply into the snow, and resistance from the snow makes it turn. Your tracks should form gentle curves rather than in straight lines. The only effort you needed was to angle a ski against the snow, perhaps by moving your knee laterally a few inches.

In this wedge turn you used the inside edges of your skis. These are the edges on the big toe sides of the feet. The inside edges control turning at all

deep snow, short-radius turns, and in bumps. Right now you don't need an extreme, tiring knee bend, but you do need a slight one.

You can take advantage of other turning factors beside pivoting. Due to their shape, skis are designed to turn, not to run straight. You may have noticed that a ski is narrower under your foot than at the tip or tail. Thus when it is tipped up onto an edge and weight is applied, it tends to run in the resulting curved arc, rather than a straight line.

Turns from edged skis. On a gentle slope, stand in a wider-than-normal stance, with your feet about eighteen inches apart. Put the right ski up on edge by standing on the big toe side of that foot, flexing the right knee inward, to the left. Keep the left ski flat on the snow and weight equal on each foot. Push off down the slope and feel your right ski dig in to carve a gradual smooth left-hand turn. Repeat, edging the left ski while keeping the right ski flat on the snow and make a gradual turn to the right.

If you look at your tracks, you'll see the ski edge

Edging one ski will make it turn.

levels of ability. Consider them as your power edges. You found that the right ski controls the left turn, and vice versa. Now you know why your skis sometimes want to cross each other! Rather than trying to remember "right ski for left turn, etc." just use the ski pointing in the direction you want to go to make the turn. This directing ski is the "outside" ski of each turn, so named because it is farther from the turn center. Thus, the inside edge of the outside ski is the power edge for each turn.

That may sound confusing until you think it through, but it's an important concept and is the basis for advanced skiing.

Perhaps you moved your body a lot to edge. If so, you should obtain a better idea of controlling edges from your legs.

Feeling skis edge. On a gentle slope leave your poles aside and ski with your hands on your knees. Start in a gliding wedge with weight equal on each foot. Turn

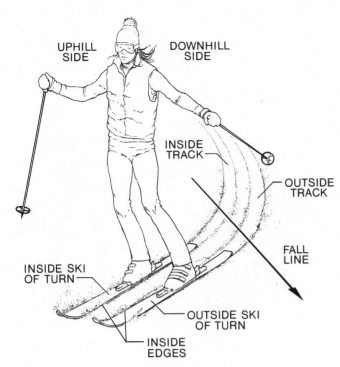

UPHILL SIDE

DOWNHILL SIDE

INSIDE TRACK

OUTSIDE TRACK

FALL LINE

INSIDE SKI OF TURN

OUTSIDE SKI OF TURN

INSIDE EDGES

Turn terminology.

by pushing one knee inward and forward. Then bring it back outward to a flat ski and push the other knee inward so that you go in a new direction. Try linking one turn after another. Once you have the feeling, stand upright and make the same turns from a normal stance with invisible hands pushing your knees.

You've been flattening the inside ski by moving that knee away from the other and edging the power ski by moving that knee toward the other. This is the same direction, and simplifies another way of thinking of your edging. Just roll both knees in the direction of a turn.

Moving edges at the same time. Start in a wedge on a gentle hill. Edge each ski equally so you are in a small braking wedge. Keep weight equal on each foot. Now change edging by moving both knees right slightly. You'll turn to the right. Change edging by moving both knees left until you're turning left.

If some of your earlier straight braking wedges actually made you turn, the skis probably weren't edged equally. When one ski is edged more than the other it becomes dominant and turns you the way it is headed. You're now taking advantage of this concept for faster turns by removing edging from one ski and edging the other at the same

time. Thus the skis aren't fighting each other to go in their separate directions.

So far we've talked pretty much about being on edge or not being on edge. As with anything black and white, there are many shades of gray, and the amount of edging affects your turns. You may want to experiment with this degree of edging in a straight run first.

Varying edging in a wedge. While in a wedge assign values to the amount of edging. Call a flat ski a "zero." A slight edge is "one," more edge is "two," and the maximum is "three." Change these values as you ski straight down the fall line, and feel how a "three" digs in most to slow you the fastest.

Now you can use variable edging in your turns.

Varying edging for turns. Ski in a gliding wedge in the fall line of a gentle slope. When you reach a comfortable speed edge one ski a minimum amount, your "one" value. Hold that same edge all the way around. Note your track to see the size of the turn radius. Now repeat at the same speed, but this time increase to your "two" value, a moderate edge. Notice how much sharper your turn is. Now go to maximum edging for the sharpest turn.

Increasing the edging tightens the turns. They still may not be as quick as you'd like. If your ski made a sharp turn at slow speed, it would be very tricky to control when you want to go fast and make a large turn. For slower speeds and for tight turns you'll want to use pivoting also. Now we'll add the third skill, pressuring, to help your turns.

While walking, your weight transfers pressure smoothly from foot to foot without awkward body contortions. The same holds true for skiing.

Weight transfer in straight runs. Ski down the fall line on a very gentle hill. Run straight with your skis flat on the snow. Stand first on one ski and then the other. Note how little body movement is required to go from foot to foot. Now step sideways one ski at a time while sliding forward. Step to flat skis to avoid edge engagement.

Of course you don't need pressure control in skiing just to move forward, as gravity does that for you. But you do need pressure to resist gravity and make turns or stops. While practicing turning with edging skills you needed weight on the edged ski to make it bite into the snow. A ski must

(1) Less edge makes a larger turn.

(2) More edge makes a sharper turn.

be both edged and pressured to cause a turn. Now we'll vary the pressuring to improve turns.

Wedge turns by weighting. Ski down the fall line on a gentle hill. Use a braking wedge with weight equal on both feet. Now pressure the right ski while reducing weight on the left ski, but be sure to keep the edge angles the same. You will turn to the left. Immediately pressure the left ski and reduce weight on the right and you'll turn right. Continue to make rapid small turns by stepping from foot to foot.

You are now turning by pressuring one inside edge more than the other. This weighted ski bites more forcefully into the snow and takes you the way it's pointed. If you're ambitious and have good balance, you could take this exercise to an extreme by lifting one edged ski off the snow, putting it down, and lifting the other. It's obvious you'll go where the ski on the snow is pointing.

It is important to transfer weight from one foot to another to change direction. In fact, ski design uses pressuring to help you to make your turn.

Skis seek the fall line. Ski straight across the hill in a gliding or slightly braking wedge, with more weight on the downhill ski, as though a turn has just been made. Now, transfer some of your weight to the uphill ski, so that both skis are weighted equally. Allow the skis to turn gradually into the fall line by themselves. Finish the turn by pressuring the outside ski more.

Although you did not increase edging of the uphill ski or use pivoting, equally weighted and equally edged skis will seek the fall line. Instead of working to turn the skis you can just stand on them, and they will slowly turn to point downhill. Of course, you'll need pivoting, edging, or increased pressure to finish the turn, and applying those skills at the start of the turn will speed up the whole process.

Besides standing harder on the big toe side of one foot or the other, where you place that pressure relative to toes or heels is important. You can experiment to see the differences.

Pressure one ski to make it turn.

Balance in wedge turns. Choose three positions: one pressuring your heels, one the whole foot, and one just the toes. Now make a series of turns pressuring each of these areas and note that a neutral stance gives the best results throughout a turn.

It's a natural tendency to lean back as your skis start into the fall line. But they are accelerating and you must move forward to keep up with them. This is the same as getting off a chair lift, where you must lean forward or risk a fall on the fanny. When you're balanced in a neutral stance you can pivot the toe and heel in different directions for easy turns. If you're too far back, you can only twist the toes, an inefficient pivot. The old advice to "get forward" applies to most skiers, as very few

are too far forward. In later technique we'll find how to use subtler pressure shifts away from the neutral position.

You now have the three skills in their basic form to apply to turns. No one turn should be done by using only one skill. Combine them to make the ideal turn for each situation.

FROM HERE TO THERE

The Traverse

Although your general path is downhill, there are many instances in which you'll want to go somewhere that is not directly down the fall line. You'll often ski across the hill from one place to another without turning. You could get there in a wedge, but it's less tiring if you let both feet point the same way you're going. This parallel position is called a *traverse*. It's similar to a straight downhill running position, but instead of being on flat skis you now ride on the two uphill edges.

Traverse position. Stand as though sidestepping on a slope. Put your poles in front to keep from sliding as you point both ski tips slightly downhill. Remain balanced on your edged skis, remove the poles, and let your skis slide forward in a traverse. Make sure your uphill ski is ahead of the downhill one by several inches. Use a braking wedge to come to a stop. Turn around and traverse across the slope in the opposite direction, keeping your new uphill ski slightly ahead of the downhill one.

The traverse position is not static. It's a basic athletic stance in which you're ready to move and respond. In the traverse you edge your skis and stand in balance on their uphill edges. Generally you won't have too many traverse problems on the gentle beginner slopes, even though they may seem like cliffs at times. Learn a proper stance for when the hills do get steeper. You must stand on two uphill edges to resist sliding sideways down the hill, just as you do in sidestepping. The steeper the hill, the greater the angle needed between skis and slope. You can easily increase the edging by pointing your knees uphill. To keep balanced over your feet you'll bend sideways slightly at the waist and angle your upper body out over your skis. (A technical term for this is *angulation*.)

Your main problem as the slopes become steeper will be wanting to "hug the hill." Instead of angling out over your skis your natural inclination will be to shy away from the steep hill. This puts you onto the uphill edge of the uphill ski, a perilously balanced position.

Balancing in motion. While traversing, slowly side-step uphill. Keep each ski lifted in the air as long as you can. See how secure you feel balanced on the downhill ski, and how delicate your balance is on the uphill ski.

You're also learning an important principle of pressuring, that your weight should be primarily on the downhill ski in a traverse. Whenever it's on the uphill edge of the uphill ski you're likely to fall over to the uphill side. I didn't say "fall down" because skiers rarely fall downhill—they fall uphill.

In order to edge easily you should get in the habit of keeping your uphill ski ahead. Whenever it lags behind the lower ski you're likely to have a stiff lower leg, which makes edge control difficult.

Pressuring one and then the other ski in a side-step is useful to change a traverse line.

Stepping to a higher traverse. While moving in a traverse, pick up the uphill ski and step it uphill parallel to the lower ski. Then pick up the downhill ski to match the upper. Continue stepping uphill as you move forward. Now try stepping downhill, lower ski first. Repeat for several yards downhill.

Stepping in a traverse is an excellent way to avoid obstacles (skiers or other nuisances) in your original path as well as a fine balance improver.

The steeper your traverse, the faster you'll go. You can easily control this traverse angle by pivoting one ski at a time.

Stepping to change traverse angles. From a traverse, bring your skis to a stop by stepping uphill, moving first the uphill ski tip outward, then matching it with the downhill ski. You are now in a shallower traverse. Keep repeating until you have skied uphill to a stop. Now from a traverse, step the tip of the lower ski downhill and match it with the upper ski. You are now in a steeper traverse. Vary between steep and shallow traverses. On a gentle hill, keep stepping across the fall line until you have changed your traverse direction entirely and are going the opposite way.

When you step through the fall line and traverse in the opposite direction you also change the

Stepping a ski into a new traverse angle.

edges on which you ride, a basic principle of turns beyond the wedge. Actually, you just made a stepped turn. However, much skiing is done without all that tiring work involved in picking up the skis. You can also vary your traverse by changing the amount of edging.

Changing a traverse by edging. Ski in a moderate traverse. Increase edging by rolling your knees uphill. Keep weight on each foot constant by also angling more over the downhill ski as you increase edging. Your traverse will turn into more of an arc. Decrease edging and your traverse will be more of a straight line.

Now you're beginning to see that a traverse is really part of a long turn whose radius you can change. You can also add pivoting to increase the change.

Varying a traverse by pivoting. Ski to a stop by changing your traverse into a curved track pointing uphill. To do this simply pivot your feet and knees to drive the tips uphill. Repeat from steeper traverses, until you are starting almost in the fall line.

Once you have traversed across a hill you may want to make a turn, rather than a stop. To do this you'll return to a wedge.

FALL LINE

Pivot the skis uphill to stop from a traverse.

Traverse to wedge. Traverse across the hill. To make a wedge, pivot the toes toward each other, spreading your feet apart slightly. Feel your lightly weighted uphill ski change from riding its outside edge to riding its inside edge. To resume a traverse pivot both feet to point straight ahead, letting your uphill ski go flat and then to its outside edge.

This may give you a little problem, as you're changing an edge. Think about making a ski flat first. Then you can easily slide it on the snow. We'll work on this shortly in "Changing Edges."

About Face

Several times in each run you'll need a breather and will stop, generally intentionally. However, upon stopping, the hill ahead may suddenly seem steeper than you'd like, or your path may be blocked by trees. You need a way to make an abrupt about-face, a 180-degree change of direction.

You already know the bullfighter turn, in which you place your poles downhill with arms straight while you step around in place. This is fine for gentle slopes, but on steeper hills can be awkward and hard on the arms. It's easier to change direction with a turn.

Turn to change direction. While standing across the fall line pivot out your uphill ski into a wide wedge. Put that uphill ski onto its inside edge. Now push forward with your poles, and immediately transfer most of your weight to the uphill ski. You'll feel your ski edge bite into the snow to turn you sharply 180 degrees. Aid the turn with strong pivoting from your knees and feet. You'll end up facing the opposite direction a few feet below your starting point.

To make this quick turn, point the uphill ski down the fall line and pressure it. Any weight left on the original downhill ski will increase the time needed ·to turn. Also, try placing your downhill pole basket in the snow one to two feet below your lower boot. Lean on it for balance and pivot about this point for a short-radius turn.

Sometimes your about-face area is too confined or the slope is too intimidating for a turn. In these cases the kick turn will change your direction without any forward movement. Although it will be most useful on a steep pitch, master it on a flat or very gentle pitch first!

Kick turn. Keep your skis directly across the fall line and on their uphill edges throughout this turn. Start by facing your upper body downhill. Place your pole baskets on each side of you above your uphill ski. Use the poles for balance as you transfer all your weight to the edged uphill ski. Kick out the lower ski so that its tip is straight up in the air, with the tail resting on the snow where the tip used to be. Swing the elevated tip around to touch the snow where the tail used to be. Be sure it ends up directly across the fall line. As soon as it touches the snow, immediately put your weight onto this edged ski and in one smooth flowing motion lift the uphill ski and corresponding pole, swinging them around 180 degrees. The uphill ski becomes the new downhill ski as it is placed across the fall line.

This is definitely a situation in which actions speak louder than words. Visualize this exercise as one continuous movement, then try it. The key points are to face your upper body downhill and to kick out the downhill ski first. This keeps you comfortably on your uphill edges. If you need

A kick turn.

To change direction from a standstill, step a ski into the fall line and pivot, edge, and pressure it around in a short turn.

extra "oomph" to kick out your downhill ski, wind up that leg by first drawing it backward, as though kicking a football.

Shorter skis make this turn considerably easier than using old-fashioned seven-foot boards, but the principle is the same. I guarantee this kick turn (K.T. to those in the know) will save your day sometime. Every advanced skier has a tale to tell of venturing into unexpected nasty snow and getting down a slope only by traversing and kick-turning the whole way. Once you know the standard kick turn, ask an instructor to show you the so-called ladies' kick turn or the Asian kick turn. They're both exotic ways to tangle your legs into pretzels.

The herringbone.

Up and Down Faster

With your increasing ability you'll find that often you'd like to get from here to there faster. For going uphill you already know the sidestep. As you use it more, you'll take larger and faster steps. If you're really ambitious, you may even hop from one ski to the other in a rapid sidestep.

Another way to get up a moderate hill rapidly is in a reversed wedge, known as a herringbone.

Herringbone. Facing uphill, put your tails together and spread the tips so your skis form a V. Push the knees inward so you are standing on the inside edges. Now lift one ski at a time uphill, staying on the inside edges for grip. As you duckwalk uphill, balance with the pole baskets in the snow downhill of your skis and thrust with the palms on top of the grips for support.

You can see why this maneuver is called a herringbone when you look at the tracks your inside ski edges leave. This is a fast way up a gentle slope, although it's not particularly graceful. Your skis are pointed backward down the fall line, so alternate supporting poles to keep from sliding downhill.

To cross flats you know how to push with your poles or to slide one foot at a time. You can also skate rapidly across a level area on your inside edges.

Skating. On a level area stand in a herringbone position with tips outward and tails together. Flex downward, bending in the right ankle and knee while also increasing edge on the right ski. Extend rapidly, pushing off the edged right ski. You'll coast on the left ski. As your speed slows, flex and edge the left ski. Extend rapidly to push off the left ski to coast on the right. Skate in a constant rhythm from foot to foot. Get additional thrust from your poles, pushing from the right pole at the same time you push from the right foot.

Skating is a dynamic action, and the more you put into it, the more speed you'll get out. You'll have to lean forward in the direction you're going, just as you would lean forward when jogging. Of course, skating isn't confined to the level. It's just an active herringbone and will work on a slight upgrade. It's often used on a downgrade, particularly by racers as they near the finish line.

To increase speed in the fall line, you can use another racing maneuver, the tuck.

Tuck to increase speed.

Tuck for speed. Choose a gentle slope free of people and bumps. With feet apart and parallel, compress your body into a tuck by bringing your torso down toward your thighs which are almost parallel to the ground. Make sure to keep your hands in front, your chin up, and your weight centered over your feet. Let 'em go! To slow down, stand up to catch the wind.

The tuck is really a very stable position, as you lower your center of gravity toward your feet. It is helpful for crossing a flat area at the bottom of a slope, and it's also a great thrill now and then for extra speed. For maximum velocity, make your shape as egglike as possible to reduce wind drag. Your thighs will be parallel to the skis. An extreme folding at the waist brings your back almost parallel to the skis also. Hands are well in front and poles close to your sides. Your neck will ache from craning your chin upward to see where you're going. Be sure to keep your skis perfectly flat and pointed ahead, as drag from edging will slow you down.

Now that you're really enthralled with speed you'll want to rush out and buy some 220cm skis, a skintight suit, a crash helmet, curved poles for less wind resistance, and good accident insurance.

Better Balance

The faster you're skiing, the more important it will be to look ahead, and your balance center works best when you see a horizon for reference.

Looking ahead for balance. Ski while looking at your ski tips, then simply raise your head to look down the slope where you are skiing. Your stability and confidence will improve when your eyes are well ahead.

A major reason for looking ahead is simply that no matter how good your reaction time, you still need adequate warning of what is coming. Even at ten miles per hour, you're traveling almost fifteen feet per second. If you still find yourself watching your skis, pick out a visual goal down the hill.

Target skiing. Center your eyes on a target well down the slope, such as a friend holding ski poles in an X, a tree, or lodge. This will keep your head up, improving your balance and reaction time.

Ski with your eyes ahead and chin up. Use peripheral vision to keep track of your ski tips and free your eyes to look at more interesting objects, such as people, scenery, and fast-approaching trees.

THE SIDESLIP

Despite your best planning, you may suddenly ski up to a section of trail that is simply too steep for comfortable skiing. You may wish you could sprout wings, but you'll need a practical way down. You could always take off your skis and walk, but that's tiring and dangerous on slick slopes, not to mention embarrassing. Kick turning and traversing would work on a wide slope, if you don't mind endless zigzagging, but they are not practical on narrow or heavily skied trails. One alternative is sidestepping. You already know how to place the skis across the fall line, digging in the edges to step uphill. You could sidestep down, a safe but tedious procedure. Let's apply that edging skill to learn an effortless way to actually ski down that steep section of trail or any steep hill anywhere in the world!

In sidestepping the edges prevent gravity from pulling you downward. However, now you'd like to go downward slowly. All you have to do is reduce the edge angle until the edge bite won't hold your weight anymore. This is called *releasing* the edges. The skis will begin to slide sideways down the fall line. To stop the slide, the edge angle can be increased until the skis dig in enough to stop the slide. This is sometimes called *engaging* the

Flatten the skis to sideslip and edge them to stop.

edges. The net result is a controlled slide sideways down the fall line, called a *sideslip* (as opposed to a sidestep).

Sideslip. Sidestep up a few feet near the bottom of a steep hill covered with firmly packed snow. Keep your skis directly across the fall line. Roll your knees outward to flatten the skis until you start to slide sideways. To stop the slide increase edging by rolling knees uphill. Slide between your upper and lower poles the first time, then slideslip without poles in the snow. Repeat to the other side.

Skis sideslip easily on steeper hills. On very gentle hills there may be too much friction for gravity to pull you downhill even when you're on a flat ski. Also, to avoid snow friction, try sideslipping first on ice or very firm snow. As the snow gets softer the ski edge bites in more. All the snow piled up against the ski bottom then prevents sliding sideways.

You may find your skis have a tendency to start tip first down the hill. If so, pressure the ski tails more by placing additional weight on your heels.

Learning an open stance for edge control with a partner.

The sideslip is a parallel maneuver, meaning that you're on two uphill edges. You should not attempt it from a wedge position, as the uphill ski's lower edge will dig into the snow if you slide sideways in a wedge.

If the inside edge of your uphill ski catches even though you start parallel, it's probably because you are facing uphill. While sideslipping it's important that you face slightly downhill. This means your uphill ski should be slightly ahead of the downhill one. In fact, every part of the uphill side of your body should be slightly ahead of the downhill side, in what's known as an "open" stance. A good way to get an exaggerated feeling for this stance is by extending your pole baskets to a friend down hill of you.

Sideslip with a friend. Stand on your edges across the fall line. Hand the baskets of your ski poles to a friend standing directly downhill from you. Weight your heels and have your friend pull you directly toward him or her until your skis start sideslipping. Drive your knees uphill to increase edging to stop. Repeat with a gentler pull, helping the sideslip by reducing edging as your friend pulls the poles. Finally, try with no pull at all, but still facing downhill.

If you don't have a friend nearby you can get a feeling of facing downhill by pushing with your poles.

Sideslip with pole push. From a sidestep position, place both ski pole baskets just uphill of your skis. They should be shoulder width apart, one by your uphill toes and the other by your uphill heel. Push on the poles to start your sideslip. Stop the slide by increasing edging. Repeat but push less by flattening your skis first. Continue until no push is needed to start the sideslip.

At first you may find the sideways motion a little strange. However, it gives you absolute control by aiming the full length of your skis across your direction of travel. Sideslipping is an important application of your edging skills, as you'll soon incorporate it with turns as well. Of course, skiing is symmetrical, so I'm sure you'll practice all these exercises in both directions. (If we were intended to slideslip in only one direction we would have been made with one leg shorter than the other.)

For straight sideslipping, edging is most easily controlled with the knees. Ideally, it would be the ankles, so if you prefer to think of ankle control,

that's fine. Rigid boots transfer most ankle movements into knee movements. Knees uphill will engage edges and knees downhill will release them. These two directions are often referred to as knees "in" and knees "out," respectively.

Edge control in sideslips. Stand on a steep, packed hill with your skis across the fall line. Roll your knees out until the edges release, then roll them back until the edges grab and stop the sideslip. Rapidly release and engage the edges down the slope, sideslipping perhaps a foot between stops. Repeat to both sides.

Increasing the edging abruptly is often called *setting* the edges. You may find little sprays of snow flying out from your edges as they dig in to stop your slide. Edging from the knees in this manner is quick and has a minimal effect on your balance. If you're having problems, check your stance to be sure it lets you angle both ski edges equally. Releasing only one edge doesn't work. Make sure you are centered over your skis, without the fanny sticking uphill and with both legs equally flexed. For best balance place more weight on the downhill foot by bending sideways slightly at the waist (an angulated position).

Once you have the feel of edge or no edge, you can refine the skill to encompass different degrees of edging. This controlled edging varies your speed throughout a sideslip and lets you handle long sections of slope.

Long sideslips. On a steep hill release edges just enough to allow you to sideslip at a comfortable speed. Gradually increase the edging so that you slow down, but not enough to stop. Decrease the edging and see how fast you can sideslip while remaining in control.

Fast, long sideslips are great fun. They let you zip down steep slopes without worrying about turning into the threatening fall line. But anytime you're sliding sideways your skis are brushing across a lot of snow, although there may also be rocks or stumps poking through the snow. These are hard on your edges and even harder on your balance, as they tend to stop you suddenly. Another problem is soft snow. Sideslipping from ice into a pile of loose snow also slows you down very rapidly.

You can avoid obstacles while sideslipping by changing your path. You probably already found out how critical weight placement is during side-

WEIGHT
BACK

WEIGHT
FORWARD

Placing weight forward or back carries your sideslip in those directions.

slipping. Too much on the toes, and you side-slipped forward and down. Thus you can vary the forward-and-back pressure on the skis, called *leverage*, to control the path of your descent.

The falling leaf. Sideslip down a smooth, steep slope. Place your weight toward your toes to make your skis sideslip forward. Then weight your heels and side-

slip while going backward. Transfer your weight fore and aft to make a falling-leaf pattern in the snow.

Not too many skiers are even aware of these results from changing pressure. Yet the falling leaf will come in handy later on, especially during mogul skiing. For now, utilize leverage to sideslip without having to follow the fall line.

So far we've been using the sideslip only to get directly down a steep slope. Actually a sideslip is a specialized example of a skid, which is skiing forward while also sliding sideways on the uphill edges. Now we'll combine a slideslip with a traverse.

Skids in traverses. Traverse across a steep, packed slope, edging enough to leave two distinct tracks across the hill. Now roll out your knees to decrease edging until your skis sideslip while you continue to ski forward. Increase edging to stop the skid and resume a pure traverse. Repeat with rapid edge releases and edgesets.

Looking at your tracks, you'll notice how a skid gets you downhill at the same time you're going forward. Whenever you want you can release edge grip to skid in the fall line. This has a very obvious practical application to avoid obstacles.

Sideslipping to avoid obstacles. Ski in a traverse toward an imaginary (or real) obstacle. Avoid running over it by skidding to a lower traverse.

This is a great "graduation" exercise to test your edging skill.

You're now discovering another dimension in skiing. Your direction of travel is not always the same way your skis are pointing, but can be sideways as well.

CHANGING EDGES

Up to now you've made turns from a wedge. In this position you stay on the inside edges, which are the power ones for turning. However, you've found that it's very comfortable to traverse standing on uphill edges. That's the way we're constructed, with both feet parallel or pointing in the same direction. In the traverse the lower ski is on its power edge, but the upper ski is on its outer edge. To ski from a traverse to a wedge you must "change an edge."

That may sound complicated, but it just means changing from riding an outside edge to riding an inside edge. You've already gone from flat skis in a straight run to edged skis in a wedge and back. Possibly you were even able to go from a traverse to a wedge and back without too much effort. We'll explore a means of changing one edge at a time through a stem, which means pivoting the tail of

one ski outward into a wedge. Although both feet may be pivoted to move the tails farther apart, we'll be concentrating on moving the uphill ski tail. Technically the maneuver is an "uphill stem," but to simplify we'll just call it a stem.

A stem position. Stand on a level area with ski bases flat on the snow. Pivot one ski tail outward to a small stem, brushing that ski base on the snow as you do so. You'll place that ski onto its inside edge. Now pick up the ski to pivot it back parallel.

Repeat the stem, but this time as you pivot back parallel, don't lift the ski. Instead make the base flat on the snow and brush it across the snow surface as you pivot it inward.

Repeat on a gentle hillside. Keep most of your weight on the lower ski. First step the upper ski tail out to place the ski on its inside edge and step it back to its uphill edge in a parallel stance. Then slide it out on the snow without lifting by flattening the ski first and pushing the tail out. Slide it back again by flattening the ski base first, then pivoting the tail in.

The stem is a simple maneuver, combining pivoting to rotate the tail with a lateral leg movement to edge the ski. You found two ways to change the edge. One way is to physically lift up a ski to push it outward. This is a very dynamic action, but it requires more demands of balance to stand on a single ski, and it also requires extra work to lift the heavy ski and boot.

The other way to change edge in a stem is by gliding the ski always on the snow. While pushing out into a stem you would "catch" the outside edge unless you first flattened the ski to get it off that edge. Moving the upper knee downhill takes the ski off the outside edge. Then the ski tail is pivoted outward. When returning to a parallel stance you would "catch" the inside edge unless you first flattened the ski. This is done by moving the upper knee uphill, then pivoting in the tail. Having the "wrong" edge dig into the snow is a common problem. As a progressing skier you should always be ready with the phrase "I caught an edge" to explain away any spills not caused by snow snakes.

Keeping the ski on the snow is a good way to learn refined edge changes you'll need for later turns. But if you're on a steep slope or if your stem is too large, you'll probably need a stepping motion. Also, if your bone structure is not matched to

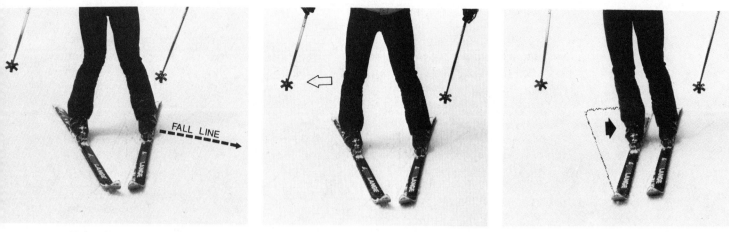

Flatten the uphill ski and then pivot it in parallel.

A stem turn.

your boots, you may find yourself catching edges unless you step. However, we'll do most of our stems by brushing the skis on the snow, to develop the needed edge awareness.

Now let's try some edge changes in motion, without making a turn. A skiing relativity law states that if you can stem standing still you can also stem while moving.

Stems from a traverse. Ski in a traverse across a gentle hill. Keep your feet comfortably apart, with the majority of your weight on the downhill ski and the uphill ski slightly ahead. Now flatten the uphill ski by angling the uphill knee and ankle toward the fall line. Pivot out the uphill tail until the ski is in a small wedge with the inside edge brushing the snow. Return the stemmed ski to parallel by angling the lower leg far enough uphill so the ski is flat on the snow. Pivot the ski tail back in. Repeat in both directions until you can stem rapidly without catching edges.

You can check your stem by examining your tracks. Only the uphill ski should have been displaced from its original course. The downhill ski stays in a single track. If you're catching edges, make sure your uphill ski is ahead and that your stem opening is not too large.

Stemming is useful to get into a turning position. A stemmed ski is starting to point in the new direction you want to go. Let's try a turn and see how you do.

Stem turn. From a traverse stem out the uphill ski. Transfer weight to that uphill ski and feel its edge bite into the snow to turn you through the fall line. Complete your turn by closing the new uphill stemmed ski. Immediately repeat a stem turn in the other direction.

One hopes that turn went smoothly. Perhaps you had a problem because in a turn the uphill and downhill sides interchange. If your left ski is the downhill ski going into a turn, it becomes the uphill one after the fall line. Imagine that a friend takes two photos of you, one when you start a turn and one when you finish the turn. They'll look the same except for left and right being interchanged. You open a stem turn with one foot, but close it with the other.

A common fault is letting the inside ski lag behind, thus finishing a turn with the downhill ski ahead of the uphill. This will catch an edge every time. To avoid this you should get into the habit of turning more with your lower body rather than twisting your head and shoulders to lead the skis.

Skiing from the lower body. Ski with a friend on one end of a slalom pole (or interlinked ski poles) and yourself at the other end. Hold the pole in front of you and keep both ends equally downhill as you turn together. To do this you'll have to ski from the waist down, keeping your upper body facing downhill.

If you don't have a slalom pole or a friend handy, you could try the above by holding your ski poles

Control the skis with the lower body.

horizontally in front of you. Automatically your uphill ski finishes a turn slightly ahead of the downhill one, and you can easily pivot it in parallel.

Another common turn problem is failing to commit to the turn. If you're hestiant about the turn and can't seem to get the skis started into it, you should practice the pressure change that's needed at the start of the turn.

Stem garlands.   Ski across the hill in a traverse, with the uphill ski ahead and your weight on the downhill ski. Glide out the tail of the uphill ski. Edge the uphill ski and transfer weight to it. When your skis move toward the fall line, release edge and pressure on the uphill ski. You will feel your skis start back uphill. Pivot the uphill ski back to a traverse. Repeat several times, then make stem garlands in the other direction.

This is a great exercise to obtain a feeling of edging and pressuring the outside ski when initiating a turn. Incidentally, the term *garland* simply refers to a series of repeated maneuvers executed without crossing over the fall line. The word comes from the garlandlike tracks your skis leave.

Once you're familiar with starting a turn, you may want to concentrate on pivoting the inside ski to complete a turn.

Pivoting the uphill ski to finish.   Ski down the fall line in a small braking wedge. Increase edging and pressure on one ski to begin a turn. Immediately flatten the other ski and pivot it in parallel. Repeat to the other side as well.

If you're still having any problem with edge changes after combining the elements of the start and finish of a turn, go back to skiing with hands on knees temporarily. You're probably trying too hard and are making exaggerated upper body movements, rather than keeping your upper body centered over your feet. Also try adding some speed, and the turn will start and finish more smoothly.

As you ski faster, you'll find that you can turn with smaller wedges.

Decreasing wedge size.   With increasing speed, reduce the size of the stem used to start your turn. Feel the turn result from edging skis and from transferring weight rather than from the physical size of the edge. Choose gentle, smooth slopes to make wide, round turns at moderate speed. Bring your skis parallel sooner

by pivoting the inner ski parallel as soon as you cross the fall line.

With some speed you'll find you don't have to hold the wedge until the very end of the turn. Your skis will pivot back in parallel sooner by simply relaxing the upper leg muscles which hold you in a wedge.

Relaxing muscles to finish turns.   Stand in a wedge and lift the uphill stemmed ski off the snow. As you hold it in a wedge, you'll soon discover the aching muscles that control the outward pivot. Put the ski down to rest a few seconds. Then pick it up, but this time hold it up parallel to the other ski. These muscles no longer ache. Apply muscle relaxation to the finish of a turn. Let those straining muscles of your lightly weighted inside ski relax, swinging the ski in parallel.

It takes a lot of effort to hold a stem longer than needed, and if you're a typical skier, as I am, you won't want to do extra work. Relax and ski with feet both pointing the same way after a turn.

Sometimes we're so fascinated at successfully completing one turn that we forget one good turn leads to another. Turns should be connected, linked events.

Linking turns.   Station a friend down the hill to act as a human metronome. He will constantly wave his ski poles to one side or the other, and you must ski in the indicated direction. Have him gradually vary the rhythm of his pole waves from slow to fast and match your turns to his rhythm.

You can also develop your own rhythm in stem turns by counting out the cadence.

Rhythm in stem turns.   Ski straight down the fall line of a gentle run. Pivot out the tail of one ski to a count of one. Apply pressure and let the ski guide you into a turn. Pivot the inside ski to match, to a count of two. To a new count of one, pivot out the tail of the new uphill ski. Pivot the new inside ski to match to a count of two. Continue making small turns pretty much in the fall line, getting the two to come right after the one. Keep up a one-two rhythm as long as you can.

This rhythm exercise also promotes a good feeling of pressuring first one ski and then the other. Without a definite weight transfer you'll be saying, "One thousand and one, one thousand and two . . ." instead of "One, two . . ." Be conscious of this pressure change from foot to foot.

Pressure flow. Without exaggerating any actions, feel your weight flow from one ski to the other during a turn. Start a turn by pushing off from the downhill ski. Let this weight flow upward to gradually settle onto the other ski. As it does, slide the inside ski in parallel. Keep the pressure flowing back and forth constantly.

You'll need some extension and flexion, an up-and-down motion, to transfer pressure smoothly, just as you would in walking. With weight primarily on the power ski the unweighted ski will slide in parallel quite early.

When you're feeling really ambitious try a "stem turn without a stem." Instead of rotating only a tail outward, place the whole ski outward to change an edge.

A nonstemmed "stem." At moderate speed flatten the uphill ski with a downhill knee movement. Slide the ski farther uphill, away from your body, keeping it parallel to the lower ski. When it is on edge transfer weight to it and let it take you around the turn. Pivot your feet to help the turn. Flatten the inside ski and slide it in parallel as early in the turn as you comfortably can.

Move both tip and tail outward to start this higher speed turn.

You'll need a little speed for this exercise. Don't worry if you can't do this one just yet. It's a stem so small you can't see it—a type of parallel turn. Now you're really discovering that the wedge and stem use the same principles as "advanced" turns.

SLOWING DOWN

"Damn the torpedoes—full speed ahead." That's fine advice for naval warfare, but now and then we like to slow down while skiing. Once you have confidence in your ability to stop whenever you desire, you can truly enjoy speed.

Round Turns

You already slowed with a braking wedge on very gentle slopes. It's a great use of edging, particularly in level confined areas, such as skiing into lift lines. But as the slope steepens, that wedge simply won't hold you. If Isaac Newton had skied, I'm sure he would have come up with some brilliant law of physics describing gravity and the skier. It would state that skis pointing down the fall line accelerate, and skis across the fall line decelerate. Basically, to go faster, keep your skis in the fall line; to slow down, resist gravity by turning out of the fall line.

Skiing uphill to slow. Choose a smooth hill, but one with a steepness near the limit of your ability. Point yourself straight downhill in a narrow wedge, bracing yourself against your poles. Take a deep breath and let yourself go. When you reach a comfortable but not quite toe-clenching speed, turn your skis back uphill, say, to your left for the first time. Let your skis run in a long arc, like the bottom half of the letter S, and see how far back uphill you can go before coasting to a stop. Practice this stop to both sides.

Look at your tracks to be sure you really made an arc, rather than an abrupt turn and a traverse. Once you feel confident that skiing uphill will stop you, change the size of your turns out of the fall line.

Speed control in various arcs. Experiment with varying the radius of your uphill stops, pivoting a more abrupt arc uphill to slow down sooner, or a more gradual one when you have more room. Pick out a target (a person, tree, two ski poles, etc.) across the slope and downhill from you. See if you can turn your skis in one round

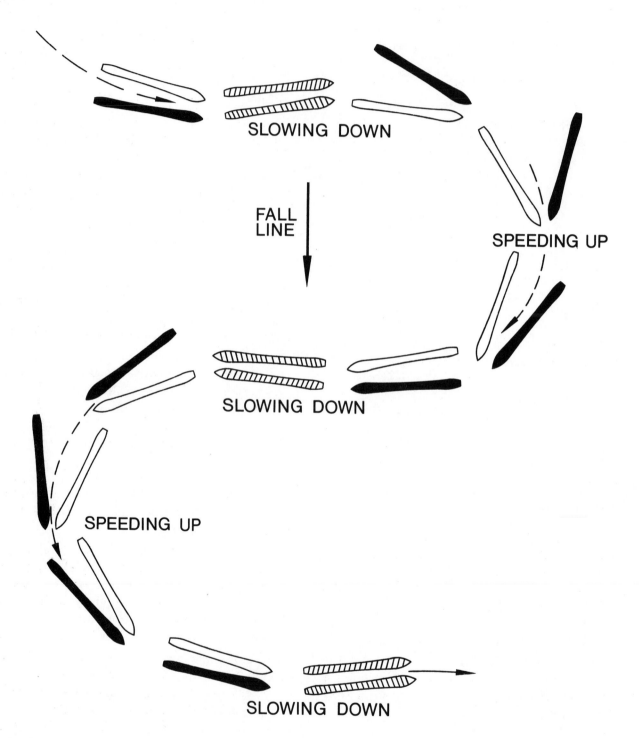

SLOWING DOWN

FALL
LINE

SPEEDING UP

SLOWING DOWN

SPEEDING UP

SLOWING DOWN

Slow down with round turns.

arc and come to a stop right at that object, merely by losing momentum traveling back uphill.

Your stopping distance will vary with differences in slope pitch and snow conditions.

Of course, most skiing is more than making one turn and stopping. Rather, it's a series of connected slowings. You'll want to ski uphill just enough to slow down instead of coming to a dead halt.

Slowing down by making round turns. Ski back uphill out of the fall line until your speed is moderated. Then make a turn in the other direction. Link one turn after the other, so that your tracks make a series of connected S shapes. Try this on slopes of varying steepness. To slow down more on a steeper pitch, your S track will be more curvy, and on a flatter pitch will be closer to a straight line.

You'll have to learn how much to ski back uphill without losing momentum for the next turn. If you don't slow enough, you'll gain too much speed. Completing a rounded turn to control speed is known as finishing a turn.

Rounded turns are great ways to slow down at any level of skiing. However, look at your tracks to make sure they form an S and not a Z. Too often skiers are so anxious to get past the fall line that they forget about the crucial center portion of the turn. This is also the part where you'll accelerate the most. You'll have a certain average speed, but this average speed is made up of fast and slow segments within each turn.

Speed changes. Assign a speed value to your skiing: one being slowest; two, moderate; and three, fastest. On a slope where you feel comfortable, link a series of turns, and call out the number corresponding to your speed. With good round turns to control speed you'll be calling out, "One-two-three-two-one-two . . ." as you accelerate into the fall line, decelerate out of it, and accelerate into it again.

The rush of speed in the fall line is one of the great thrills of the sport. Learn to enjoy it without hurrying your turn. As long as you can ski uphill to slow, the fall line speed will be invigorating rather than frightening.

Skidding

Unfortunately, there's not always enough room to ski back uphill to slow down. The slopes may be crowded or too narrow, or you may just need to put on the brakes and stop rapidly. Yes, you did buy skis equipped with power brakes—they're your edges. Anytime a ski is slightly across your direction of travel, its edge brushes against the snow. That friction will slow you down. You can increase the slowing by pivoting the ski more against your direction of travel and by edging more.

Let's start with a variation on the familiar wedge. Imagine you're traversing across a slope and need to slow down without turning uphill. To wedge you would pivot out both feet. However, the uphill foot is largely unweighted and won't slow you. It's the downhill foot that bites into the snow in this wedge. So we'll simply do a half wedge with only the lower foot, called a *downhill stem*, or just a *downstem* for short.

Downstem to slow. From a moderate traverse, pivot out the tail of your downhill ski. Follow this ski with your upper body to keep pressure on it. Immediately your speed will slow as the edge bites into the snow. Repeat, increasing the edge angle gradually to emphasize slowing.

You'll need weight on the skidding downhill ski. Flex your lower knee and angle your upper body outward as you pivot the ski outward. You may have to experiment with how rapidly you edge the downstemmed ski, as that inside edge also wants to turn you uphill.

This downstem can bring you to a complete stop, if you so desire. While you're slowing or stopping, you can use both skis, rather than leaving one hanging back uphill.

Downstem to parallel. From a traverse, downstem the lower ski to start slowing. Then pivot in the lightly weighted uphill ski to match the lower ski. Use a count of one to downstem and a count of two to match the upper ski. See if you can bring the one-two very close together.

Pivoting in the upper ski is the same as closing an uphill stem after a turn. You can pick up that ski or else first flatten it on the snow and then brush it across the snow without lifting it. The advantage of going to a parallel stance is that you're in a more relaxed, natural position and also that now you can slide sideways on two uphill edges, rather than just one.

Downstem across your direction of travel to slow.

Downstem one ski and pivot the other to match.

The parallel slowing position is really the same as the sideslip position. They are both skids on the uphill edges. They slow you down because the edges are across your direction of travel. We'll apply that skidding idea to the finish of each turn. First, practice getting into a skid from the fall line.

Finish turns with skids. Ski in the fall line at moderate speed in a small gliding wedge. Pivot your skis in a tight arc out of the fall line, as though finishing a turn, letting your uphill ski pivot in to match the lower. You'll be skidding sideways in addition to finishing the turn up the hill. If necessary, stay on flat skis and overturn your skis until you get a feeling for the skids.

Actually, you may have already been skidding to finish the turns, which is great. However, some skiers resist the sideways motion until they realize it has a valuable function—to slow down. You'll find that at higher speeds and in shorter turns it's very easy to skid. Centrifugal force is greater in these turns. It tries to pull you out of the turn, adding to the gravity force already fighting your edge hold.

Enough physics! These skids were developed in the last century to control speed. A skid is often known as a "christie." It's named in honor of the city of Christiania (now called Oslo), in Norway, where the christie originated. The christie just means skidding on two uphill edges to slow down.

Skidding in turns. As you turn across the fall line, keep your skis flat enough to allow the edges to slide sideways on the snow. Help them to skid by pivoting the lower ski outward, in a downstem, more than you normally would. Let the inner ski slide in parallel to match, so that you christie. Open a small uphill stem to start the next turn and link skidded turns down the slope.

Now you're starting to see the values of skids. They both slow you down and get you down the slope in a partial sideslip. Consequently, you can make fewer turns.

Skidding to cover distance. Pick a long moderate slope and ski it at one constant speed, at first without skidding. Traverse, turn, and traverse all the way down, counting the number of turns required. Now go back up and ski the same slope at the same speed, but skid as much as you can after each turn, so that you are sideslipping downhill while still going forward. See if you can decrease the number of turns required by half.

Skidding is controlled by the edges, but to use them you must flex in the ankle and knee joints. Too frequently skiers come around a turn with a stiff lower leg.

Bend zee knees, five dollars, pleeze. As you finish your turn, see for yourself if your downhill knee is really bent or not. While crossing the fall line to skid a turn finish, bend sideways from the waist and feel the back of the downhill knee with your lower hand. If it is bent, that's terrific. If not, then bend it by pushing in the back of your knee. Straighten up fully after feeling the knee, and immediately start another turn. Sink down while crossing the fall line to feel the back of the new downhill knee. Straighten for the next turn and continue this sequence down the hill.

Feeling the knee will also get you more used to the idea of flexing and extending for each turn, which we'll work on soon.

You won't want to skid every turn. Sometimes, you won't need to slow down with a christie. Don't forget that skiing a round turn back up the hill controls speed best. If you're racing or on flatter terrain, you may not need much slowing, and in marginal snow conditions you'll want to avoid much sideways motion. But for most of your skiing, round turns with skidding will be part of every turn. They are not only useful, but fun too, and you can't ask for more than that.

DOWNSTEM TURNS

You've already used a downstem to slow your speed. Now we'll emphasize its use in turning. The downstem is similar to the uphill stem, but it has more dynamic edging and pressuring.

You'll recall a downstem (sometimes referred to as an "abstem") simply means pivoting out the tail of the lower ski. This angles the ski across your direction of travel. Applying edge and pressure in this skid slows your speed. This sharp edgeset can also aid turns.

Downstem turn. Make turns at moderate speed. Upon completing each turn, pivot out the lower ski into a downstem, and pressure its edge. Transfer weight to your uphill ski and ride it around the turn. Complete the new turn by flexing while pivoting out the lower ski and pressing against it to rise onto the uphill for the next turn.

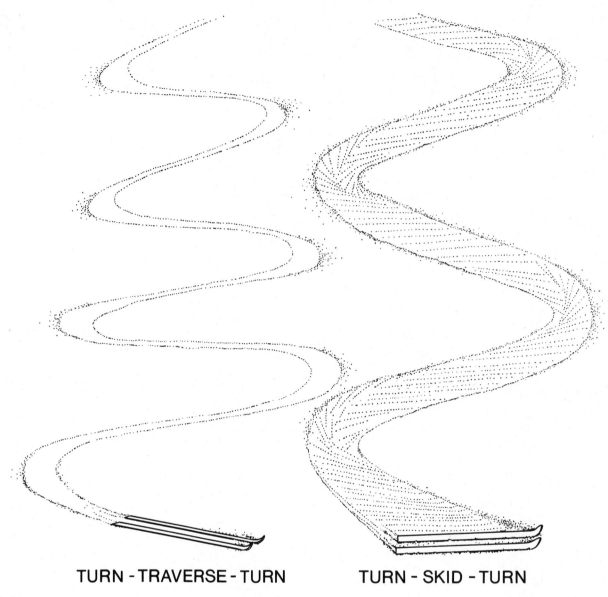

TURN - TRAVERSE - TURN   **TURN - SKID - TURN**

Skidding reduces the number of turns needed.

Pivoting the lower ski tail outward also gives you the advantage of changing the uphill edge. As your upper body follows the lower ski, it moves away from the uphill ski. That ski then changes from an outside to an inside edge. However, at this stage some skiers feel comfortable downstemming the lower ski while also matching the upper ski to it in a christie. If you do, that's great, but you may need to pivot the upper ski outward into a small stem to start the new turn.

One hopes that you are able to throw out a spray of snow from your downhill ski when you edge and pressure it abruptly. This rapid edge bite is called a *check*, because it retards, or checks, your speed. You can easily push from this check to transfer pressure to the upper ski, starting a new turn.

Pressure change in a downstem. From a steep traverse, downstem to slow your speed. Push up off a sharp

FALL LINE

Plant a pole with the edgeset in this downstem garland.

edgeset. Let your weight flow upward to settle back down onto the other ski which you are pivoting into the fall line. Apply this weight to the new ski and sharply downstem it. Feel your weight flow from foot to foot as you link turns near the fall line.

You pressure one foot and then the other, just as in walking. Combine that with a good edgeset, and you will find turns quite easy to make.

Up to now you've used your poles mainly for cleaning off the boots, getting up, or spearing lost candy wrappers and trail maps. If you have a feeling for the pressure transfer from foot to foot you can also start to plant the poles. They will help your timing and balance right now.

A pole plant just means touching the tip to the snow. When your hands are ready and out in front only pivots of the forearm and wrist are needed to direct the tip. For the time being, plant your pole a foot or so down the fall line from your toes with the pole shaft "growing" straight up from the plant. Most importantly, use the right pole for starting turns to the right, and vice versa!

Downstem garland with a pole plant. Traverse across a hill at moderate speed. Vigorously stem out the lower ski. As the edge bites in, touch the snow below the downhill boot with the downhill pole. Immediately push off the edge and flow your weight to the uphill ski. As you start to turn toward the fall line, christie back to the original traverse angle and downstem again. With each edge engagement of the lower ski, plant a pole and push off the lower ski.

The garland was an exercise to get you familiar with the timing of the pole plant without making turns across the fall line. The pole plant occurs at maximum edging, when that little spray of snow flies out from your power edge. It signals that you should push off immediately from that lower foot, extending to the upper foot. The pole plant must be an integral part of your pressuring action and not a separate step. If you have the rudiments of a pole plant, go ahead and use it in a turn. If the pole plant confuses you, forget about it for now. We'll be using several different approaches to pole plants later on.

The downstem edgeset is dynamic and you can apply it to a very active turn, a downstem wedel.

Downstem wedel. Stand on a gentle slope in a braking wedge. Without moving forward, establish a rhythm by pressuring your weight entirely onto the inside edge of one ski and then shifting it to the other ski's inside edge. When you have a good rhythm going, switching weight about once a second, push off down the fall line. Feel yourself turn from side to side. Let the unweighted foot relax each time to flow with the turn.

The wedel (pronounced with a V as "vedel") is simply one short turn after another in the fall line. You may even make some basically parallel turns as you relax the inner leg of each turn, letting it swing around to join the downstemmed ski. If you're feeling good about these turns, you're finding that motion and rhythm are essential to skiing. Try the downstem wedel with a gentle pole plant at the time of each edgeset. Remember to use the right pole with the right ski's edgeset, and vice versa.

You've probably run into some small moguls by now. The downstem helps you to handle these gentle bumps easily.

Downstem in moguls. Approach a small mogul at slow speed in a shallow traverse. Downstem, so that your lower ski pushes against the uphill side of the mogul. Immediately transfer your weight to the uphill ski and turn around the mogul by edging and pivoting that ski. After a bit of practice, touch your downhill pole to the mogul crest just as you push off from the down-stemmed ski to start turning.

The downstem slows you down, a reassuring feature when you don't know what's hiding on the other side of a bump. The maneuver also sets you up for the next turn. The big secret is to downstem against the uphill side of the bump, rather than waiting until you're past the summit. Then the bump's shape will draw you right around it for a turn. Of course, you can also use this technique on any rounded terrain, such as a convex ridge. Armed with this knowledge, you're ready to go out after bigger game, the intermediate slopes!

Downstem against the uphill side of a bump (partially hidden here by snow flying from the dynamic edgeset).

16
Intermediate Technique

Intermediate is a nebulous term. Some skiers like to call themselves intermediates after two hours on skis, and others retain the phrase for years. Many try to subdivide the classification, prefixing "lower" or "advanced" in front of "intermediate."

This chapter is designed for skiers who are ready to venture onto the "more difficult" slopes. It's also for those who already ski these blue square trails but aren't ready to tackle the most difficult runs.

You should feel comfortable on the "easiest way down" trails before delving into this chapter. Most of your turns are started with a small wedge and finished in a parallel christie. You'll learn techniques to improve your stopping ability, to start your turns with parallel motions, to control pressure better, and to handle mild moguls. Mastering these skill refinements will open up a huge expanse of the mountain for your ski enjoyment.

BETTER TURNS

As you move onto intermediate slopes, you'll ski longer runs on steeper terrain. This calls for improved speed control and better turning ability. You'll need to develop sensitivity to the snow, to

make your motions fluid, and to retain a good body position.

Improving Your Senses

Your primary sense of vision is a major factor in maintaining balance. You should allow for your reaction time by perceiving what will happen in the future. Focusing on your ski tips only shows you where you've been by the time the sight registers in your brain. Even at fifteen miles per hour you'll cover twenty-two feet in just one second. With increasing speed you must look far enough ahead to prepare mentally and physically for all those bumps and trees rushing to meet you.

For additional vision tips, you may want to read the section on storms in "The Elements" and also review goggle selection in "Gearing Up."

Sometimes we depend too heavily on eyesight at the expense of our other balance sensors. If you've been fortunate enough to watch a blind skier on the slopes, you'll understand what I mean. Try closing your eyes to increase your body sensitivity to the snow.

Skiing with closed eyes. On a very gentle slope have a friend ski near you to warn you of unexpected skiers or obstacles. Close your eyes and push off in a straight run, balancing to stay over your feet as they accelerate. Link turns and find the perfect balancing points throughout each turn. Next, ski over some gentle terrain changes or small bumps with your eyes closed, feeling with your feet and knees when the snow surface rises up and when it falls away.

The body can only "feel terrain" when the joints are allowed to flex in response to varying pressures. Avoid skiing with tensed muscles, which inhibit motion and sensing. Stay loose and relaxed.

Your body must actively balance for speed changes throughout each turn and for terrain variations. This requires sensitivity in your feet to what your skis are doing. Nerve endings in the feet, ankles, and lower legs respond to pressure changes from the boots. To feel the changes, stay centered in your boots rather than hanging too far back or forward. Allow your skis to become extensions of your feet, with your toes stretching to the tips and your heels to the tails.

Increasing foot sensitivity. Unbuckle your ski boots and make turns on easy terrain. Feel your whole foot sole against the boot bottom and become aware of the balancing movements your body makes to keep the entire foot pressed to the ski.

Become conscious of how the snow feels under your ski tips. They are twenty to thirty inches in front of your boot and will give you advance warning of terrain changes. Eventually, your skis and boots will become a vital part of your sensory apparatus. Cold or numb feet lose their ability to sense, so adjust the boot buckles loose enough for blood circulation and to avoid pinching nerves.

Another good way to improve your runs is to awaken and use all your senses.

Using all of your senses. Make runs concentrating on senses other than sight. For instance, on one run, identify all the sounds you can, such as birds, squirrels, wind in treetops, the scrunch of your skis in the snow, your parka flapping in the breeze, or other skiers. On another run, smell the pine trees, the burgers frying in the cafeteria, the perfume of suntan lotion or the freshness of the air. For touch concentrate on the boot pressures, the lightness or heaviness of your body during turns, the wind on your face, or the feel of a pole plant. For taste recall the breakfast you had, the hot chocolate you're looking forward to, or stretch out your tongue to catch a snowflake.

Becoming Fluid

You've noticed that good skiers are not stiff. They are fluid and graceful, in constant motion. You will also be fluid if you're relaxed.

Of course, it's easy to say, "Stay relaxed," but it's hard advice to follow when faced with an icy slope that resembles the north wall of Everest. If you have any yoga training, a personal mantra, or a favorite prayer, you might try those. However, there are several other positive ways to relax your mind and body.

Visualizing a run. At the top of a run look down the slope and visualize yourself skiing it. See yourself make perfect, fluid, controlled turns all the way down. Then immediately push off and make the same run you just visualized.

Stiffness is a major enemy of good turns. When muscles are tensed rather than loose they don't respond. Before starting a run you should "get the kinks out" by stretching.

Stretching. Before each run loosen up your muscles, particularly after a cold lift ride. Twist and stretch from head to toe until you feel some pull, but do not bounce.

Movement is at the heart of relaxation. During your run keep moving to stay loose. To avoid paralyzing your muscles, try exaggerating movements, jumping, swinging your arms, or touching your toes.

Tenseness in one part of the body affects all the muscles. One common cause is simply gripping the poles too hard.

Relaxing your pole grip. While skiing, relax your clenched hands by merely uncurling the index finger of each hand. Let the finger straighten out. Immediately your grip relaxes, and this relaxation spreads up your arms and throughout your body.

Another way to keep motion and to give needed oxygen to muscles is to remember to breathe. Often skiers are so engrossed with getting down the hill that they actually hold their breath all the way.

Breathing with rhythm. Before starting a run, concentrate on inhaling and exhaling. Continuing to breathe as you ski, try to time your breathing to your turns. Inhale to start a turn and exhale to finish a turn.

Rhythm is really a key word in skiing. It's the factor that makes it graceful. Rhythm comes into play when you link a series of turns down the slope. One way to start thinking beyond just one turn is to associate musical rhythm with skiing rhythm.

Singing in the snow. Sing, whistle, or hum your favorite tune while skiing. Synchronize your turns to the beat of your music. Try a slower tune on a gentle slope and a lively tune on a steeper one, matching your turns to the beat.

Helpful hint number 243—don't try Ravel's "Bolero" on trails called "Free-Fall Plunge."

Another good way to think of skiing as connected turns is to ski a slalom course which forces you to turn rhythmically through the gates.

Slalom courses. Set up a fun race course consisting of slalom poles in a straight line. If you don't have poles, you can substitute paper cups, snowballs, or food coloring spots. Ski constant round turns through the course. When you have the feeling, ski imaginary slalom courses, linking continuous turns all the way down the slope.

Often rhythm is inhibited simply because we think too much about the next turn. Overanalyzing a turn keeps it from happening. You will overcome this tendency with spontaneous turns.

Following in tracks. Ski in the tracks of a more skilled skier. Match the turns of the lead skier, and you'll automatically copy his or her rhythm without even thinking about it.

Another way to develop spontaneity is to turn when another skier directs you.

Turns on command. Have a partner ski behind you. Your friend will signal you to turn by shouting, "Turn" or by clacking his or her ski poles together. The signals should be continuous, but in a varying rhythm.

Body Position

Your feet are unbelievably smart. If you'll give them a chance, they will turn your skis. However, at this stage too many skiers are hampered by an awkward, contorted body position. This prevents easy turns and causes loss of control on the steeper slopes.

The athletic stance you've been using relies on feet comfortably apart, back mostly upright, and hands slightly in front. If you've been feeling undue muscular strain, you're probably off balance, or bending at the waist and sticking the derriere out. When the pelvis is tilted downward in this stance you'll have a curved, hollow spine— your elbows are pulled back, your legs are stiff, and your weight is on the heels. To correct this stance, imagine a belly dance routine where you thrust the pelvis forward and upward by drawing the abdomen up and in. Once your pelvis is comfortably tilted up your seat will tuck in and your balance improves immensely.

Most skiers are surprised to see how they really look on videotape or film. You can get a good idea simply by watching your shadow.

Watching your shadow. On a sunny day, ski down a slope where the sun is at your back. Your shadow shows how you look. Try to make the shadow relaxed, smooth and graceful.

One hopes your shadow looks relatively quiet, although not static, as you make fluid turns. If you use a great deal of twists, bends, and contortions of the arms, head, and torso, you're probably fighting for balance. Graceful and smooth experts ski quietly. Their skis interact subtly with the snow to do their bidding.

Generally your upper body should be a balancing mechanism, gently reacting to changes in your skis' speed or direction. The main turning should take place at your feet. They are attached directly to the skis. If you turn the arms or hips, that motion has to transfer all the way down to your feet to do any good. We'll use the upper body for additional turning force, but right now let your feet take over. The following exercise is highly recommended for skiers of any level. If you're stuck in a permanent wedge, it may get you parallel, and at more advanced levels it may increase your edge control on steep slopes.

Quiet upper body. On a gentle slope hold your poles as though carrying a tray in a cafeteria. Wherever your upper body faces the tray also faces. Point this tray straight down the fall line and keep it there as you ski. Imagine that any time you twist the tray you spill the food. Make continuous linked turns down the fall line, concentrating on keeping your upper body quiet and forgetting about your feet. Have a partner watch you from below in the fall line to see if you are keeping your upper body quiet.

The "tray" is merely an indicator of where your upper body is facing. You should be exaggerating by keeping it directly down the fall line. Your feet will find the easiest way to turn, without your brain having to analyze the hundreds of actions needed to get you safely down the hill.

FALL LINE

Make short turns from the lower body.

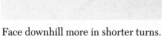
Face downhill more in shorter turns.

Keep working at this exercise until you have it! Don't cheat by facing only your arms down the hill instead of your whole upper body. Check to be sure your hips are quiet too and still centered over your skis. For this exercise, think of your hips, upper body, and head as being locked in one position, with your legs and feet absolutely free to twist beneath you.

By facing your body down the hill your skis will probably end up parallel after each turn, skidding on their uphill edges. If you twist to face back up the hill, you fight this christie.

Tip crosser. Make a slow wedge turn. As you cross the fall line to finish the turn, point your "tray" back up the hill. Immediately the uphill ski lags behind the lower one and tries to cross over. Repeat the wedge turn with the "tray" pointed downhill all the way through the turn. Automatically, the uphill ski comes out ahead and slides in parallel on its uphill edge.

Whenever you face uphill in a wedge position, you force the uphill ski onto its inside edge, and also pressure that edge. Rather than becoming parallel, that ski tries to cross the lower one.

You don't see good skiers in this extreme tray-carrying position all the time. However, you do need to face downhill somewhat in wide turns, and decidedly so in narrow turns.

Facing downhill in various size turns. Stand at the top of a smooth moderate slope. Imagine a large narrow upside-down V with the point where you are standing. It culminates at the bottom of the slope, where it is

perhaps ten yards wide. Serve a tray and ski down the slope, just touching the outside boundaries of the V in your turns. As your turns get wider and the tray begins to feel awkward, aim your upper body more in the direction your skis point.

In wider turns you can comfortably face your ski tips more, but you must still keep the uphill side of your body ahead of the downhill side.

Even when holding your poles normally be conscious of where your upper body is facing. Your edging is increased by lateral leg motions uphill and decreased by lateral motions downhill. You will be able to adjust the edge easily only when you're facing downhill.

Angulation and edging. Stand comfortably on a steep hillside with your uphill ski, knee, hip, shoulder, and hand slightly ahead of the downhill ones. Increase your edging by first moving your ankles uphill. Return them to their original position and move your knees uphill to increase edging. Angle your upper body downhill at the same time to maintain balance over your feet. Next move your hips uphill, again compensating for balance by angling your upper body outward. Now advance your downhill ski, knee, hip, shoulder, and hand ahead of the uphill ones. Try to increase edging from each joint. You'll find it's not possible to increase edge and also to retain balance in this stance.

An angulated stance just means standing comfortably on your uphill edges. Your joints then have freedom to make lateral edging movements. As you increase edging, for example, by driving your knees uphill, you would fall uphill without a slight sideways-forward flex at the hips and waist. This flex allows your upper body to tilt slightly outward. Your weight balances over your feet, especially over the uphill edge of your downhill ski. During maximum edging an extremely angulated stance is sometimes called a *comma position*. Remember that this articulated position is not a static one and is used only at the time you need the edge.

Anytime the uphill half of your body falls behind the downhill half, your stance becomes "blocked." This means that you can't increase edge and still balance over your feet. That's why you were cautioned in early lessons to keep the uphill ski ahead. Obviously, the uphill foot will also be ahead, as will the uphill knee. But too frequently skiers forget about the uphill hip and come around a turn with the downhill hip leading. Perhaps this happens to you as your lower leg becomes perfectly straight. No matter how hard you try, that lower knee just won't bend. This position is caused by turning your torso back uphill, and your hips follow to face uphill. Even letting your uphill hand drag behind you can cause a chain reaction destroying body position.

Keeping the hips unblocked. Put your poles aside and ski with your hands on your hips. You can feel the hip position. Bring the hips back to an open position facing downhill whenever you feel them rotate excessively to point uphill.

Of course you'll normally ski with poles, but a visualization aid is often helpful to keep you in a good stance.

Facing downhill. Imagine a flashlight beam shining out of your navel. Whenever the beam strikes uphill of your ski tips, your body position is ruining your edging capability. Always keep the beam shining to the downhill side of the ski tips.

You can also visualize this concept by imagining an arrow coming out of your navel. It always points to the downhill side of your ski tips.

Now that you understand the value of a good stance, you can have some fun as a critic of other skiers.

Observing body position. While riding the chair, take advantage of the time to observe skiers on the slopes. Watch those in trouble—you'll see excess upper body movement, and as soon as they "grab for the hill"

A flashlight beam from the navel should always point downhill of the ski tips.

This skier is making problems for herself by facing uphill.

FALL LINE

114

by turning their upper bodies back uphill drastically, get ready to see a spill. Contrast them to smooth, controlled skiers with quieter upper bodies.

In short, stand comfortably over your uphill edges, facing downhill somewhat. Your feet will take over and ski for you.

PARALLEL STOPS

You've generally been finishing turns in a relaxed stance known as parallel, where both skis point in the same direction. Skidding on the uphill edges then slows you down. However, you've probably gotten into this parallel position by turning first one ski and then the other. That's fine, as it's a sequential action, the same way legs are controlled in walking. Now we'll begin turning both skis at the same time, in a simultaneous action. This is what many skiers mean when they say "parallel."

First, we'll concentrate on the finish of parallel turns and learn a useful stop at the same time. It's called a *hockey stop* and is named after the way ice skaters make a sudden stop. With long "skate" edges and soft "ice" you'll find this stop much easier on skis than on skates.

Parallel stop from traverse. Traverse across a smooth hill with feet comfortably apart. Start from a high, upright stance. Abruptly flex downward, simultaneously forcefully pivoting your skis across your direction of travel, tips uphill. Gradually angle the ski bottoms against the snow so that they bite in and stop your slide. Repeat at higher speeds and from traverses in both directions.

You're combining pivoting and pressure control at the same time. Rapidly flexing downward in the ankles and knees temporarily reduces weight on the skis. This makes them easier to pivot quickly. You may find that after you pivot applying weight more toward the heels prevents the skis from turning rapidly up the hill.

Of course, the hockey stop isn't only done from traverses. That's a special case in which you stay on the same set of uphill edges. Now you can try going from flat skis to the uphill edges.

Hockey stop from a straight run. Ski straight down the fall line, on flat parallel skis. Flex downward, simultaneously pivoting your skis underneath you. Increase

edge to a stop. Again ski in the fall line, but this time stop to the other side.

In an ideal hockey stop you should travel in one direction both immediately before and during the stop. The only difference is that before the stop your skis are pointing in the direction you're going and during the stop your skis are skidding across your direction of travel.

In these stops it's important to keep your upper body facing in the original direction of travel for maximum edge control. Just pivot the legs and feet underneath your upper body. You'll want to pivot to flat skis, then increase edges to stop. The quicker you edge, the faster you'll stop, but the more critical your balance, as momentum tries to throw you headfirst over your skis.

Edgesets in stops. From a moderately steep traverse flex downward, pivoting your skis uphill. Using careful knee action, try to skid on a flat ski for a long distance before coasting to a stop. Repeat, this time edging abruptly after pivoting your skis. See if you can "hit" the edges hard enough to spray snow and stop quickly.

You should feel a great deal of pressure on your feet as you increase the edging. The stop begins with less than normal weight on your skis as you flex downward and concludes with a greater than normal weight. This pressure change will be an important part of future turns, so get used to the feeling.

This abrupt edgeset is the classic parallel stop with style and flair. It's a great maneuver to practice for the flashy impression it will make on your friends, not to mention the utilitarian value of stopping quickly. You may be tempted to use the hockey stop to spray your friends with snow, but I'd advise against it. If your skis stop quicker than you anticipated during an abrupt edgeset, you could be catapulted headfirst downhill. This is also called *catching an edge*, and can happen to the best. One famous incident occurred to an Olympic champion, who showed off with a hockey stop in front of a restaurant deck. He ended up sliding headfirst across a picnic table, collecting all the food on the way.

When you have a feeling for the edgeset you can add a pole plant.

Pole plant in hockey stops. At the end of the skid in a parallel stop, plant your downhill pole just as you

Applying more edge stops you faster.

A dynamic parallel stop with a pole plant.

make the final edgeset and come to a stop. The tip of the pole should end up a foot to a foot and a half down the fall line from your lower boot toe.

The pole plant is an excellent habit to develop for future turns. It's simply a touching of the tip to the snow at the finish of the stop. Planting down the fall line from your lower boot keeps you facing downhill for good edge control. The plant should be a distance away from your boot for two good reasons. First, it aids your angulation and gets you out over the downhill ski in a balanced, aggressive position. Second, if the pole is too close to the skis and you should happen to mistime your edgeset, you'd ski into it, a proven way to do a sideways cartwheel.

Skiing down a slope isn't really a series of stops, but rather a series of "almost stops," as the skier slows down after each turn. Now we'll use the hockey stop to control speed at the finish of a turn.

Linked skids. From a moderate traverse flex downward and initiate a hockey stop. However, before your edging has stopped you, touch your pole to the snow and rise up to the same angle of traverse. When your speed has built up again parallel skid to slow. Repeat in steeper traverses so that your skids come closer together.

Instead of a traverse, we'll now apply the parallel skid to its most useful application, skiing in the fall line.

Fall line skidding. Ski in the fall line and do a hockey stop to control speed. Touch your downhill pole to the snow when you've slowed enough and immediately rise up, pivoting skis back into the fall line. Again, do a hockey stop, but this time to the other side. Repeat down the hill alternating skidding to each side. Stay in a very narrow track, perhaps ten feet wide.

For this exercise you should not be traversing, but rather going from a sideslip on one side to a slideslip on the other. What connects the two sideslips is a pole plant, which signals you to rise back up and get into the fall line. The pole plant says that it's time to get off the uphill edges and onto flat skis. One hopes that as you plant the pole and rise, your skis both pivot into the fall line at the same time. If not, try to make the stem very small. We'll be working soon on starting the skis simultaneously into a turn.

As with any turn, you should be pressuring the power ski. This means that your weight goes from foot to foot as you skid from one side to the other. It always ends up on the downhill ski as you finish

117

Controlling speed with parallel skids in linked turns.

a turn or complete a skid. If you get a feeling of rapidly pressuring from one foot to the other, you'll have a good rhythm going.

Hockey stop wedel. Start from a very narrow wedge in a steep fall line. Keep your poles in front to prevent sliding forward while you get a rhythm going. Flex to pressure one inside edge, rise up, and flex to pressure the other ski's inside edge. Also press harder on the corresponding pole. Change from edge to edge perhaps once a second. Take your poles out and ski, so that you are skidding primarily on one foot, rising up, and flexing down in a hockey-stop action to skid on the other. Let the unweighted ski swing around so that it matches the skidding one. Make dynamic edgesets to control speed and use a pole plant at each edgeset to signal a new turn.

This is a dynamic, rhythmic exercise. That wedel (with the *v* pronunciation) means one turn after another. This is really the same exercise you did with a downstem in the previous chapter, only now with emphasis on a parallel stance.

You may find yourself drifting to one side of the trail or losing rhythm during these connected skids. It's because everyone has a favorite, stronger side to stop on. If you do have a weaker side, practice stops on it. Your problem may be in your body position, so be sure you're not swinging your upper body around in one direction. Go back to "holding a tray" in front as an aid to see what you're doing.

The finish of every turn doesn't have to be a dramatic parallel slowing. It can be a gentle, parallel finish with almost no skidding. But once you know how to make it dynamically, you can temper the amount of skidding to suit any slope.

STARTING TURNS PARALLEL

You'll recall that parallel means both feet pointing in the same direction, but not locked together. When you traverse a hill in one direction you ride on two uphill edges. Traversing in the other direction, you ride on the other two edges. Somewhere during your turn you have to change edges. If your feet point the same way during this edge change, you've made a parallel turn. If the skis are not

Dynamic edgesets control speed in short-radius turns.

Stepping out the tip and tail equal amounts to start a turn.

matched during the turn and instead are closer at the tips than tails, you've made a wedge or stem turn.

You're probably finishing your turns in a parallel stance. In "Parallel Stops" we worked on turning both legs at the same time to complete a turn. Now we'll work on starting those turns by rotating both legs simultaneously.

In a stem you first start one ski into a turn and then follow with the other. A parallel turn is not necessarily superior to a stem turn. However, you're approaching speeds at which a parallel turn is easy. At a higher speed you don't want to place a stemmed ski suddenly across your direction of travel. It would dig in and you'd fight for balance as your direction changed rapidly. Unless you really enjoy making angels in the snow, you're using very small stems by now, rather than large ones.

As a stem becomes small enough we could just call it parallel. This leads to a popular turn many skiers enjoy.

Sequential edge change "parallel" turn. At moderate speed, move out both the tip and tail of the uphill ski, placing it farther away from the downhill one. Keep this uphill ski parallel to the lower one as you put it on its inside edge. Transfer weight to it and turn, helping by pivoting your feet. Finish the turn in a skid, bringing the skis closer together. Repeat by moving the new uphill ski outward to change its edge.

In this turn you're still first changing edge on one ski and then on the other, as in a stem. However, the feet are pointing in the same direction all the time. It's a sort of hybrid parallel. We're going to work on this idea extensively in the next chapter when you step turns dynamically. Right now we want to concentrate on changing both ski edges at the same time, rather than first pushing one ski outward. This is the type of turn most skiers think of as "parallel."

You've already done many simultaneous leg maneuvers. This is a good time to review a few, since you'll need them to start parallel turns.

Simultaneous edging. Traverse across a shallow, packed hill. Release edges to start a sideslip. Go back and forth from flat skidding skis to edged traversing ones.

Ski the fall line on a very flat hill, keeping skis parallel. Start on flat skis. Then edge both skis simultaneously to their left edges. You'll start a gradual curve to the left. Reduce edging on both skis so they flatten onto the snow at the same time. Edge both skis simultaneously to their right edges, starting a gradual right curve. Repeat, feeling your ski bases go flat on the snow at the same time.

Simultaneous pivoting. On a shallow packed hill, ski in the fall line, with feet comfortably apart and parallel. Pivot both skis slightly to one side while staying on a flat ski. Pivot the skis simultaneously the other way, still on a flat ski. Make many small turns down the slope.

You can now combine the simultaneous edging and pivoting to get a feeling of starting a turn.

Turn starts. From a moderate traverse flex downward to skid on both uphill edges. Plant your downhill pole and rise up to flatten the skis. Simultaneously pivot both skis toward the fall line. Again flex to pivot skis uphill and skid. Repeat rhythmically across the hill. Then do a series in the opposite direction as well.

In this garland exercise you practice the elements of a turn start and finish without actually crossing the fall line.

You may be able to make a complete parallel

Start turns by flattening the skis and pivoting them toward the fall line.

turn from just these elements. However, many skiers get hung up crossing the fall line because they fail to transfer pressure from ski to ski. Even in your wedge turns, you found that a push or stepping action from one ski to the other helped start the skis into a turn. You're always pressuring the dominant ski to make a turn. This power ski is the outside ski of the turn. It happens to be the lower

ski as you complete a turn out of the fall line. You could instead weight the inside ski of a turn, but, as the next exercise will show, that position is precarious for balancing.

Pressuring the outside ski. Stand across the fall line on a moderate hill. Have a partner down the fall line pull hard on your ski pole baskets while you resist by

Maintain an upright stance by balancing against the outside ski.

Balancing against the inside ski is precarious.

pressuring against your downhill ski. Let your partner suddenly release the pull at his or her discretion, and you'll automatically balance by weighting your uphill ski. Now have your partner repeat the pull, only this time you will resist by pressuring against your uphill ski, a position you'll find awkward for balance. When your partner suddenly releases the pull you'll probably fall uphill.

Your partner in the above exercise has been acting as centrifugal force. This natural force tries to pull you to the outside of every turn. The sharper your turn radius or the higher your speed, the greater the pull. You balance best against this force when you pressure the outside foot of each turn. This places your center of gravity inside the support base of your feet.

At the start of each turn you are no longer resisting a centrifugal force pulling you downhill. If you were to keep weight on the downhill ski, you would really be off balance, as that ski becomes the uphill ski after you cross the fall line. I hope you're not totally confused with up and down. I'm just saying the power ski changes as soon as you start into a new turn direction, and not when you reach the fall line.

This points out a big difference between most stem turners and parallel turners. In a stem turn weight transfers slowly from one foot to the other. After the stem is opened weight gradually goes to the stemmed ski until finally enough pressure is off the inside ski to change its edge and match the skis parallel. In a parallel turn this weight transfer is frequently more pronounced.

At the crucial start of a turn, the outside or power ski is the uphill one temporarily. To facili-

tate a turn you must transfer weight very early in that turn.

Early weight transfer in turns. Make medium-radius turns on a packed surface. Exaggerate your weight transfer by keeping the inside ski of each turn lifted in the air. As you finish one turn, you will have only the downhill ski on the snow. Plant your pole as you place your uphill ski down parallel on the snow, firmly weighting it. Immediately lift your downhill ski and ride the new outside ski around the turn. Repeat for each turn. Discover the feeling of first weighting and then turning each new outside ski.

Lifting a ski into the air is extra work and isn't normally done. However, this exaggeration is a good learning aid to force you to commit your weight early to the outside ski.

Lifting the inside ski also shows where you are standing on the skis. Sometimes skiers revert to wedge turns simply because they are standing so far back on the skis they are having trouble pivoting them. If your lifted ski comes cleanly off the snow, or even higher at the tail, then you are keeping up with your skis as they accelerate into the fall line. If your ski tail is dragging, you're too far back, and your own tail will be dragging in the snow fairly soon.

While you're lifting the inside ski you can convert this exercise into a trick to impress your friends.

Javelin turn. Just for fun, while you are picking up the inside ski throughout a turn, cross it in the air over the outside ski to form an X. Uncross the inside ski, put it on the snow parallel to your downhill ski and immediately start another turn, picking up the downhill ski and crossing it above the new outside ski as you turn.

122

FALL LINE

Transfer weight at the finish of one turn and the start of the next.

This is sometimes called the *Iron Cross turn*. You may find yourself riding a good edge in this trick, as the position forces you to increase your angulation. As you bring the ski back parallel and set it down, you decrease edging, otherwise known as deangulation. This helps flatten your skis to start the next turn. In a normal, nontrick-type turn, lateral knee motions often control the edging. Flexing downward to christie makes additional knee drive available for edging. Upward extension takes away the edging to flatten the skis again for turning. You'll apply this concept in the "Unweighting" part of this chapter.

After all these exercises it's time to relax and make a series of easy parallel turns.

Parallel turn with weight transfer. Start in the fall line of a smooth moderate slope. Finish a turn with a christie. At maximum pressure on your lower ski plant the corresponding pole, rising to flatten the skis. Pivot them into the fall line as you pressure the uphill ski. Repeat, making smooth, round turns.

This relaxed parallel turn is especially great for larger-radius turns on open slopes. You can modify edging and pivoting to help vary the radius. You'll know when you're doing this turn well, as it feels terrific.

Skiers often complain that they are stuck in a small stem, which prevents their making a pure parallel turn. In fact, the problem is so common ski instructors often classify them as "RSers," instructor language for "residual stem turners." As a matter of habit that unweighted ski tail is pushed outward and then weighted. The cure is to weight

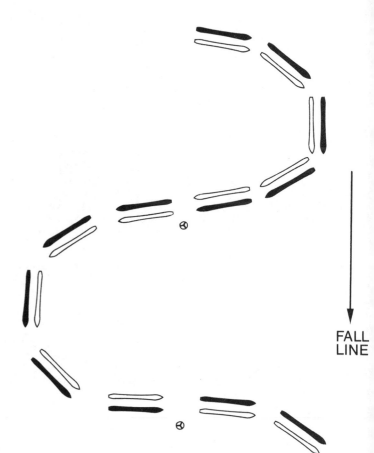

FALL LINE

Weight transfer occurs at the change of direction.

the ski *before* it is turned. A ski with weight on it then becomes difficult to stem. Think of weighting the new outside ski first and then turning.

Time of weight transfer. Imagine that your ski tracks trace a round outline into which you set a huge old-fashioned clock face. Try to make your weight trans-

An easy parallel turn.

fer occur at the same point where your turn starts; that is, at the twelve o'clock position. Have someone ski behind you watching your track to see when the weight transfer happens. If your weight transfer doesn't occur until one or two o'clock, it's coming much too late.

Once again, the key point is to *transfer the weight early.*

Another way to avoid that residual stem is to round out your turns. Frequently, skiers are in such a rush to get through the fall line without picking up speed that they stem just to get the turn over with. You'll have to learn to enjoy some speed and to let your skis take you down the slope in a linked S course rather than a panic Z one. The first part of your turn should be a float, or a free-fall waiting phase before you cross the fall line.

Count to five. As you start to change edges for a new turn, begin counting from one to five. So you can't rush the count, say, "One thousand and one, one thousand and two . . ." Round out your first part of the turn so that you're not in the fall line until you're at the three count. Right after the five start a new turn with one.

Let's hope you didn't take the ten count on that one. We'll be working on increasing turn speed soon enough, but your turn will still be rounded.

A pole plant is integral to parallel turns. It helps timing and rhythm by signaling the start of a new turn. But the pole plant also provides a valuable balancing aid when transferring weight from foot to foot.

Poles for balance. Stand across a steep hill as though you are completing a turn. Take the ski pole baskets out of the snow and lift your uphill ski. Now step to the

uphill ski, lifting the downhill one. This will be awk-ward and hard on the balance. Repeat, but this time plant your downhill pole. Lean on it slightly for balance as you step from the downhill to the uphill ski. Your weight will transfer smoothly.

Thus the pole plant is also a stabilizing factor. It should be planted when you are ready to transfer weight to the new power ski. That transfer occurs at the bottom of one S as you get off the edges and pivot toward the fall line. The sequence is plant, push. To get a feeling of the plant, try actually pushing off it to help your lower leg extend.

Let your pole plant be a natural action. If your hands are in front, as they should be, the plant will be smooth without excess motions. Only a slight cock of the wrist and a forearm movement are needed to place the pole tip on the snow. Remem-ber to retain a good upper-body position by keeping your uphill hand ahead of your downhill, pole-planting hand.

You can play a game with a friend to sharpen your pole plant.

Figure eights. Find a slope with snow soft enough to leave ski tracks. Have your partner ski ahead of you making round turns. Ski half a turn behind your partner, but crisscrossing in the opposite direction, so that you make a figure eight out of his tracks. Plant your pole where you cross his track, which is also the point at which you start into a new half of an eight.

Even without a partner, you should strive to make imaginary figure eights. Your turns in either direc-tion should be mirror images of each other, punc-tuated by a pole plant. A European Olympic skier

A pole plant is a natural motion.

I once worked with phrased this idea best in his limited English by saying, "Your turns to the left and your turns to the right are exactly the same, but just the opposite."

Mirror-image skiing applies to a direct fall line route. Once in a while you'll ski a double fall line, a sidehill trail in which your route and the fall line are different.

Rhythm on a sidehill. Ski at an angle across the fall line. Maintain your course by making short turns into the fall line. Turns out of the fall line will be long. Establish a repeating rhythm of "quick" on one side and "drawn out" on the other.

With variable rhythm and parallel motions you're starting to dance on skis, flowing from turn to turn. Keep it up!

Left and right turns are mirror images.

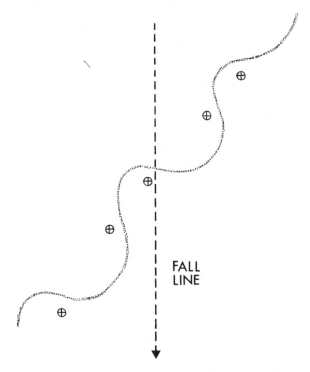

FALL
LINE

In a double fall line turns to each side are of different duration.

MOGULS

On the intermediate slopes you've begun to hit (only figuratively, I hope) small fields of bumps, known as moguls. Contrary to popular belief, these are not sculptured by secret crews of sadistic mogul-makers who do their dirty work in the dark of winter nights. Whenever the snow is even slightly soft, a little loose snow flies up from the ski edges as skiers skid and turn. A mogul forms from numerous skiers turning in the same spot.

Moguls are intimidating at first, because you're worried about running into them, getting stuck in them, or bouncing over them at Mach 1. However, they really make your turns easier if you use your skills on them. In this chapter we'll examine the smoother bumps you'll be likely to encounter on the intermediate trails. In the advanced chapter we'll take on the huge bumps, the "man-eaters."

Your first concern in bumps is making quick turns. You'll want to practice pivoting rapidly, and you'll recall that a lower stance helps you twist your skis easier.

Gorilla turns. Hold the poles out of your way, or discard them. On a very gentle smooth slope exaggerate a low stance by flexing deeply in the knees. Bend forward from your waist just enough to keep your weight centered over your feet. Now, while keeping your skis flat, see how rapidly you can pivot your skis back and forth in short turns.

Gorilla turns are also a good test of balance, as you must be centered over your feet to pivot the skis. You may make two turns a second if you pivot efficiently. If you can't turn rapidly, try moving your weight forward over your feet. Just moving your hands forward a few inches can help. The idea is to pivot about the axis of your lower legs, so that the ski tips and tails swing equal amounts. If your weight is too far back, you're trying to pivot from behind the ski's center point. This means the tip has to swing a greater distance. Without going into the physics involved, it's a tough way to turn.

Efficient skiing also means skiing from the lower body. Gorilla turns make you do just that and avoid time-wasting upper-body movements. Naturally, we don't see people skiing continuously in this low stance, as it is very tiring on the muscles. However, it's good to know that when needed in the bumps, you can swivel your feet rapidly by increasing your flex.

The pole plant you've been practicing so much is especially valuable in the moguls. Besides aiding timing and balance, it can provide a support point, helping your skis pivot easier.

Pivoting around a pole plant. Stand across the fall line on a moderately steep bump-free hill. Place your downhill pole in the snow about eighteen inches directly below your lower boot. Lean on the pole. Now put your weight forward onto the toes and flatten your skis by pointing your knees downhill. Pivot your skis so that they immediately head into the fall line. Let the pole come out of the snow as your body passes it. To finish the turn, flex downward and skid to a stop on your uphill edges.

Without the pole this short-radius turn would have been harder to do. The pole supplies an anchoring point to help you deflect your skis. It's somewhat like standing on a scatter rug on a slick floor. You can swivel your feet very forcefully if you hold onto a table for support.

Maybe you're starting to become convinced about your ability to make short turns. However,

Flatten skis and press forward to pivot about a pole plant.

the best is yet to come, as the moguls themselves actually make pivoting easier. A bump reduces friction between the skis and snow if you turn on a rounded part of it.

Choosing terrain for pivoting. Find two gentle bumps and stand in the trough between them. Note how difficult it is to turn in this spot. Now stand on top of a gentle bump so that your tips and tails are off the snow, with your feet over the top of the bump. Using the downhill pole for balance, swivel your feet rapidly back and forth.

The convex terrain effectively turns your skis into shorter ones by reducing friction at the tips and tails. Parallel turns are extremely easy to do on bumps.

You will find rounded terrain in places other than mogul fields. Think about always "cheating" your turns by making them in the easiest possible spots. Look for miniature hillocks on which to start turns, or find transitional terrain where the slope suddenly steepens. Another good spot is a ridge, where the ground drops away to either side.

(1) Turning is difficult between two bumps. (2) With tips and tails off the snow you can easily pivot your feet.

At first it may seem scary to think of turning on the bumps, but stop and look at a mogul field. The tracks in between the bumps are frequently icy bobsled runs where you would be taken for a ride. Snow is softer on the bumps themselves, and turning is easier when the tips and tails are off the snow. In addition, skiing up a bump slows you down. This doesn't mean you have to ski to the very top of a bump. For small bumps you could, but larger ones generally have a convex ridge on their uphill side where you can easily pivot into the next turn.

After all these encouraging words, it's time to turn on a bump.

Turn from a mogul crest. Turn from a stopped position by standing on a convex area of a bump. Face your upper body downhill and plant the downhill pole about a foot and a half down the fall line from your boots. Lean on the pole, weight your toes, and pivot your feet. As you cross the fall line of the bump, flex and christie to a stop on the bump's back side.

That may sound fine for one bump, but in a field of them that resembles a tank proving ground you'll want to do one thing besides turn quickly—that is to slow down quickly. Actually, you have already perfected the needed edging skill. In bumps you don't have much room to ski uphill for speed control, so you must skid on your uphill edges. This is the same as the sideslip, christie, and hockey stop. The skid both slows you down and lets you lose elevation until you find another convenient convex spot to turn. Now you're ready for linked turns.

Turns and skids in the moguls. In a gentle field of moguls, ski up the uphill (front) side of a mogul. Plant your downhill pole below your boots as you pivot your feet on the rounded crest. Rise as your skis swing through the fall line and around the bump. Flex and skid to slow down as you descend the lower side of the bump. Control the skid and forward traverse so that you end up on a convex part of the front of the next bump. Turn and skid down its back side. Control your speed with skids so that you can ski a narrow fall line path.

Without the skids you'd probably gain too much speed and not have time to plan your turning spots. Remember to turn on the uphill side and skid to slow before your next convex turn point.

If you're having any problems, go back and examine your basic stance in the bumps. Because they may be intimidating at first, it's easy to start shying away from them. However, you must be over your skis to turn them well. Get a little more aggressive in the bumps. Inhale before one, and exhale or shout at them as you go over them. Yell, "Turn!" or "Hah!" or whatever inspires you. Your pole plant should be well downhill of your boots. As you stab the little devils, you can now shout, "Take that!"

Your stance should also include a quiet upper body to edge most effectively in these short turns. (In the next chapter we'll discover another reason for this position.) If you face back uphill with your head, chest, or hips, you'll be in deep trouble. Take the pole out of the snow as you ski by it, so that the hand that planted the pole (now the uphill hand after the turn) stays ahead. Sometimes the fall line can be confusing among all the miniature mountains you're skiing over. Think of the general fall line down the slope, and keep your upper body facing that way.

It's possible you may find your ski tips crossing

Pivot on the crest and skid to slow.

Turn and skid.

Leverage controls the skid direction in bumps.

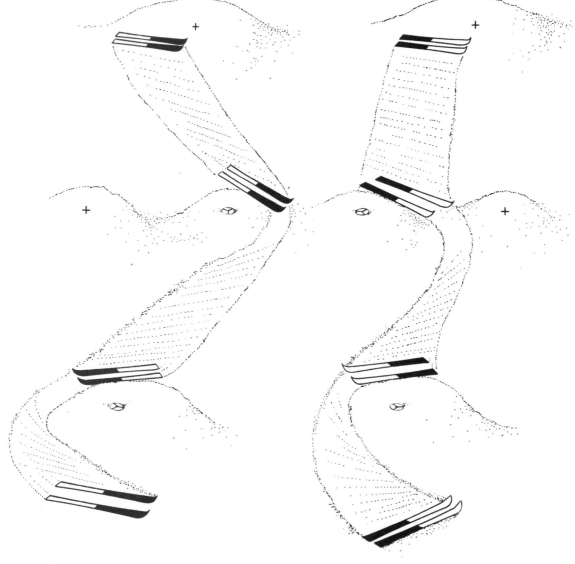

WEIGHT ON TOES   WEIGHT ON HEELS

as you pivot on the bumps. This is because most people have more strength to pivot a toe inward toward the other foot, rather than outward, away from the other foot. However, in each parallel turn the outside toe of the turn pivots inward and the inside toe pivots outward. (Did you follow that?) Thus the outside ski may cross. You'll soon learn to compensate by applying extra pivoting force to the inside ski.

Mogul skiing is a series of controlled slowings. Ski the bumps as though linking hockey stops, with the turn between each hockey stop taking place on convex terrain. It's a good idea to stay in a narrow fall line path. There's no such thing as the perfect mogul, so it won't do you any good to traverse back and forth across the whole slope looking for it. Once you start traversing across bumps you've lost your turning rhythm. Plus there's usually some bomber cruising down the fall line at ninety-seven miles per hour who will cream you if you're traversing.

You can vary your path by changing how you apply pressure in your skids. If you remember the falling-leaf exercise from "The Sideslip" in Chapter 15 you know that weight forward causes a forward sideslip, and weight back a backward one.

Each leg functions independently.

Let your knees flex when riding up a bump.

Leverage to control skids. Stand just past the crest on the backside of a mogul and sideslip down it. Move your weight forward and backward from the ankles to produce a forward or backward motion in the sideslip. Aim for where you want to turn on the next mogul and skid right to that spot. Keep skiing moguls, using leverage in your skid to help control your direction. Turn on each bump and stay in a narrow path down the hill.

Once you gain confidence you'll start skiing the bumps faster. However, you'll find they have a disconcerting tendency to throw you in the air. You can reduce this inclination to fly by relaxing your legs to soak up the shocks.

The legs as shock absorbers. Ski at slow to moderate speed across a series of small bumps. Imagine your head traveling in a straight line and your feet moving up and down with every variation in terrain. Allow your knees to flex up and extend down like shock absorbers to join your feet and head.

This is another major reason to ski in a flexed stance. If your legs are stiff, they can't absorb shocks and terrain changes. Without flex your

Flexing to absorb the bump places the skier in a powerful turning position.

head would bounce up and down all day, which is no fun even when it's not New Year's Day.

Even though you're skiing parallel, each leg still works independently in its shock-absorbing capacity. Thus, if one ski hits a bump or rut, that leg can respond. Avoid skiing with your legs locked together where they could not work separately. Letting each leg function as needed is known as independent leg action.

Now you can ski the moguls letting your shock-absorbing legs keep you on the snow rather than in the air.

Mogul turns with absorption. Start from a high body position heading for a bump. Relax your knees and let them fold under you as you approach the crest. Plant your pole and pivot your skis at the crest. Allow your legs to extend through the fall line to stay in contact with the snow. Absorb the next one, skidding to slow before you turn on the crest.

Absorbing the mogul puts you in a low, deeply flexed position near the mogul crest. Handily, that's also your strongest position for pivoting. If you had not absorbed the shock, you'd be thrown in the air and also unable to turn as fast. As the bumps increase in size, you'll find that instead of climbing to the summit and planting the national flag, you can just turn on the uphill portion before the crest.

I hope you're starting to look upon the moguls as friends. We'll meet a great many of them in the rest of our technique and travels, so learn to like or at least to tolerate them. When you approach a series of bumps, stay loose and remember the old groundhog expression, "Gopher it."

UNWEIGHTING

I'm sure you've idly twisted your skis left and right while riding the chair lift and thought how great it would be if you could turn that easily on the snow. Well, you can, almost. Even without next year's antigravity skis, you have the ability to control your weight on each foot. In fact, you do this frequently already as you step from foot to foot or flex downward to a parallel stop.

We'll concentrate on reducing the total pressure on both skis so that they can be easily started into a turn simultaneously. The emphasis will be on

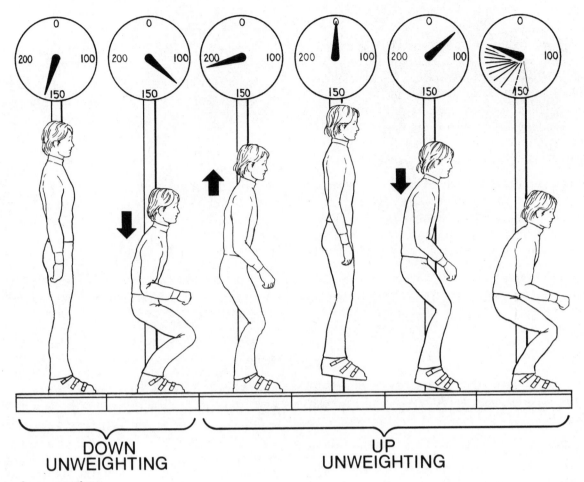

DOWN
UNWEIGHTING

UP
UNWEIGHTING

Down and up unweighting.

reducing weight at that critical point where one turn finishes and another turn starts. Unweighting here reduces friction, so that you can pivot the skis with less effort, just as you did on the chair lift. Also, taking pressure off the uphill edges lets you easily change to the new power edge that makes your turn.

Positive and negative pressures are tied closely together, as one must be used to create the other. For example, stand on a bathroom scale. The scale registers your normal weight while you stand quietly. If you suddenly lower your body by flexing rapidly in the ankles and knees, the registered weight momentarily decreases. This is an unweighting—technically, a "down" unweighting. When you stop the downward movement, the scale briefly registers more than your normal weight. This is a weighting action. You can increase this weighting by forcefully extending your legs to raise your body. When you stop the upward motion the scale swings below your normal

weight. Again, this is an unweighting—technically an "up" unweighting. If you extend upward powerfully enough to hop off the scale, you would experience total unweighting, and then a forceful weighting when you crash back down on the scale. With continual controlled flexion and extension you could swing the scale smoothly from high to low readings, a motion that you'll want to apply to skiing. This is one reason we've emphasized rhythm so much. Anytime you stop constant motion you lose the ability to vary pressure effectively and thus lose the ability to fully control your skis.

If all this sounds esoteric, think about normal walking. That consists of pressuring one foot while unweighting the other, accompanied by constant flexion and extension of the legs. If you attached a bathroom scale to a foot, it would register a continual change in pressure from a high value to zero and back again.

You've already encountered momentary un-

Push off the bump, angle your skis to match the landing area, and flex to absorb the shock.

weighting during a jump, perhaps even intentionally. You can get airborne by skiing fast over a bump. This miniature ski jump launches you into space. Technically this is called *terrain unweighting*. There are two ways you can get higher off the ground. One is by skiing faster over the bump. The other way requires that you actively push your body into the air to help terrain unweighting.

Jumping. Flex in the knees while skiing up a bump. Then, just before the top, begin a rapid rise. Time your jumping motion so that you reach full extension just at the crest of the bump. When you land, let your ankles and knees flex deeply to absorb the shock. For maximum height on the jumps, also plant both poles on the crest and push upward from them as you extend.

Jumping is a playful expression in skiing. So that you don't end up shorter, be sure to land with slightly flexed knees, and rapidly compress to absorb all that impact, which is actually the weighting phase after an active unweighting. Also lower your hands to help absorb the landing shock.

In your pursuit of getting higher ("More air!" is the skiers' expression), don't forget that your skis take off at an upward angle but land on a downward slope. A common fault of inexperienced jumpers is landing with their tips up and falling backward. While airborne you should angle your skis downward and get your body forward so your skis touch down along their whole length.

You can take advantage of this momentary free flight to turn your skis effortlessly.

Airplane turn. Ski off a small bump, planting one pole as you rise up the bump. As your skis near the crest begin turning them in the direction of your pole plant.

Continue to pivot to that side in midair. Land and complete the turn.

Midair direction changes are fun in moderation. Balance is tricky if you overdo these airplane turns, as your skis take off in one direction but land in a different one. If you edge too rapidly upon landing, your direction changes very quickly.

By now you've realized another reason we made turns on a convex part of a mogul at slow to moderate speeds. Each mogul pushes you upward, unweighting your skis so they will pivot easier.

Unweighting in moguls. Be responsive to pressure changes in the moguls by traversing across a series of them. Note how light you are at the crests, and how heavy you feel while skiing up to a crest. Take advantage of this by turning at the areas of least pressure.

Whenever you ski down a slope and start up a bump you are fighting inertia and the pressure on your skis increases. (This also happens when you ski uphill at the finish of a turn.) As you approach the crest of this convex terrain, the steep rise gives way to less steep terrain. This change of angles is known as a slope transition. If you happen to be going fast enough when you hit this transition area, you'll become airborne. These transition points are easy places to turn, because the ski tips and tails may be off the snow and because the skis' pressure is momentarily lightened.

Turning at the transition points makes skiing very easy. Be on the lookout for little bumps or ridges on which to start your turns. You can also take advantage of unweighting on large changes in terrain, as in a long gully with walls rising steeply on each side, for example.

Convex terrain in a gully. Ski down one wall of a gully, across the trough, and up the other side. Turn on the gully wall where the slope starts to level off and you feel lighter on the snow. Swoop down through the trough and up to a turn point on the other wall. Maintain your speed and keep your turns round.

You might consider the gully walls as a huge mogul on either side of you. Skiing gulches in this manner is exhilarating and quite effortless. You'll feel confident going much faster than you normally would. Look for runs that contain "gulch" or "gully" in their names. Sometimes "bowl" runs have gullies too. Since you'll be covering a lot of slope in going back and forth, try to ski these runs during uncrowded hours when less experienced skiers won't be fighting their turns straight down the concave center.

It would be great if there were tiny bumps wherever you wanted to turn. Although there aren't, you can simulate them with more body motion. You already do this during rapid parallel stops.

Down motion in hockey stops. Ski the fall line of a moderate hill. Start in a high stance and flex downward slowly to initiate a hockey stop. Then repeat, but this time flex rapidly. Note how much easier it is to pivot your skis across the fall line when you flex rapidly.

This rapid downward movement is a down unweighting. The faster you flex, the more you unpressure your skis, and the easier they can be pivoted. Also, if you start from a high stance and flex, the unweighting is greater than starting from an already flexed stance, which limits the total range of downward motion.

Down unweighting is a rapid way to unweight. Your skis are lightened the instant you start to flex. You can aid the flex by pulling your feet up toward you. Down unweighting is used primarily for stopping actions and seldom for initiating a turn on smooth terrain. (However, when we talk about the man-eating moguls in the next chapter, we'll use the down unweighting action to control pressure during turn initiations.)

The longer the period of unweighting, the more time you have to start your skis effortlessly into a new turn. As an example, imagine holding a huge snowball. If you let it drop (down unweighting), it lands relatively quickly. But if you first heave it into the air (up unweighting), it takes considerably longer to land.

You can learn up unweighting with a little exaggeration, lightening your skis so much they come off the snow even without the help of bumps.

Hopping a turn. Ski in the fall line on a very gentle slope. Flex downward, then rapidly extend upward to hop your skis off the snow. Try to lift them so that both tips and tails leave the snow. Absorb the landing by smoothly flexing downward. Plant your pole, at the same time beginning an extension to repeat the action. When you have the rhythm, also pivot your skis slightly in the air. Alternate directions of turning on each hop. Make numerous small turns down the fall line, planting your right pole as you extend to initiate a right turn, and your left pole for a left turn. Push lightly on the poles to help your hop.

Hopping the skis into the air makes them easier to pivot.

Lower the hips toward the feet when flexing.

Hopping helps you get the feel of unweighting. It's a vertical motion: first down, then up, then down again. Sometimes instructors simply call it *down-up-down.* You might pretend you're bouncing on a trampoline to get the rhythm and timing. The unweighted period comes as you stop pressuring the edges during your extension. This is when the new turn starts. By sinking after the up motion you extend the duration of the lightened phase, get into a stronger edging position, and prepare for another hop.

Skiers learning pressure control sometimes fail to flex at the ankles when lowering the body. This leads to dropping the hips back or bending at the waist.

Lowering hips to flex. Visualize imaginary walls extending upward from the front and rear of your bindings. When you flex you must remain within these walls. Bend forward at the ankles as you flex your knees to lower your hips toward your feet.

The pole plant triggers the up motion, and in this sense it aids your timing as well as your balance. The sequence is to plant and immediately rise up. If you're having a problem with the pole plant, try leaning on it a bit to aid your lift in the up motion. Then you'll find it helps in the unweighting only if you plant it prior to your extension. The sequence is plant, push.

You seldom see anyone actually hopping their skis in the air, as it's just too much work. Generally, you want to retain contact with the snow to avoid a temporary loss of control. Therefore, unweighting motions are usually more subtle, just forceful enough to lighten the skis.

Smooth unweighting. Stand at the top of a uniform slope and decide how frequently you'd like to make continuous turns on it. Flex down and extend up in this desired turn rate. When you are continuously moving down, up, and down in rhythm, push off and start a new turn with each up motion. Keep the motion continuous, with no pauses.

Your vertical unweighting should always be fluid and never jerky. Avoid holding a static pose throughout a turn and then at the finish of it deciding to suddenly flex and extend. A good skier uses continual down and up motions throughout the whole turn. If you're not as smooth as you'd like,

A smooth upward motion starts this turn.

Unweighting in linked short turns.

think about coordinating your vertical motion with continual breathing.

Unweighting by breathing. Imagine that each time you inhale, your lungs fill with a lighter-than-air gas that almost lifts you off the snow. Every time you inhale you rise up and start into a new turn. At the fall line you begin to exhale, and your body collapses to a low stance as the air leaves your lungs. Then the cycle begins again as you start inhaling for a new turn.

You've made short-radius turns before, while concentrating on the stopping motion. Now let's redo a series of hockey stops, with emphasis on up unweighting to start each turn.

Unweighted wedel. Imagine a ten foot fall line path down a smooth, steeper slope. Before starting out, begin a rhythmic down-up-down motion in your knees with perhaps one second between each down. Then push off, maintaining this rhythm. Skid as you flex down, and then turn during the light period following the up extension.

If you're thinking too hard about vertical motion and getting confused, ask a friend to help you find the rhythm.

Directing vertical motion. Station a friend down the fall line. Have him rhythmically raise and lower his arms. Match the height of your body to his arm height. Each time he starts to raise them from the lowest point, plant your pole to begin a turn.

You shouldn't get locked into any one rhythm. Too frequently skiers get so used to turning at a certain rate that they never change. These skiers look half alive and mechanical. You should vary your turns at will by using pronounced unweighting for shorter ones and subtle unweighting for the big swooping round ones.

Various-radius turns. Ski on a slope with a constant pitch. Start out with wide turns and gradually shorten the radius until you are making them extremely short and close together. Increase your amount of unweighting with additional up-and-down motion as your turns come closer together.

Changing your turn radius gives you the ability to control your speed. As the turns become shorter, you'll go slower, a useful feature when the slope steepens. Your amount of vertical motion helps control your speed on steeper terrain by increasing the number of tight, round turns you can make.

Varying turn rhythm. Choose a slope with a gentle start followed by a steeper section. Decide on a moderate speed at which you'd like to travel and plan on maintaining this speed all the way down the run. On the gentle section use small vertical unweighting motions to aid your turns. On the steeper section use vigorous unweighting to tighten up the turns and thus keep your speed constant.

In the shorter turns unweighting by upward body motion is quite useful. Only a gentle upward motion is needed in the longer turns, where there's plenty of time for edging and subtle pivoting to guide the skis through the turn.

The amount of pressure on a ski is not constant. Rather, it gradually increases throughout a turn, until at the turn's finish gravity and centrifugal force are combining their pulls in about the same direction. You must relieve this large pressure on the edge of the power ski to change edges for a new turn. The simplest way to relieve pressure is by releasing edges. That's simply rolling the skis off their edges, going through a flat ski phase, and rolling onto the new edges.

Rising up at the finish of a turn realigns the body joints to a straighter position. This deangulation takes the skis off their edges and flattens them, the first requirement of a turn. In fact, deangulation is a primary means of unweighting skis. Although they don't jump in the air, the pressure has been relieved and they can be turned in a new direction. Flexing downward during the turn allows you to angulate and edge. Unweighting by deangulation and by vertical body motion are combined nicely in an exercise you already did, in which you skated on the flats. Let's advance a little to skate down a grade.

Skating down the hill. Ski a gentle slope by skating down it. Flex and pressure the inside edge of one ski. Extend upward, pushing off the snow to glide to the other ski. Place that ski on its inside edge as you flex, turning through the fall line. Extend off that edge, pushing your weight back to the first foot and turn that ski into the fall line. When you have an up-and-down rhythm going, add a pole plant, pushing from the right pole at the same time you extend upward to push off the right foot and vice versa.

Use the skating motion to rise into each turn. It's possible to flatten the skis without rising by just driving the knees. However, a constant low

The outside ski is pressured into the snow near the turn finish.

stance tires the body and causes a loss of rhythm. Whenever you lose vertical rhythm you must combat inertia to get it going again.

The pressure changes show up clearly if you examine your ski tracks in soft snow. You'll see the outside ski carving a deeper and deeper trough in the snow as the skis cross the fall line and finish the turn. Where the edges are changed the track becomes momentarily straight as the skis ride flat on their bases. The track will also be faint here, as pressure has been reduced in this area. Then the track begins to turn toward the fall line and the new outside ski starts to lightly carve into the snow. It carves in deeper as you cross the fall line and head toward maximum pressure again at the turn's finish.

You can also listen to these pressure changes as you ski. It's a great way to heighten your pole plant timing. (Turn off your portable stereo for this exercise.)

Pole plant with pressure changes. Listen to the sound your skis make. As you finish a turn they swoosh loudly in the snow. Then at the start of a turn they are almost soundless. The noise level builds up as you again finish a turn. Plant a pole at the junction of the loudest and the softest sounds.

In conclusion, use vertical motions to control pressure on the ski edges. Now that you know the ins and outs of ups and downs you're getting ready to move on to bigger and better slopes.

LET THE FORCES BE WITH YOU

As your skill level improves, you're finding a thrill and challenge in skiing faster. You've realized that speed doesn't hurt—it's those sudden stops against trees that smart. However, you've practiced your parallel stops enough that you have the ability to make a planned stop whenever you need to bail out.

Use caution when looking at photos of speedy skiers. A photo shows a single instant of a moving, dynamic action. You wouldn't look at a photo of a jogger leaning inward while rounding a street corner and think you could stand at that angle without moving. Similarly, realize that you can't assume a static pose of some of the positions you see in photos. You also must be in motion.

Inclination

At higher speed and on steeper slopes your basic techniques won't change, but certain new forces enter the picture for which you'll have to compensate. One of the major refinements you'll need is adjusting your body position to balance for speed. At beginner speeds you learned to keep your body "over" your feet. Now you'll be balancing the pressure through your feet, although your body may not be truly over them. It's like riding a bicycle. At a very slow speed you turn the handlebars where you want to go, but at higher speed you lean your body into the turn direction. In fact, inward lean is needed in any sport whenever direction is changed with speed. This balancing against centrifugal force is called *inclination*.

You can feel the needed inclination during turns at moderate speed.

Leaning in turns. Ski in the fall line at moderate speed. Place both skis on their same edges so that you turn out of the fall line. Lean uphill to balance against those edges. As you complete the turn, drive both knees in the opposite direction to change edges while simultaneously tilting your head, torso, and hips across your feet in that direction. Use a pole plant to aid your balance at this critical point of edge change. Feel your body lean inward even more to balance on the edges as you complete the turn.

Without this lean toward the turn center you could not balance on the edges. Your skis would flatten and you'd be in an uncontrolled skid.

Incline into the turn at higher speeds.

How close together you keep your feet affects how much inward lean you'll use. With a wide stance you will not need a great deal of inclination. Try placing your feet together while getting the feel of these leans. This is a good time to point out that parallel turns are difficult to accomplish at two or three miles per hour. Allow yourself enough speed to make your turns easier. If you incline your body into a turn without enough forward velocity, you'll fall over, as there will be no centrifugal force to support your lean.

The necessary amount of inclination depends upon your speed and how short your turns are. Near the finish of a turn there is a great deal of force pulling you down the fall line, as gravity and centrifugal force combine. You can best balance against these forces in a low, very angulated stance. Racers often round a gate this way, with feet well downhill and bodies near the ground. When the skis are flattened the turn is stopped and you can move "over" the feet again as you start your new lean. Centrifugal force is not very great yet and temporarily pulls uphill, so you won't need much lean here. A comfortable upright stance rests those aching muscles. Then as you get into the heart of the turn and your speed builds up, you increase flex to edge and balance.

Steve Mahre balances on his edges by leaning his upper body well inside the turn. (Photo courtesy Lange, USA)

The direction of lean changes at the start of each turn.

The changeover point occurs at that critical area where one turn finishes and the other starts. Here your balance is most precarious going from a lean uphill to a lean that's momentarily downhill. Thank goodness for the pole plant! It gives you extra stability just when you need it. Planting well downhill makes you lean into the new turn.

Another way of thinking of inclination is that you have a center to your body, known as a center of mass. It's roughly behind your navel, and it must cross back and forth like a metronome over your skis at the start of each turn. You can appreciate this if you deliberately ski on the "wrong" ski, the inside ski. After all that practicing to ski on the "right," outside ski, you may have to try this one a few times.

Turns on the inside ski. Ski a moderate hill with small turns, but use your inside ski for each turn. To go left, stand on the left edge of the left ski. To change direction, step to your right ski and use its right edge. You'll have to exaggerate your inclination from side to side to balance on these edges.

I hope that being on the inside edge felt strange. Now you know why we worked so hard on using the outside ski of a turn. However, it's not a crime to be on this ski. In fact, knowing how to use it will sometimes make a recovery possible if you

A pole plant provides support during the change of inclination.

Banking is a relaxing way to stand upright and ski open terrain.

A "royal christie" is another fun way to appreciate inclination.

lose the power ski's edge hold on a patch of ice or in a rut. Actually, balancing on that wrong ski is the basis for much trick skiing. Since you did so well, you may as well have some fun with this exaggerated leaning.

Charleston. Ski the fall line of a gentle hill. Make small, rapid turns, always staying on the inside ski. Kick out your outside ski in a Charleston dance step with each turn.

The Charleston may take a little practice, but it's a great one for rhythm and balance in addition to inclination.

Another popular trick, a "royal christie," is based on the same idea of leaning in balance. It's a great one to impress your friends, but practice in private before you spring it on them.

Royal christie. Make wide turns at moderate speed on a gentle slope. Start each turn riding on the inside edge of the inside ski. Lift the outside ski up and backward so that it is parallel to the ground. (If you have very long skis, be careful not to kick yourself in the head!) Put the ski down as you complete the turn and repeat on the opposite skis in the next turn.

Inclining from one turn to the next also changes

edges. Some interesting turns are made by using body inclination only.

Banked turns. Cruise on wide open terrain. Maintain an upright stance and initiate a turn by simply leaning your body into it. Let the skis carry you through the turn, then reduce your edging by leaning out of the turn and banking toward the next turn. Feel your edge angle increase as your lean increases.

In these banked turns the side-to-side motion of your body to balance centrifugal force is quite apparent. These are easy turns to make, especially when you want to rest your muscles, as you can stand upright without any flex. You'll fly down the mountain on autopilot on these loose and lazy banked turns. (By the way, don't confuse banking your body with banking just the ski bottoms.)

You have to be careful not to overuse banking, however. In pure banked turns balance is rather critical, as your center of mass is high and placed well away from your feet. If you should lose edge hold momentarily on ice, or hit an obstacle that deflects your skis, your delicate balance is disrupted. Often before you can lean your whole body back toward your feet to recover you're in a perfect noseplow. Normally you would ski in an angulated stance, with flexion and sideways artic-

An angulated stance permits quick edge control without disrupting balance.

ulation at the ankles, knees, and hips. Although it's more tiring than an upright stance, angulation allows rapid lateral edging motions from the joints when needed.

Another major disadvantage of banking is that you are dependent on your skis' sidecut to determine the turn radius, as your upright position eliminates much edge control and pivoting force. A modest rule of thumb is to bank turns on smooth, open terrain when your muscles scream for a rest but when you still want to ski.

You'll become aware of how much easier it is to edge by angulating rather than by banking if you narrow your support base to the width of only one ski.

Skiing on one ski. Hold one ski in the air and ski on the other one. Use the left edge of that ski to make left turns and the right edge to make right turns. Make both quick turns in the fall line and longer-radius turns. Switch feet and repeat.

I hope you didn't back out on this one. Skiing on one ski really makes you aware of changing edges and teaches you how to ride on an edge with inclination. Plus you'll use a pole plant for balance. Surprisingly, turning on one ski may even have a practical application sometime in your ski career. I once broke a ski on Red's Run in Aspen. Rather than having to walk up or down through deep snow to get to a lift station, I was able to ski to the bottom thanks to this exercise.

Balance for Speed Changes

With an increased average speed you're encountering greater accelerations and decelerations. Your basic stance must be fine-tuned to balance against these forces. Your neutral position should allow leeway for forward or backward movement when you need it.

Jumping in balance. While straight running on a gentle slope, flex down and extend up with enough force to lift your skis off the snow. Repeat these hops rapidly and have a friend observe if the entire ski comes off the snow, as it should if you are in a balanced stance. When you find the balance point, then deliberately move your body forward to hop off just the tips or back to lift just the tails. Note the muscular strain in these less stable positions.

Skiing through changing snow conditions re-quires planning to stay balanced. When you suddenly ski from firm-packed snow into loose snow your skis will slow rapidly. To avoid a head plant you'll have to lean back from the ankles. In addition, you'll want to flex, as a good bend at the knees lets you "push" your body against the skis. If you're upright, you don't have this muscular force available. When you ski from deep snow to firm pack your skis will suddenly speed up. So that you're not left behind in the fluff, you have to lean forward at the transition.

Balancing by leaning forward or backward is a skill you use all the time. Imagine you're standing up in the aisle of a city bus. When the driver tromps on the gas you'd go tumbling to the back of the bus unless you leaned forward. Conversely, when the brakes are applied you'd be sitting in the driver's lap unless you flexed downward and leaned backward to brace against your feet.

Your skis also slow rapidly when skiing up a bump or uphill. You have to slow your body also, by flexing and leaning back into a more seated position. Your skis accelerate when going over the top of a bump or skiing onto steeper terrain. At this point you must get forward again.

The same speed changes happen during every turn. Each time you change direction you head into the fall line, which is the same as a steeper hill. You must get forward to stay balanced through your feet as your skis head toward the speed of sound. After crossing the fall line your skis slow down, both by skiing uphill and by skidding. The sharper your turns, the more rapidly they slow. You must flex and lean back slightly during those turn finishes. This forward-and-backward movement is in addition to the side-to-side movement used for inclination. If it were possible to hop in the air at any time, your skis should still come cleanly off the snow. Even though you are moving your body you remain in dynamic balance directly through your feet.

A critical point occurs when you change from slowing down to speeding up. While slowing you have been braced back against the deceleration. When pressure is taken off the edges to flatten the skis for a new turn your skis accelerate forward. Bracing by "pushing" against your feet makes them speed up. It's as though the skis "jet" ahead. As you might guess, the sudden spurting ahead of

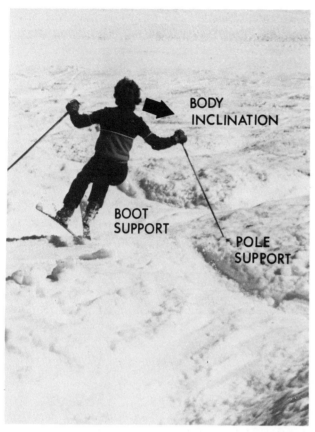

Catching up to skis that have "jetted" ahead at the turn start.

Even though you're generally balanced against the center of your skis during speed changes, you can deliberately increase pressure on the tips or tails to vary your skis' response. You've used this leverage concept to help direct skids. It also affects the way skis turn.

Leverage for turns. Experiment with leverage in a moderate traverse. Start by standing neutral on your skis. Then flex forward from the ankle to pressure the tips, without changing the edge angle. Your skis will curve uphill. Flex back to pressure the tails, and the skis will run straighter. Use these results in turns by pressuring forward to help sharpen a turn when you start into the fall line.

All skis react to leverage in different degrees. Generally, skis have a softer flex in the tip area. When pressure is applied to this section they readily bend to start into a turn easier. This is useful during a turn initiation, as sufficient centrifugal forces have not yet built up to flex the whole ski in a turning arc. In addition, the ski is always widest at the tip, and this accentuates the natural turn radius when the ski is edged and weighted.

Pressure the tip area slightly as you start each turn. By the time you reach the fall line you should be riding the whole ski, with weight even between toe and heel. At the finish of the turn place your weight back slightly on the heels. Now you'll be in balance against deceleration as the skis slow, and also you'll be using the stiffer tail section of the ski to maintain a constant-radius curve. This area generally doesn't flex as easily under the greater pressure experienced at the turn finish. The tail is also narrower than the tip to effectively reduce the rear sidecut to retain a more uniform turn radius.

The use of leverage is a subtle one, with only small changes of pressure required along the length of the ski. If you're too far back at the turn initiation, your skis react sluggishly and stay in the fall line longer than you'd like, particularly on steep slopes. If you pressure forward too long in the turn, your tails wash out and your tips abruptly hook as you cross the fall line.

By now you are skiing relatively fluidly on three-quarters of the trails at most mountains. You're doing great, but before you get too complacent, we'll move on to those black-diamond runs.

the skis is called *jetting*. On bumps it's a dramatic sight, with ski tips out in midair way ahead of the skier.

Your big task now is to catch up to your skis, since you should be forward on them at this point. The pole plant is very helpful here. You remembered to plant it just as the turn was finished, didn't you? High-speed, short-radius turns are almost impossible without good pole plants. The pole provides a support point to move your torso forward. Also, you can muscularly pull your feet backward, slowing them slightly.

Incline your body into the turn to catch up to your feet also. When your upper body is inside the turn, it takes a shorter, quicker path than your feet.

The high, stiff backs on your boots also aid getting forward. They prevent your leg from angling backward at the ankle. This gives you a leverage point to boost yourself forward. In the next chapter we'll mention two more aids to balance when your feet try to jet ahead of you—extension and stepping.

17
Advanced Technique

This chapter is for everyone who is ready to move onto the most difficult trails at ski areas. You should feel comfortable on the intermediate runs, where you start and finish most turns parallel. Before beginning this chapter you may want to review "Better Turns" in "Intermediate Technique," as the ideas there regarding balance, rhythm, and body positions apply equally well on advanced terrain.

The black-diamond trails are generally steep, sometimes quite narrow, and may develop huge moguls. With higher speed you'll find liveliness from your skis, the terrain, and your body. You'll ski dynamically but with optimum efficiency. Skill refinement will enable you to ski off the groomed runs, where you'll encounter powder and ice. You'll venture into steep chutes and through the trees now that the whole mountain will be open to you. Go out and enjoy it!

DYNAMIC TURNING

The terms *advanced* and *dynamic* could be synonyms. One of the characteristics of expert skiers is their effortless skiing. It's almost as though their skis are alive and magically turning for them.

We'll add extra pivoting and unweighting power to initiate each turn easier. We'll also trigger these turn starts with a better pole plant.

Anticipation

Facing downhill increases your edging ability. However, there is another reason for twisting the upper body relative to the skis. This position will amplify your pivoting force, a definite asset for quick turns. A twisting of the upper body toward the fall line is called *anticipation*, since your head, torso, and hips seem to be anticipating the turn your skis will make. You can observe anticipation in the quiet upper bodies of expert skiers.

Watching anticipated turns. Watch an expert skier making short-radius turns in the fall line of a steep hill, in moguls, in gates, or in powder. Put out your hand at arm's length to block your vision of the skier's lower body. The skier's upper body will be so quiet you'll have difficulty telling which way his skis are turning.

You can easily discover how anticipation aids pivoting while riding the chair lift. Be sure to co-ordinate this one with your chair partner.

The untwisting force. Sit in a chair lift and swivel both toes left and both heels right, so that your skis are twisted at least forty-five degrees at both tips and tails. Feel the muscular tension needed to hold the skis in this position. Now simply relax your muscles, and your skis will swing back so that your feet point straight ahead. Again twist your skis, but this time help them swing all the way around to the other direction. Feel how quickly and powerfully they can twist from side to side.

Anticipation helps these shorter-radius turns.

A twisted position is not a resting one. When you twist the feet you stretch muscles that want to return to their normal resting status. Imagine that you were to accidentally fall out of the chair lift while your feet were twisted. If you resist the temptation to flap your arms and just relax, your feet and body would untwist to face the same direction.

You can feel the power of anticipation in short turns.

Anticipated turns. Choose a fall line path about ten feet wide down a moderately pitched smooth slope. Make some turns in this tight path while not anticipating, that is, while always facing your ski tips with your

upper body. You'll probably stem or need violent unweighting to turn. Now ski the same path, but this time keep your upper body constantly facing down the fall line. Your turns will be easy and fluid.

Instructors often compare anticipation to a Popsicle stick. If you put one hand on top and one on the bottom and twist lengthwise, there's a lot of resistance. Let go of one end and it whips back to normal. The upper and lower body also work in opposition to twist like the Popsicle stick.

Upper-lower body separation. Borrow a bamboo slalom pole and have a friend hold one end as you hold the other. Make parallel turns down a smooth slope,

Twisting feet beneath the body.

FALL LINE

FAST

FALL LINE

SLOW

Complete turns across the fall line for additional speed and control.

keeping the pole even out in front. Your upper body will be quiet while your skis turn back and forth.

Another common analogy likens anticipation to a spring. Your anticipated body resembles a twisted spring, ready to uncoil. The more you wind up, the more powerfully you can pivot into a new turn. Skiers often forget this fact on steeper runs because they are so worried about getting their skis into the next turn they don't finish the previous one.

Speed control by finishing turns. Ski close behind a friend on a smooth, moderately steep slope. Your partner will wedge straight down the fall line. He or she controls the speed by varying the amount of braking. You must make short-radius parallel turns to match the speed. When going slower you'll need to finish each turn farther. Keep your upper body anticipated in the fall line to obtain extra turning power.

We're anticipating to gain additional extra turning power in short-radius turns. A twisted body is awkward and unnecessary if you're traversing or making large-radius turns. The amount you'll need to anticipate will increase as your turns get tighter. A quiet upper body aids your anticipation, but it is not rigid. Let all parts of your body always be loose and relaxed.

Pole plants perform a vital function in anticipation. They stabilize the upper body, preventing it from untwisting in the direction of the skis. This utilizes the full muscular potential of your antici-

pated position. Avoid reaching too far forward with the pole plant, as this could drag your upper body around, destroying the twisting power.

Anticipation also provides extra turning force for certain isolated turns. If you suddenly need to make a quick turn that normal leg pivoting won't provide, you can also rotate your torso into the turn. This is sometimes seen in heavy snow, when skiers "punch" their outside arm around in the direction of the new turn. This rotary impetus transfers to the lower body and helps the turn. The technique is called *rotation*, and you probably already use it now and then.

Rotation. Face your upper body toward your ski tips in a steep traverse. Make a turn by rapidly twisting your upper body toward the fall line. When your rotation stops your skis will swing into the fall line also.

Rotation used to be a common mode of turning, but nowadays it's rather inefficient. However, the more ways you know how to apply the skills, the better skier you'll be. There are definitely tricky situations besides the "crud" snow times when you can use rotation. You may find it valuable when you're thrown off balance, where rotating your upper body around into a new turn could prevent a spill.

You can have some fun with rotation and also learn a trick guaranteed to impress by turning a complete circle.

Rotating the upper body toward the fall line helps pivot the feet.

The three-sixty. Look for a convex piece of terrain located on shallow terrain. Approach it in a traverse, but prior to reaching it wind up by twisting your upper body downhill. Unwind forcefully by twisting your body uphill as you reach the convex point. Pivot rapidly around 360 degrees on flat skis and engage the uphill edges to resume the run in your original direction.

The three-sixty also requires good edge sensitivty to remain on flat skis without catching an edge. With practice you can do it on smooth terrain, but while learning use a convex area to keep your tips and tails off the snow. When you're really daring you can combine the three-sixty with a jump to perform an aerial three-sixty or "helicopter." This takes great timing so that you don't end up doing an aerial two-seventy and a cartwheel ninety!

"Counter rotation" is another body action that can increase pivoting. It was a brief fad as a major turning method, but it is grossly inefficient for directing the skis into a new turn. It's essentially the opposite of anticipation, and it's applied when the skis are unweighted. Imagine you are in free flight, perhaps having jumped off a huge bump. While the skis are not weighted you'll find that if you twist your upper body to the right the lower body and skis twist to the left. (That's conservation of angular momentum from elementary physics.) If you're into long jumping you may want to try this in midair as a trick. Counter rotation can be useful when you've momentarily lost snow contact coming off a bump. To turn your skis in one direction, you'd swing your shoulders into the reverse direction. You can also counter rotate when down unweighting to a parallel stop, twisting the skis in one direction and the torso in the other. Frequently an anticipated position is referred to as a

A rebound from skis in reverse camber unweights the skier.

Rebound Unweighting

As your turns become tighter and faster, your skis become livelier. You need less active unweighting, as the skis almost spring you into the air. This springboard feeling has been designed into the skis and shows that you are learning to use them effectively. This upward spring is called a *rebound*.

Spring from reverse camber. Stand with your ski tips and tails on two bumps (or use piles of books in your living room) and your boot section suspended in air. Flex downward and stop. When you stop the skis will bend into reverse camber and then unbend to push you upward. Repeat by flexing downward and then immediately extend your legs forcefully. The skis are pushed into greater reverse camber and will then spring you even higher into the air.

Skis are somewhat like a trampoline. If you put positive pressure into them they'll flex into reverse camber and rebound you upward. Standing with only tips and tails on the snow to feel a rebound is obviously an exaggeration. However, in normal skiing the skis are pressured during turns. The hourglass shape of the sidecut allows the center of the ski to be bowed into reverse camber if

"countered" one due to the relative twist between the upper and lower body.

the ski is both edged and weighted. Centrifugal force in tight, fast turns increases the pressure, causing even greater reverse camber. The soft snow yields, allowing the ski edge to penetrate even deeper underfoot, which also increases the potential rebound.

A ski in extreme reverse camber at the finish of a turn.

As soon as pressure is released from the ski, it rebounds back to its normal shape. This resiliency helps unweight the ski so it may be pivoted more easily. Some skis are designed to be livelier than others, so the amount of rebound you actually obtain will vary among ski types.

An edgeset quickly flexes a ski into the reverse camber needed to rebound.

Edgeset rebounds. Ski at moderate speed in a traverse. Hop your skis off the snow several times while maintaining a straight traverse. Note how strenuous the hops are. Now traverse at the same speed, but this time as you flex downward to start a hop, also pivot your skis uphill and set the edges quickly enough to make the snow fly up from them. At the same time plant your pole and extend upward, pivoting the tips downhill to resume the original traverse. Make a series of these quick edgesets to see that unweighting is much easier with the rebound.

The edgesets momentarily slow you down, greatly increasing the pressure on the skis and pushing them into extreme reverse camber. As soon as you relieve the pressure the reverse camber becomes a powerful upward force known as rebound unweighting.

If you anticipate during this traverse by always keeping your upper body facing slightly downhill, you'll know when you have a good rebound. Instead of forcefully pivoting your skis back to the traverse, they will automatically swing into it, as they align with your upper body. In fact, each edgeset and rebound may put you into a steeper traverse. Your body resembles a spring that's both twisted and compressed, just waiting to spring open and untwist. Your skis want to turn!

You can readily take advantage of anticipation combined with rebound unweighting to make rapid fall line turns. To avoid complications, go back to the basics and turn from a wedge, concentrating on the spring at the finish of each turn.

Wedge rebound. Ski the fall line of a moderate hill. Start in a braking wedge. Abruptly edge and pressure one ski so that snow flies out from the edge. Plant your pole at the same time and immediately transfer weight to the other ski. Sharply edge that ski, while planting the pole, and rebound your weight to the first ski. Step rapidly and dynamically from ski to ski, controlling your speed in the fall line with edgesets. Let your skis gradually become parallel while maintaining the rhythm.

With a definite weight transfer you'll find it difficult to maintain a wedge. The unweighted ski swings into each turn if you relax the rotator muscles in your leg.

The edgesets control your speed. They also

A rebound from an edgeset.

pressure your skis into extreme reverse camber for rebound unweighting. Sharply setting an edge is often called *creating a platform*. If you look at your tracks, you notice that the outside ski digs deeper into the snow at the point of maximum pressure. In softer snow you'll see the platform, an imprint of the whole ski bottom, at this point.

In the wedge exercise you essentially down-stemmed first one foot and then the other, rebounding from foot to foot. Now try it starting from a parallel stance, making hockey stops, first to one side and then to the other.

Hockey stop rebounds. Stand high and start out straight down the fall line of a steep hill. Flex low, pivoting your skis across your direction of travel and sharply setting the edges at the low point of your flex. Plant the pole at this point and rebound, pivoting your skis in a turn during the extension. Immediately flex and set your edges in the other direction. Make snow fly up from your edges and then turn again. Continue to alternate sides, using a series of abrupt hockey stops in the fall line.

Instead of just skidding to slow in a christie, you're now making a definite edgeset. This occurs with a final downward pressure as you stop flexing, accompanied by a sharp edging. This final "hit" of the edges is brief and powerful and should be accompanied by a pole plant at this instant.

You may especially enjoy making sharp skidded edgesets in ideal packed powder. The snow billowing out from your ski edges is a pretty sight. However, it's not always necessary to skid on the edges to increase ski pressure prior to a rebound. If you ride the skis around on their edges without skidding, it is called carving. In a tighter turn the ski pressure increases dramatically due to higher centrifugal force. During short-radius turns this force places the skis in extreme reverse camber at the finish of a turn. You may need quite a low body position here to angulate enough for adequate edging.

It's crucial to keep the turn going during the sharp finish. The arc back up the hill is sometimes called a *preturn* or a *fish hook*. Anytime your skis go straight you're back to only normal body weight on them, reducing their rebound potential. Check your tracks now and then. They should show constant arcs with deep pressure marks just prior to changing direction, followed by a light touching of the skis to the snow as they start the turn. If the tracks run straight after crossing the fall line you're not finishing the turn enough to take advantage of any rebound.

The carved preturn is most useful in shorter-radius fall line turns, in which rebound unweighting helps you start the skis quickly into each new turn.

Shortswing. Choose a narrow path defined by imaginary boundaries on a steep, smooth slope. Ski within this path, using continuous short, round turns and rebound unweighting. Finish each turn with a dynamic pressuring of the skis and feel them push you into each new turn. Maintain a constant dynamic rhythm of "pressure, release, pressure, release" to the bottom of the slope.

The shortswing is a dynamic version of the wedel. It's a good way to make many turns on a steep slope. With adequate edging and turn finishes you can keep your speed quite low despite the extreme pitch.

Your skis may momentarily leave the snow after hard edgesets. If so, relax and extend your legs after the edgeset to maintain contact with the snow.

Rhythm and timing are important. Don't get locked into one rhythm, because with changing terrain you'll need to vary it.

Shortswing in varying terrain. Choose an advanced slope with several changes in pitch. Pick a fifteen-foot-wide fall line path. Ski straight downhill in this path until you reach a comfortable speed, then make one round rebound turn after another. Maintain your original speed all the way down the hill. You'll need frequent short-radius turns on the steep terrain, and more relaxed wider turns on the flatter.

Pole Plants

You've already planted the pole for many purposes, including balancing when transferring weight from foot to foot, stabilizing your upper body in anticipation, supporting your body during inclination, and deflecting your direction. Now we'll concentrate on pole plant timing, which is critical to fluid skiing at higher speeds.

Your pole plant triggers all the necessary actions of rising upward, changing edges, and pivoting in a new direction. To appreciate all this synchronize your skiing with a partner.

Shortswing using anticipation and edgeset rebounds.

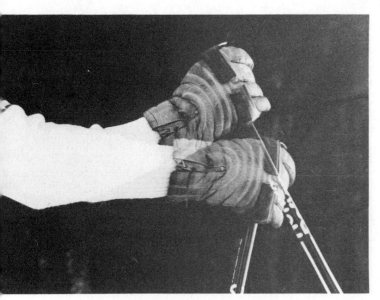

An efficient pole plant is quick and effortless.

Synchronized skiing. Ski with a partner who makes fluid turns. Synchronize exactly with his turns by matching your pole plant to his. Try matching without watching his pole plant, and you'll lose his rhythm.

This is a great exercise if you have a group of people behind one leader. When everyone plants their pole at the same time it looks like the Rockettes on snow!

The pole is planted with a flick of the wrist and forearm at the junction of two turns. Keep your hands in front of your body, always ready for the next pole plant. Anytime a hand drops out of sight behind you it takes extra time to bring it forward. Losing even two-tenths of a second at fifteen miles per hour carries you forward an additional four feet.

The location of the plant is somewhat a matter of preference. However, common mistakes are to place it too far ahead, so that you have to ski around it, or to place it too close to the skis , so that you skid into it. For shorter-radius turns make the plant at least a foot down the fall line from your toes. In steeper terrain where you radically complete turns this will be almost equidistant

(1) A stabilizing pole plant.

(2) A deflecting pole plant.

The pole is planted toward the center of the new turn. To concentrate on this, make it a focal point of some turns.

Pole plant slalom. Imagine that wherever you plant your ski pole a real slalom pole springs up out of the snow. Choose a straight line down the fall line where you'd like to run a slalom. Alternately plant each pole on this line as your body skis around these slalom poles.

Look at your tracks to verify that your pole plants ended up in a straight line and your skis curved around the basket marks. Tracks are your signature on the canvas of snow and show you're beginning to ski like an expert.

CARVING

Skis are actually precision tools, which is one reason why they are so expensive. Using this ski design to its maximum is the secret to effortless, efficient skiing. Imagine that you were to cut up a turkey with a long, sharp knife. You could hack away at it as though you held an axe, or you could slice it with firm, smooth strokes. We're going to fine-tune the use of the ski's sharp edges in a type of smooth skiing, which is in fact called *carving*.

A carved turn is simply one in which there is no skid. After all the effort you devoted to controlling skids, you may rightly question why you'd want to

Plant the poles in a straight line down the hill in this imaginary slalom.

Skidding versus carving.

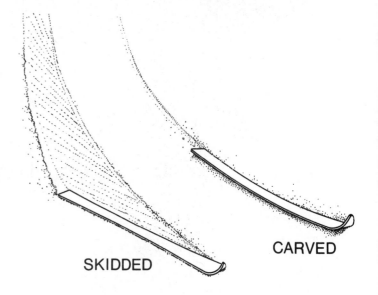

SKIDDED

CARVED

from the tips and tails. In gentler terrain the turns are not completed as much, and the pole tip ends up nearer the ski tip, but it's still down the fall line from the toes.

An upright pole plant stabilizes your anticipated upper body and provides a balance point for weight transfer or inclination. An angled pole plant, where the palm is somewhat up, provides deflection and can slow down your upper body while your skis pivot into a tight turn. In either case, avoid locking your elbow into your ribs.

FALL LINE

Step continually to an edge in the "thousand steps."

156

do away with them. Skids slow you down by brushing edges sideways across the snow. However, if you want speed in a race or on easy terrain, you would not want to skid. If the snow were sparse, you'd also want to avoid skids, as the edges could catch on rocks or bare patches. On ice skids are hard to control and result in chattering skis. In rough broken snow skis catch edges during skids, making balance difficult.

You already know how to make the skis skid, by pivoting rapidly or by reducing edging so centrifugal force pulls you out of the turn. To carve, all you have to do is tone down the pivoting and keep adequate edging. Instead of skidding to slow down after crossing the fall line you'll increase edging to carve sharply uphill in a preturn. Let's start by feeling a carve.

Natural carve. Ski on flat skis down the fall line of a moderate hill. Place both skis on one set of edges and let them carry you around. Balance on the edges, flexing to increase edging and to maintain a carve as your speed increases. Look at your tracks to make sure you left two sharp arcs in the snow.

Another way to think of carving is that each crystal of snow touched by the front of your ski edge is also touched by the rest of the ski edge. Your tracks are a dead giveaway as to whether or not you carve. If you're leaving a wide, mushy track, you're skidding. You'll be able to feel the difference. Carving feels crisp and fast. While skidding, loose snow is sprayed sideways from your edges. However, loose snow flies backward from your edges while carving.

When you're on flat, pivoting skis you have minimal tracking ability and may be pulled out of the turn's arc by centrifugal force. Therefore, a secret of carving is to edge early, well before the fall line. In fact, on ice, where friction is at a minimum, you'll want to ride an edge all the time. It's time to get used to balancing entirely on an edge, rather than on a flat ski. Stepping on your edges throughout a turn is good practice for this balance.

Thousand steps. As soon as you cross the fall line in a turn, begin stepping uphill from foot to foot, always riding on the ski edges facing the inside of the turn. Once you're feeling confident in this, also begin your turns by stepping to the new edges. Continue with rapid, small steps right through the fall line. Place only the edges of your skis on the snow. See how far up the hill you can climb at the finish of a turn before starting the next stepped turn.

Carved tracks must be round, as an edged ski is designed to turn in an arc. When you look at a ski you'll find that it's narrow in the middle and wide at the tip and tail, a feature called *sidecut.*

Edging and Ski Arcs. Take a ski and place it on a smooth floor. Tilt one edge up and slightly off the floor. Due to the sidecut the edge only touches the floor at the shovel and tail. As you'd normally be standing on the ski, pressure the boot area until the entire metal edge touches the floor. Trace the edge now and you'll find that it forms a slight curve. If you were on the snow, the ski would track in this arc of a circle. Raise up the elevated edge even more, to increase the edging, and again press the boot area to the floor. This time it requires more force to make the entire edge touch. The arc now becomes more curved, or part of a smaller-diameter circle.

Increasing the edging thus gives you an easy way to vary the turn radius, without having to pivot your skis abruptly.

Increased edging in carves. Traverse across a steep hill at moderate speed. Suddenly flex and increase edging. Your skis instantly shoot uphill in a tight turn.

For short-radius carved turns you may need a good deal of edging, which requires a very low, angulated stance at the finish of a turn. This is the point where you are completing the bottom of your *S* turn and resisting a large centrifugal force trying to pull you downhill in a skid. You can obtain an idea of the magnitude of edging required by having a partner pull you downhill.

Maximum edging. Stand across a steep slope and extend your pole baskets to a partner standing down the fall line. Have him or her gradually increase the downhill pull on the poles while you resist the force by increasing edging. As the pull increases, note how you use a combination of inward body lean plus hip-and-knee angulation for maximum edging.

Now you can see why racers round a gate in a low stance, with their feet well downhill for maximum edge hold. You can also understand why your thighs become tired, as you support more than your normal weight due to the g forces at a turn finish.

Discovering maximum edging for a turn finish.

Minimal edging is needed at a turn initiation.

LESS EDGE

MORE EDGE

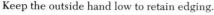

Keep the outside hand low to retain edging.

When one turn is completed and the next one starts the direction of centrifugal force changes. This is analogous to your partner in the previous exercise suddenly releasing the pull. At this point you change edges and begin the new turn.

Edging at turn initiation. Stand across the fall line on a moderate hill. Have a partner stand above you in the fall line. Remain facing downhill but extend your pole baskets to your partner and have him or her pull gently uphill. You can easily balance against your partner in an upright stance with minimum edging.

Once again your partner has represented centrifugal force. At the very start of the turn this force acts uphill, which is to the outside of the new turn. However, the force is small at this point and a more upright stance provides all the edging you need for carving. Think of the needed edging as exposing more of the ski base throughout a turn.

Ski base messages. Pretend you have written a message such as "Hi, I'm a super skier!" on the bases of your skis. As you carve your turns, no one can read this message at the turn's start. In the fall line phase, spectators to the sidelines may begin to see it. However, at the finish of the turn, the message is clearly displayed to spectators downhill of you.

Sometimes the maximum edging a skier could achieve is lessened by poor body position, which destroys angulation. You should think of your uphill side being higher than your downhill side. This particularly applies to the hands. Raising the outside hand in a turn could raise the arm and shoulder. This deangulates the body, reducing the edging and causing a skid. As you finish a turn, keep that lower hand down, close to your boot.

Test yourself to find how well you can hold an edge by momentarily returning to a wedge turn, but this time with carving.

Edge locks. Ski in a gliding wedge on a gentle slope. Sharply increase edging on one ski so that it bites into the snow. Briefly ride that edge in a carve, without skidding. Then sharply increase edge on the other ski while simultaneously flattening the first ski. Immediately you'll carve in the other direction. Repeat rapidly from inside edge to inside edge. Look at your tracks to verify that your edges left sharp distinct marks in the snow. Now try it on steeper terrain.

This exercise is sometimes called the *crabwalk*, since your motion is predominantly sideways. It's a great one to see if you can articulate your body

Track from the "crabwalk."

Be nice to your partner and don't suddenly let go of the poles while playing tug-of-war, as you'll both slingshot into the trees. You'll zip right along, so choose a gentle slope.

Carving is a great sensation. You'll know when you're doing it as you enter controlled flight down the hill. Even your skis sound happy, as they slice crisply through the snow. You'll be pleased to know that after spending so much money on high-performance skis they're finally paying you back by doing what they do best.

STEP TURNS

A few years ago an expert skier was distinguished by his ability to rotate both legs simultaneously into a turn. Nowadays, an expert skier is one who is versatile enough during turns to apply independent leg movements also. This is essentially what you did in your first wedge and stem turns. However, now we'll make dynamic turns using your refined skills.

In a step turn you transfer weight early to a ski that has been picked up and moved sideways. The outward step of the new power ski is the turn's distinguishing characteristic. Because weight is transferred left to right, or laterally, to the new ski, this variety of turns is frequently referred to as "lateral projection." A more common name is *racing turns* because they are used extensively in racecourses.

A tug-of-war to test carving.

sufficiently to carve without losing an edge.

In addition to increasing edging, you can also sharpen a carved turn by increasing the pressure on a ski. If you have pressure on two skis, you can place it all on one. This enhances that ski's reverse camber and tightens the turn radius.

Pressure effect on carves. Traverse at high speed across a steep hill with weight on both feet equally. Then stand entirely on the downhill foot, and your track becomes an uphill curve.

This is one of the reasons that racers often stand on just the lower ski near a turn's finish.

For a little competitive fun, you can measure your carving ability against that of a friend.

Tug-of-war. On a very gentle hill hold on to a partner's ski pole baskets while he or she holds on to the grips. Start off equally in the fall line and apply edging to try to turn away from each other. The better edger will complete the turn and pull his or her opponent with him.

Stepping from foot to foot.

The stepping action has several advantages, one of which is changing a path. Suppose you were cruising along and a mature maple tree popped up in front of you. Despite all the cartoons showing one ski track on each side of the trunk, I guarantee you'd rather step both skis to one side. Of course, that tree could have been a rock, a racing gate, or even a mogul. A few other advantages we'll discover to step turns are that they help your balance, they keep you riding on an edge, and they initiate turns quickly.

As a warm up to independent leg action, practice some stepping.

Stepping. On a gentle hill make a mark down the fall line by laying out some ski poles. Start above and to one side of the poles. As you approach them, step both skis over the poles. After you can do this, visualize an imaginary, long fall line mark. Step both skis back and forth over this mark with one modification. Both skis must go to left and right of the line. However, when on the right side of the mark you must keep most of your weight on the right foot, and when on the left side keep most of your weight on the left foot. Step to the power edges rather than to a flat ski, and you'll be making step turns.

I hope you felt a rhythmic pressure transfer back and forth over the fall line.

There are many variations on step turns. One of the most useful is a step to an inside edge. While carving on the outside ski you change the inside ski's edge with an uphill step. When you place weight on that ski it immediately starts a new turn.

You continuously carve on an edge without a flat ski phase, which could skid.

Step turn to the inside edge. Ski at moderate speed on open terrain. At the finish of one turn, step your uphill ski about a foot farther uphill, placing it on its inside edge. As the uphill ski touches the snow, extend upward and sideways to brace against it. Immediately you'll be in a turn. Lift up the lower ski to match it with the uphill. Cross the fall line, complete the turn, and continue to initiate turns by stepping the inside ski laterally uphill while at the same time changing its edge. For high-speed longer turns make the step parallel. At slower speed, or for quicker turns, step the tail out more than the tip.

This step to an inside edge starts your new turn immediately. To make that turn extra sharp you can step to a stem position, which is often called a *converging step* because the skis point toward each other. You won't want a large stem at higher speed, as the sudden direction change would cause a skid.

You may find that with cruising parallel step turns you forget to plant your pole! If so, that's fine, as you have discovered a better way to balance without it. Previously you inclined your upper body across your feet into each turn. Now you are inclining by stepping your feet away from your upper body as you start a turn. Your center of gravity is thus automatically placed inside the new turn radius. The step to an inside edge has eliminated the precarious balance at the change of inclination. That's why these turns feel so smooth.

A parallel step facilitates a smooth carved turn.

This skier has come too wide on the gate. His converging step changes direction quickly.

Perhaps you wonder why the ski is stepped rather than slid across the snow as it was in earlier turns. It's because on the steeper slopes and in the higher-speed turns you are skiing, a considerable angular ski change is needed to go from edge to edge. The uphill knee would hit the lower leg before the edge could be changed. Therefore, to get on the inside edge, the ski is picked up and moved sideways up the hill. This is edging predominantly from the hip. With the two skis farther apart and with a large angular difference in their edging, the new inside ski must be picked up and matched to the new outside ski during the early part of the turn.

Stepping also helps eliminate skidding. You can emphasize this carving advantage while making tight turns.

Running Gates. Set up a slalom course in the fall line of a moderate hill. If you don't have bamboo gates, use snowballs, food dye spots, or paper cups. Ski the course without stepping. Go back and ski it with stepping. Time yourself both ways to see how much faster your run is when you step. To further develop mobility from foot to foot, run imaginary gates, or ski around the shadows cast by each chair of a lift.

Step turns leave discontinuous tracks. That is, the tracks have a lateral gap between the finish of one turn and the start of the next. Each turn does not

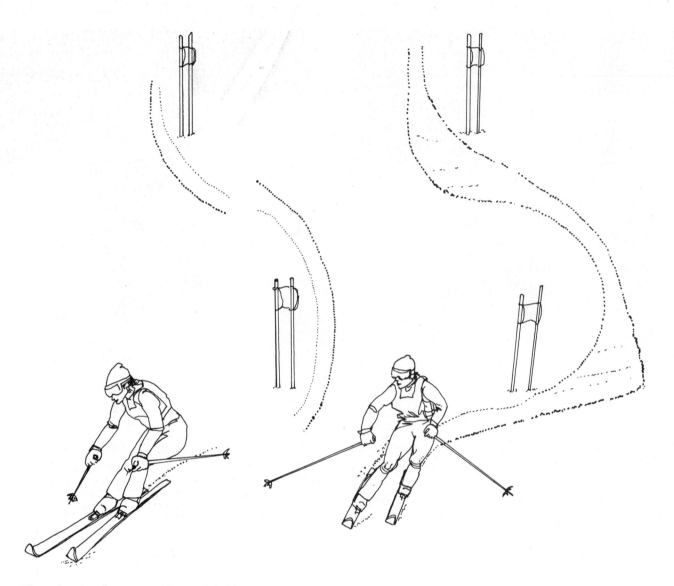

The wider arcs of a step turn eliminate skidding.

have to be as curved, and a skier can make wider-radius turns. These larger turns provide better edge hold and more time in the fall line for extra speed. Step turns are invaluable in racing gates, where the nonstepper often skids and loses time trying to negotiate the sharp turns of a course. For the same reason, step turns are also great for reducing skids on ice.

Step turns to an inside edge are used to gain speed in racing. Instead of merely stepping side to side, you can thrust forward. This is known as an "accelerating step" and is really a skate step.

Accelerating by skating. On a gentle slope skate dynamically from foot to foot. Flex deeply in one leg and push by extending diagonally forward onto the other ski, which is flat or slightly edged. Flex onto the inside edge and repeat. Next, try it on a steeper hill, and then in the gates.

As with any turn, you still have to move your body forward as you head into the fall line. Try driving your hands ahead as you skate to help bring your weight forward.

The step turn provides an easy turn entry after a rebound.

Stepping from a rebound. From a steep traverse sink into a hard edgeset. Let the rebound help you step the upper ski out and forward onto its inside edge. Immediately pressure it into the turn, stepping the new inside ski parallel. Continue to turn with a rebound and step.

This racer skates off his right ski to gain speed.

As with other step turns, the unweighting is projected laterally uphill to the new ski, rather than straight upward.

You can also step laterally to a flat ski or to an uphill edge. Riding a flat ski or an uphill edge will momentarily delay a turn until you change edges by inclining into the turn.

Diverging step turn. Near the finish of a medium-speed turn step the tip of your upper ski more uphill. Transfer your weight to the uphill edge of the stepped ski as soon as it is back on the snow. Change that ski's edge by leaning your body downhill, and the ski will start into a turn.

This step turn to an outside edge is also called a *scissors turn*, from the way the skis spread apart. You could step parallel, but stepping to an angled ski takes you more sharply uphill. This is especially valuable when racing, to gain elevation coming into a gate.

In the diverging step you balance on the "wrong" edge momentarily. To get off that edge and onto the power edge you have to lean into the new turn. If you find yourself rushing this turn, you can practice by deliberately delaying the edge change.

Delayed edge change. At the finish of a large-radius,

higher-speed turn, transfer your weight to the uphill edge of the stepped uphill ski. Ride this edge for at least one second on the snow. Then initiate the next turn by inclining your body and driving your knee toward the fall line. At the finish of this turn again ride the uphill edge of the new uphill ski, delaying your turn initiation.

The scary part is leaning downhill at high speed and trusting centrifugal force to hold you up. Admittedly this may be difficult at first, but it's a superb exercise to test your balance and to develop your sensitivity to edge changing.

Interestingly, the diverging step turn can also be made without a step! Since you're not changing edges before the weight transfer, you can make the skis scissor apart while keeping them on the snow. Just increase the edge angle of the upper ski and let it climb.

You can play a variation on the childhood game of tag with a friend to practice stepping.

Chase skiing. Ski with a friend and choose who is to lead. The chaser tries to keep up with the lead skier. However, the lead skier tries to outmaneuver the chaser by stepping into turns and stepping uphill during the turns. The chaser wins if he can match the leader for a run. The chaser loses if he ends up lower than the leader because he couldn't match the leader's carved step turns.

165

This skier has come too low into the gate. His diverging step gains height to return to a good line without skidding.

Step turns are not the answer to all skiing situations. Frequently it's just plain fun to turn with your skis together or to throw a spray of loose snow in skids. In powder a step turn could lead to disaster. However, use step turns when you want to carve better. For variety, toss in a step here and there on easy terrain. Versatility is the key to entertaining skiing. Step turns are dynamic and lively and show that you know how to dance on your skis.

THE MAN-EATERS

Nothing strikes as much terror into some skiers as venturing out into the wild, white world and encountering a herd of hungry, full-grown, man-eating moguls. Although snow cats (snow-grooming machines) have helped control them, they are fed by such large numbers of skiers that they are not endangered. The species includes all shapes from the mellow giant round ones with humped backs to the nasty sharp-cornered ones with flat backs and sheer drop-offs for lower sides. I hope you have gained some appreciation for the fun you can have in the moguls. If not, take a glance at "Moguls" in the chapter "Intermediate Technique." Here we'll look at large moguls on steeper slopes and apply the edging and pivoting skills of our dynamic turns to them. We'll also learn to fine-tune our pressure control skill to tame them.

You must slow down and turn in this three-dimensional bumpy slalom course just as you would on any slope. Start in smaller moguls and work your way up. Everything happens ten times faster in the bumps, so you won't have time to think any technical thoughts. Concentrate on being loose and fluid.

Moguls demand efficient skiing. This means turning from the lower body and using a twisted body for extra pivoting power. Find a friendly local mogul on which to practice your anticipated turn.

Anticipation on a bump. Stand on the crest of a sharp bump so that your tips and tails are off the snow. Wind up your body by facing your upper body directly downhill and your skis directly across the hill. Flex to a low position and plant your pole well downhill of your boots. Leaning on the pole, extend upright while pressing forward onto the toes. Your skis will untwist into the fall line. Finish this single turn by flexing and skidding to slow. Keep your upper body facing downhill so that you are ready for another turn.

You should feel that the skis head into the fall line all by themselves. Your pole plant both stabilizes your upper body so that it doesn't untwist and helps your balance as you incline toward the fall line.

Slowing in the moguls is always a major concern. Rather than skidding all the way through the bumps, you can start applying more dynamic edgesets just prior to a turn.

Checking on a bump. From a steep traverse, start in a high stance while skiing to the uphill side of a bump. As you approach the bump's crest, flex downward and turn the skis under you. Make a final sharp edgeset to a stop, planting your pole with the check.

You slowed on that bump by skiing uphill and skidding to an edgeset. While turning the skis uphill your upper body remains facing downhill.

A turn with anticipation on a mogul.

EDGESET

PIVOT

Linking turns in bumps.

This is convenient, because now you're positioned for your next turn. Slowing down also sets you up for the new turn! Now you're ready for a series of not quite full-grown man-eaters.

Linked turns in bumps. Choose a moderate mogul field and pick a fall line path two bumps wide. Choose your first bump and ski straight for it, flexing as you approach. Use an edgeset on the convex uphill side to slow. Pivot and extend around the bump, all the while keeping your upper body facing downhill. Immediately begin flexing for an edgeset on the next bump. Maintain a fluid rhythm of "edgeset, turn, edgeset, turn" all the way, touching every bump in your narrow path.

The main elements are facing downhill with the upper body and slowing with edging. In rounded moguls you'll find that the edgeset can be less of a skid and more of a carved preturn.

As the bumps mature and get larger, you'll want to stay closer to the troughs, rather than skiing to the very tops. There are still convex areas on each bump on which to turn. You may not have to check your skis directly across the fall line as you take this lower path. Set the edges at an angle to the fall line against the upper side of each bump. If snow flies out from your edgesets, it will end up on the bumps, and you'll be helping to make them bigger. Drive your upper body forward after the edgeset to keep up with your skis which accelerate rapidly down the steep lower side of each mogul.

Keep your hands ready in front so a slight flick of the wrist and forearm will plant the pole. Pole plants are absolutely vital to successful bump skiing. They offer balance and deflection during

A pole plant momentarily supports the skier.

EDGESET

PIVOT

the rapid direction and pressure changes. Pole plants also help you lean into the new turn. For a moment the pole may support your body, so plant the pole well downhill for a wide base of support. Watch a great bump skier, and one day you may see him miss a pole plant. He will actually fall outward, landing downhill of his skis. Of course, if you do this, you'll imitate the great skiers by rolling over and continuing to ski as if you had planned it!

Stepping can also be useful in bumps.

Step in bumps. Check against a bump with an edgeset on the lower ski. Step the upper one out in a small stem and immediately step to it to start a turn. Check that ski against the next bump as you step out the first.

This is really a definite weight transfer and a quick edge change. Because bumps are close together you won't use a big lateral step. The pole is planted as you transfer weight from one foot to the other.

One disconcerting feature is that as your speed increases and as the bumps get bigger, they try to catapult you into the air. This is terrain unweighting. You may be bouncing into the air off one bump and crashing into the next. Even the rebound unweighting from your edgeset helps push you into the air. Passively flexing your legs isn't enough. Active pressure control is needed now, so that you keep those critters from launching you into orbit.

Jumping or absorbing bumps. Find a single large bump or a long roll in the terrain. Take one run at mod-

erate speed across it and get air off the crest. To do this flex low before the rise, then extend forcefully as you approach the crest to help push yourself into the air. On your next run over the same spot ski at the same speed, but this time avoid leaving the snow surface. To absorb the bump, approach it in a high stance and flex as you go up it, pulling your feet upward. At the crest you will be compressed with a deep ankle-and-knee flex. Forcefully extend your legs as the slope drops away to keep your skis always touching the snow.

To negate a bump's ski jump effect, you must reduce pressure on the skis while rising up the bump and increase ski pressure on the far side of it. This requires a dynamic flexion as you ski up the bump and a dynamic extension as you ski down from the crest. By actively pulling up and pushing down your feet you effectively erase, or swallow, the bump. The popular French term for this movement is *avalement* (pronounced "av-al-mahn") which in translation means "swallowing."

You should tailor the amount of retraction and extension to match your speed and each bump's size. With higher speed or with bigger bumps you must retract and extend more forcefully and more rapidly to reduce the terrain unweighting.

Avalement in bumps. Ski in a moderate traverse across a mogul field. Don't try to turn for this exercise. Instead swallow every bump by folding your body to raise your feet and extending your body to lower them. Try to maintain the same ski-to-snow pressure throughout the traverse without catching any air. Keep your head traveling in a level line without bobbing while your legs absorb the bumps. Increase your speed and see how much more dynamic you must be to stay on the

Jumping off a bump.

snow. To increase your absorption on a bump also lower your hands to your feet at the bump crest.

The rapid folding and unfolding movements use calf, thigh, buttock, and abdominal muscles. At high speed on large bumps your knees may almost touch your chest as you fold your trunk forward and downward and pull your feet upward to absorb the bump. Conversely, you'll be almost completely upright between them. Too often skiers think about being low in the bumps, but they for-

get about the importance of being upright. A full extension between bumps may be necessary to maintain snow contact and also to maximize the amount you can fold for the next absorption.

Once you know how to swallow the bumps in a straight line you'll find that turning on them is very easy. You may want to practice first on a slope without bumps.

Practicing pressure control for bumps. On a smooth, steep slope, practice the extension-retraction

Absorbing the same bump with active flexion and extension.

Traversing a series of bumps to practice pressure control with retraction and extension.

Practice folding to initiate a bump turn.

Turning with absorption on a mogul.

motions you'll use in the bumps. Start a turn by flexing downward and turn from a low position. Extend into the fall line. Then flex downward to finish and start the skis into a new turn.

This is a down unweighted turn. Occasionally you may use it on a steep slope, but the main application is on bumps. Although it's an unweighting, it neutralizes the positive weighting the bump gives you when you ski up it. Flexing also puts you in a low position. This is a powerful stance from which to pivot and also from which to change edges using knee drive.

Absorption turn on bumps. As you ski up a bump, absorb it by flexing deeply. Near the crest of the bump pivot your feet in the direction of the new turn and begin an edge change with knee drive. Extend your legs to maintain snow contact as you ski on the downhill side of the bump. Begin leg retraction after crossing the trough between moguls and starting up the next bump.

Sometimes, instead of absorbing a mogul, you'll want to emphasize its unweighting tendency by jumping off it. This would be useful where two moguls are close together. You jump from the uphill side of one with enough height to land on the downhill side of the second. There you flex to absorb the shock of landing.

Your knees sustain large stresses in the bumps. They are flexing up and down and also changing edges left and right. Rest them if they get tired and think about conditioning to build up their strength and to improve their flexibility.

Even with absorption, you can't go slam-bam through every mogul field. On the really large ones you'll cut across the bumps on an uphill ridge, carve through a trough, and go partway up the next. You might consider them as a series of minigullies, in which you only have to ski up each bump to a convenient convex turn point. Your skidding will be reduced as you carve preturns to control speed.

Much route finding in the mogul wilderness depends upon who made the bumps. Carving skiers at higher speed make rounded, well-spaced ones. Skidding skiers at lower speeds leave choppy, cliff-like bumps. You have to adapt your skills to the different bumps. Choosing a path is also a matter of personal preference in style. Many good skiers find a fall line route most satisfying, with a turn against each bump in that path. A few racers on

173

Use the natural unweighting tendency of bumps to jump from one to another.

Carving through the moguls.

long skis prefer to carve long-radius turns in a mogul field, soaking up bumps as if they weren't there. Some skiers like to take a very high route, skiing right along the crests of the bumps, throwing in an extra turn on the convex downhill ridge of each bump. Others prefer the low, fast, bobsledlike path in the troughs.

Visualization is a key to a good run in the moguls. Like the great mogul skiers you should go into a state of relaxed concentration at the top of a mogul field. Visualize your path down it as being a fluid line in harmony with the rhythm of the bumps, then push off and go for it. The journey of a thousand bumps begins with the first one, so make that one right. If you're late turning on the first bump you'll be behind for the next several.

Avoid getting locked into one turning rhythm. Be creative and versatile in the moguls. Change your pace, use different ways of turning, and vary where you turn on the bumps. That way the big mogul fields will become your personal playground.

BECAUSE IT'S THERE

The Steeps

Skiing the steeper slopes always pumps a little adrenaline. However, on steep runs skiers frequently find themselves fighting for balance. As the brain perceives how sharply the slope falls

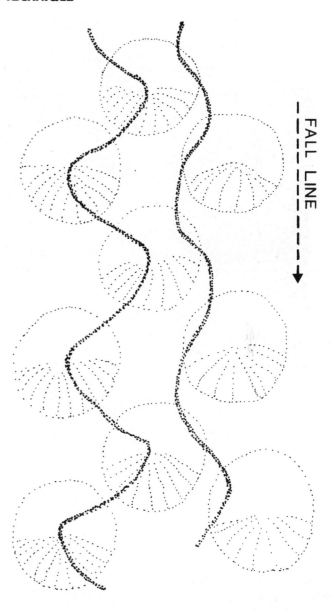

FALL LINE

HIGH LINE   LOW LINE

Looking down this mogul field, you can choose a high line across the bumps or a lower route near the troughs.

away, it often tells a skier to lean into the supposed safety of the hill. I'll give you odds that the last time you "fell down" on a steep hill it was really a fall *uphill* of your skis. There's frequently no need for this loss of balance. Remember that you want to be balanced without muscular strain.

175

and on a new power edge, ready to turn. This is also a good way to start out from a stop. Rather than traverse, step right into the fall line. That way your first turn only has to be half a turn, and you start your rhythm going immediately.

At higher speeds you can use a parallel turn. When skiing fast you must incline into the new turn and also press forward. Starting the turn should be almost like jumping out of a window. This is where panic sets in, as all of a sudden you're hanging out in space, looking down at the base lodge two miles straight down. Frequently, skiers revert to a stem for support at this point, rather than trusting to some esoteric force by the name of "centrifugal." However, you do have a great support with you—your pole. Plant it well downhill and you're automatically leaning outward toward the new turn. A common fault is planting the pole right next to the skis, so no inclination takes place. Make an effort to reach for the plant, placing the tip an extra half foot below its normal plant.

One nice feature on the steeps is that you can start turns without much unweighting. The slope drops away so quickly that all you have to do is release the edge hold and press forward. In fact, you'll want to extend your legs as you start into the fall line. This pressures the skis so that their edges bite into the snow.

Once your turn is going you'll immediately

Balancing out over the lower ski.

In a traverse across a steep hill the body weight should go through the downhill foot to the inside ski edge for most effective balance. This may mean turning off your brain, which is busy shouting, "Look out for that steep hill!" If you try to balance over the inside ski, you can't recover if you lean too far uphill, and you will fall uphill. You should instead allow your natural balancing mechanism to take over, placing you away from the hillside and *out* over that downhill foot.

Balance point on a steep hill. Traverse across the bottom of a steep pitch. Lift the uphill ski, angling your body out to balance entirely on the downhill ski. When you feel comfortable in this stance, complete turns by skiing out of the fall line onto only the downhill foot. Now try it higher up on the steep pitch.

Starting the turn on steep terrain is often a mentally difficult concept. If you've really slowed down after crossing the fall line, a stepped stem is a good turn entry. It puts a ski into the fall line

Reach for the pole plant on steeper slopes.

Stay perpendicular to your skis while accelerating in the fall line.

think of slowing down. If you've ever driven a car on an icy road, you've faced the same situation. When going around a curve you hit the brakes before the turn and again after the turn. Braking in the middle can lead to an uncontrolled skid. In skiing your brakes are skiing uphill against gravity, and also skidding on the edges. You need to retain the accelerating center part of the turn for control. During the fall line phase of the turn be sure to keep up with your skis by staying perpendicular to them.

One hopes you'll still make a round turn for best speed control. This round turn will take the skis back uphill. The big trick is to *finish your turn*. Keep skiing uphill until your speed is well under control before you start a new turn. Lose too much speed and you'll stall out. But retain too much and you'll go faster and faster. The tracks at your turn finish should resemble a fishhook, or the letter *J*.

During all your slowing you are (of course!) still facing downhill, for maximum edging ability. Anytime you face uphill of your ski tips your edging is lost, and if there's one friend you have on the steep slope, it is definitely edging. You'll need to spread your feet apart on the super steep to get adequate edging from the lower ski. That way the lower knee won't be restricted by the upper boot.

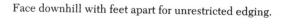
Face downhill with feet apart for unrestricted edging.

Slowing down a partner to learn speed control.

You can use the edges to drastically shorten your turn radius for better speed control.

Shortening turn radius through knee drive. Ski at moderate speed at about a forty-five-degree angle to the fall line, but in a mostly upright stance. Now suddenly flex your knees to lower your body. Simultaneously point your knees uphill to quickly increase edge angle. Your skis will shoot uphill in a rapid turn.

You'll need a low stance to drive your knees radically uphill. It's still necessary to be balanced against your feet, so think of lowering your hips toward your feet. You won't spend much time with your legs fully extended on the steeps.

The combination of facing downhill and increasing edging can be practiced easily on less intimidating slopes before going out on the steeps.

Slowing through edging. Have a partner ski ahead of you and extend his pole grips back to you to hook into your baskets. Your partner will stand with his skis parallel and let gravity pull him down the fall line. It's your job to slow down both of you, while also making turns.

The extra weight of your partner simulates your extra acceleration on a steeper slope.

A lower stance is needed for optimum edging on the steeps. This allows you to angulate by bending sideways at the knees and hips. Your shoulders will angle downward at about the same pitch as the slope. If you're having a problem flexing low enough for adequate edging, one cure is to practice with shorter poles.

Lower stance for edging. Hold your poles below their grips for a few runs. Stand in a normal upright position at the start of turns, but flex down to make your poles touch in a plant at the finish of turns.

On the super steeps shortswing works well. The rebound from a dynamic edgeset unweights the skis enough for a quick pivot. The skis swing back and forth from one edgeset to another, with almost

An angulated stance with shoulders at about the slope pitch provides maximum edging.

Hopping and pivoting about the tips for rapid edgesets.

no snow contact when the skis are pointing down the fall line. Some skiers like to put their weight a little forward to pivot about the tip area. They hop the tails back and forth in quick edgesets.

Use extreme caution on steep slopes covered with hard-packed snow. A spill could result in a long slide and a longer walk back up to retrieve a ski. Avoid icy slopes where a fall could propel you into rocks or over a cliff. If you do take a spill on the steeps, you should know how to slow down rapidly. Get your feet below you to dig in the ski edges (or boot edges and heels if your skis are off). Sometimes you may be sliding headfirst downhill. If so, dig in one hand, arm, or elbow to twist your body around feetfirst, and then you can stop easily with your feet.

Trees

If you've only stayed on the open slopes, you're missing one of skiing's great experiences—the trees. Skiing in the trees has several advantages. It opens up new terrain. Each run is different, thanks to the random spacing of tree trunks. You won't find crowds or moguls, but you may find light powder, which the trees have harvested from the wind and shaded from the sun. On stormy days your visibility in the trees will be much better than on open slopes.

Many ski areas thin certain trees, or else have a natural burned area, which has cleared some of the growth. These sections are called *glades* and are good slopes to start your tree experience. No special skill refinement is used in the trees, but some common sense is in order. Start with short excursions, maybe darting around one or two trees right next to the trail. That way you'll have a feeling of the snow without committing yourself. Most importantly, you'll know if you're up to making the necessary turns.

You can't go straight very far before a tree pops up. Trees are nature's slalom course, and the "gates" are not very yielding. Rather than try to cut close to them, aim for the center of the open space between two trees. That way you can err slightly and still miss the trunk. Another reason for avoiding the trunks is that the snow melts in a crater around the large trunks, particularly in the spring. Ask any dedicated tree skier about this phenomenon, and he or she will probably relate a story about falling into an unseen crater and struggling for an hour to get out.

Even though you will be skiing trees within a ski area, they probably won't be patrolled, so always ski with a partner. Also, there's more than trees and bears in the woods. The woods are full of boulders, logs, and debris from trail clearing. It takes a lot of snow to cover these obstacles. Wait until the snow base is plentiful before venturing into the forest. A particularly safe time to avoid obstacles is when the snow is firm enough that you don't sink below the surface.

Make sure you know where you're going. Sometimes what looks like an open path through the trees can close up, leaving you to bushwhack. Don't cross an area boundary to ski trees. It's amazingly easy to get turned around and end up in some canyon miles from the ski area.

Little unseen branches are going to whip across your face. Wear goggles or sturdy glasses for eye protection. Branches and stumps are also going to snatch at your ski pole baskets. To avoid a dislocated arm or thumb, remove your pole straps.

When you get into the woods your whole outlook changes, as you're in a new world, one that's more intimate with smaller boundaries. Maybe, like some skiers, you'll even find tree skiing almost a mystical experience.

THE DEEP STUFF

Powder. The very name brings images of fluffy snow billowing up around a skier. Skiers fly halfway around the world and charter helicopters in search of it. Nonskiers know you've gone off the deep end when you try to describe powder as "the ultimate sensual experience."

In its loosest usage, the word *powder* can be applied to any freshly fallen snow. However, new snow comes in many forms, depending on the humidity, wind, and temperature. In its lightest, driest form you can't even make a snowball out of a handful of it. In its densest wet forms new snow is aptly described by various regional names, such as Sierra Cement or Cascade Crud.

Although it's most prevalent in the Rocky Mountains, good powder can be found anywhere. It comes in many depths, ranging from the "cheater's powder" of a couple inches to the truly "deep stuff" of over a half foot. The light, untracked stage is elusive and transitory. You won't find it at two o'clock in the afternoon of a sunny day. Take the effort to try the light stuff while it's still snowing, or catch the first lift ride the morning after a storm.

At first use your regular skis for powder. Most recreational skis are flexible enough to plane in powder, although a few older, stiff models may "dive." When you become a "powder hound" you may want a special shorter, soft-flexing ski. For the deep stuff wear a retention strap. When a ski releases in a powder spill it can rocket under the

Aim for the center of the space between two trees.

Cross poles for additional support to stand up in bottomless snow.

surface for many yards. Searching for a lost ski by digging with your poles while balancing on one ski can be a long, exhausting experience. I've seen skiers give up in frustration and abandon the missing ski. If you're opposed to retention straps, attach some "powder cord" (or "avalanche cord") to each ski and stuff the loose ends up your pants legs. This brightly colored cord stays on the snow

surface indicating the location of your detached ski.

You're going to be making angels in the snow in powder. Just relax if you do take a spill. The snow is soft and refreshing to sink into. Getting up can be exhausting in bottomless snow, however. If your pole baskets sink in deeply, cross your poles in an *X* shape and place them flat on the snow. Put your hand in the middle of the *X* and push to get up. If you're having trouble putting on a ski, stamp out a firm platform in the snow on which to stand.

To become acquainted with untracked snow, find a gentle patch that hasn't been skied.

Planing the skis. Ski straight in untracked, light snow. Keep your feet close together with weight centered between heel and toe. Your skis will begin floating. Push harder on one ski and it will sink as the other rises higher. Keep weight equal on each foot to plane both skis at the same depth.

I guarantee you'll enjoy the floating feeling. Suddenly you have a third dimension to the sport, one in which your skis are part of the snow itself. At times your skis are going to be lost from sight. Don't worry about it; wouldn't you rather watch the scenery anyway?

The important things you learned are that with

Start with vertical motion and small turns out of the fall line.

speed your skis will plane and that you must keep weight equal on each foot. Think of the two skis as being one single ski and refrain from transferring weight from foot to foot. The closer you bring your feet together, the better off you'll be. You also found that you didn't go as fast as on the hardpack. This is due to the resistance of the snow against your boots and also against the bottoms of your skis as they plane at an angle upward. To generate enough speed to plane your skis, you'll want to ski steeper slopes than you normally would on the pack.

For your first turns in powder, think about rhythmic up-and-down motion.

Unweighting motions in powder. Ski the fall line in a gentle stretch of untracked deep snow. Begin a rhythmic flexion and extension, dropping to a deep flex and straightening to a very upright stance. Your skis will rise and sink relative to the snow surface. Begin making small turns to each side as your skis rise from the release of pressure. Be sure to keep your motions constant, without static pauses. Use a pole plant during your flexed position to start each turn. To stop, sink into a flex with your knees pointing uphill and keep skiing around back up the hill.

Your skis will take time to react in the deep snow. It's like the difference between jumping on a solid floor and jumping on a trampoline. You'll get in the air either way, but on the trampoline there's a delay as the material underfoot first yields downward. Perhaps this is one of the reasons powder skiers sometimes feel a slowing of time. In any event, for this reason you won't enjoy traversing and trying to make a sudden turn. Rhythmic fall line turning is extremely important.

Your balance point in powder is no different from other snow conditions in which you pressure both heels and toes. Forget the advice from well-meaning friends who say to sit back. You will flex into a lower stance, by dropping your hips toward your feet, but it's not an armchair sitting position. Your feet slow down because they are immersed in the resisting snow. You'll have to constantly push them forward. Also, your skis are planing upward but you'll stay mostly perpendicular to them. The pushing and planing makes your body only appear to be behind your feet. However, you should still feel slight pressure against the boot tongue, and not against the upper boot back.

Good powder skiers are perpendicular to their skis and balanced evenly throughout their feet.

SNOW
RESISTANCE

Pivot the skis while they are flat, then bank the bases against the snow.

Your vertical motions in powder are quite important to control pressure against the ski bottoms. It's nothing new. You're in a low position to finish a turn, a higher stance into the fall line, and back to a low flex again. You must keep these motions going constantly and exaggerate them more than you would on the packed slopes.

Perhaps you wonder how your skis turn when there's nothing for them to grab onto in the fluff. They turn the same way they would in a carved turn on the pack, by pivoting and by being bent into reverse camber. It may sound strange to talk about carving in powder. However, the same technique of using the edges applies to control turns

in untracked conditions. Snow resistance against the whole bottom surface of the skis causes a turn. The skis flex into reverse camber from the snow pressure, and they then travel in the resulting arc. You must put the ski bottoms against the snow at an angle to flex them in the direction you want to go. This is essentially the same as extreme edging on the pack. The running bases are banked against the snow with the same lateral motions you would use to edge the skis. (Don't confuse banking the ski bottoms with banking your whole body.)

Banking ski bottoms. Ski down the fall line in untracked snow. Lower your hips to flex your ankles and

Use smooth vertical motions in powder.

ways against your boots and legs that you'll flip over headfirst. Look back at your tracks. They should be continuously round, and relatively narrow. They will cut deeply into the snow in the belly of the turn after the fall line.

If the rhythm and retraction-extension leg motions are eluding you in powder, go back to shortswing turns on the pack, concentrating on the side to side motion in your legs.

Pendulum. Pick a narrow fall line path on a steep, packed slope. Imagine a pivot point at your waist. Your upper body will be upright and your lower body will

Each of these powder tracks shows continual turning, with no straight running even though they are different sizes.

The legs swing back and forth like a pendulum.

knees. Angle the ski bottoms against the snow and they will turn.

Incline your body and angulate to bank the ski bottoms against the snow for a turn. To change from one direction to the other you change the angle of the ski banking by leaning in the new direction and by increasing your angulation into the turn. That may sound complicated, but you do these motions already. Think about making linked short-radius turns, and you'll have powder turns licked.

Powder turns. Pick a moderate untracked hill and start out directly down the fall line. Flex by sinking your body down and pulling your feet up. As you do so, angle your ski bottoms against the snow to complete a turn. With a pole plant lean into the new turn, extending your legs into the fall line. Complete by retracting again and finish the turn. Keep your turns rhythmic and round.

Just as in carving, you can't rush the turn. It should be rounded, even though it's short radius. A sudden Z turn may catch so much snow side-

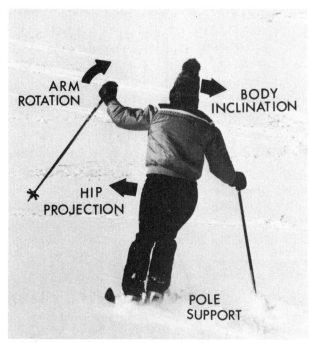

Aids to powder turns.

pivot back and forth like a pendulum on a grandfather clock. Push off and ski in rhythmic short turns so that your feet pass back and forth underneath your body.

Apply this pendulum idea to help make short-radius turns in the powder. In larger turns you'll lose the rhythm and gain excessive speed. It's also considered hoggish to make huge turns or to traverse across a slope when other skiers could enjoy a narrow fall line stretch of untracked snow.

Guide your skis into the new turn direction by pivoting. As you finish each turn in a low flex, a lot of rotary power is available. To increase this power, ski with extra anticipation, keeping a very quiet upper body facing down the fall line.

There are other aids to help your pivoting. A primary one is a good pole plant for additional deflection. If you find your poles sinking too much in powder, try some larger baskets.

Some skiers like to increase their pivoting with rotation. You can "punch" your outside hand around into the new turn to increase turning at the feet.

Projecting your hips to the outside of the new turn direction is a valuable powder aid. This swings the tails outward, pivoting the skis about their tips. That much body mass moving laterally

pushes the skis through resisting snow. Once again a firm pole plant will help this sideways deflection.

You can also throw out an anchor to one side in powder to help a pivot.

Dragging a pole to turn Ski the fall line in powder. Lower one hand and drag that pole basket deeply in the snow. You will begin to turn to that side.

This is sort of like dragging a paddle in the water, and so it is often called a *canoe turn*. It's not a very elegant turn, but sometime you may need that little extra force. Anyway, I always say that if it works, it's OK.

Skis pivot easily when they slice sideways through the snow, so that only the thin sidewall hits the snow head-on. (As a real powder fanatic, you'll buy thin skis and wax the sidewalls.) To increase pivoting, keep the skis in this flat profile longer by delaying the edging action.

Soft edge turns. Make a series of medium-radius turns on smooth, moderate terrain. However, at the start of each new turn, use a two-step method. From a flexed stance, first rotate your feet in the direction of the turn, but keep your knees to the outside of the new turn. Incline your body normally into the turn. Then partway into the turn also drive your knees inward to engage the edges and finish the turn. Feel your skis "float" into each turn before the edging is applied.

A delay driving the knees into a turn increases the pivot time.

185

A rebound in powder.

This technique is also called a *surf turn* due to its similarity to a surfboarding maneuver. Your skis are kept flat by delaying the lateral knee drive into the turn. Besides helping in powder, this subtle edge control works great in moguls to increase your pivoting time.

Sometimes it's hard to get that first turn going. When you start out in powder, ski the fall line first, rather than trying to traverse and turn. In the fall line your speed builds up to plane the skis. All you do is flex to complete half a turn, and you have your rhythm going. When you stop, step the skis one at a time into the fall line to get started again. If you really want to look as though you know what you're doing, jump turn your skis in midair from your stopped position to point them downhill. A yodel is mandatory to accompany this maneuver.

Rebound unweighting also works in deep snow, particularly during short, higher-speed turns. Without a restraining hard surface, the skis flex into deep reverse camber during turns. Just as on the pack, this flex can give you a springboard platform from which to unweight. You can help the skis reach the snow surface by also retracting your feet after the rebound to pull them up higher.

New snow doesn't stay fluffy long. It settles into a denser mass from its own weight. Sunshine can quickly turn new snow into the proverbial "mashed potatoes." Wind across the top of fresh snow compresses and ripples the surface, making

"wind pack." In very light snow you may be able to turn by simply cranking your knees to change the angle of ski banking. However, as the snow becomes denser additional vertical unweighting becomes necessary. In wind-crusted snows hop up with enough force to actually lift the ski tips above the surface to pivot them into a new turn. For extra lift, you can also bring your hands low in the flex and raise them to shoulder height in the extension or else push on a pole plant for additional upward thrust.

Once the snow is cut up by other skiers you'll find it more challenging. Your skis rapidly speed up as they enter tracked snow and slow down as they hit the untracked. Your balance becomes more complicated as your ski tips deflect off areas of disturbed snow. Control your speed by skiing tip first into remaining clumps of powder and by rounding out your turn finishes even more.

In extremely nasty snow you can pressure your tips to the surface and pivot about the tails. I'd recommend this only for muscular skiers who are skiing steep slopes covered with unstable snow. Sometimes called a *windshield wiper* turn, it consists of first moving your hips back and lifting your toes to shoot the tip out of the snow. Maintain balance with a firm pole plant of long duration. While leaning on the pole and ski tails, bank your legs and knees into the turn, simultaneously rapidly pivoting your feet. This whips the ski tips around in the new direction. Be sure to slow your

Lift the tips and pivot about the tails in a "windshield wiper."

The downstem works when nothing else will in dense snow.

speed before each turn, as you'll have to balance against sudden changes of direction.

There is an easier nonparallel turn that works well for tricky, dense snow.

Survival turn. At the finish of a turn downstem the lower leg. That ski will push against the dense snow. Use the upper ski as a feeler to gauge how much edging to use in the new turn. Step to the upper ski and pivot into that turn.

This slow-to-medium speed downstem turn works when nothing else will, hence its "survival" name.

After all these words about powder technique, I've saved the best advice for last: "think positive." Powder is a state of mind as much as technique. If you think "fall," you will. If you think "fluid and smooth," you'll do fine. How will you know when you're skiing powder well? There are two indicators—one is the snow all the way down to your Fruit of the Looms, and the other is your enormous smile.

SLICK AS ICE

Too often skiers head for home after seeing the sun glint off an inverted ice skating rink where their packed powder mountain stood last week. However, ice can be enjoyable, even if you don't have a perverse sense of humor. After all, your skis are big ice skates and are designed to handle hard snow. Plus some hot day next July you'll be sorry you didn't ski that icy day in midwinter.

Ice comes in many forms. "Firm pack" or "hardpack" still retains individual snow granules. Although smooth, it's white and your edges will throw out a spray of snow. A rough, icier surface is referred to as "frozen granular." You'll see the sun reflect off it in a diffused glare. It's sometimes called *spring conditions*, as the sun may soften

this hard surface quickly to corn and then to slush before it freezes again for the evening. Real ice isn't white anymore, and when it's thick it may show the dreaded "blue ice" color. The sun glints sharply off a true ice surface.

Just because one part of the mountain is icy doesn't mean all the slopes are. Modern grooming equipment chews up ice and spits it out in a fine consistency. Check the morning trail report to see which slopes have been groomed. Snowmaking on certain trails also covers up a bulletproof base. Ice is exposed on trails when wind whips away loose snow. If you ski sheltered trails, they may still have softer snow left. Even better, maybe you can find where all that loose snow went. It gathers wherever the wind is cut, such as in groves of trees or on the wind-sheltered lee side of ridges. On a sunny day you may be able to ski softer snow all day by sticking to southerly slopes facing directly into the sun.

While choosing trails, remember that you're going to have the afterburners on, as the snow won't slow you. Stick to slopes half the pitch you'd normally ski in packed powder. This also reduces the potential length of falls, which seem to last forever on ice.

Your equipment should be in top-notch condition. You wouldn't have much luck carving a turkey with a dull knife, so make sure your ski edges are sharp to carve into the icy surface. Any free play between your legs and the skis slows your response time and can lead to vibration. Therefore, your boots should fit well to transmit lateral edging motions instantly. Also, there should be no slack in the fit of the boots to the bindings. Your pole tip has to penetrate the ice to make a good plant. If the points are dull, have them replaced, preferably with ones designed for ice. When you start skiing ice frequently you may want to buy special skis that are longer, highly damped, and torsionally rigid.

There's one positive aspect about skiing on ice—it's easy to start a turn. In fact, it may be too easy sometimes, as rapid pivoting places the skis across your direction of travel in a skid. To apply the skills to ice, we'll concentrate on toning down pivoting and emphasizing edging and controlled pressuring.

You should always balance on an edge in your basic stance for ice.

Angulation for edging. Stand across the fall line on a very steep but short patch of ice. Facing your ski tips, increase edging by driving your knees uphill and bending sideways at the waist. Balance entirely on the downhill ski and see if you can stand there without sideslipping. To further increase the edging, lower your downhill hand toward your boot.

This is an aggressive but relaxed stance. It's not a static position, but a good neutral position from which to move. If you're accustomed to keeping your feet close together, try spreading them apart for better balance and edging. Your upper body

remains fairly square to your ski tips, without much twisted anticipation, as you won't need that extra rotary force. Your upper body should be angled outward. In fact, your shoulders may drop at an angle steeper than the slope. A common fault on ice is shying away from the outward upper body lean that is required to balance on the lower ski. Once you start riding the uphill edge of the uphill ski it's difficult to balance, and the ski slides out from underneath. Get used to pressuring primarily the power ski, as the harder the snow, the more definite weight transfer you'll need from foot to foot.

Once you feel comfortable balancing on an edge on ice, experiment to see what might cause loss of that edge.

Staying on an edge. Traverse across the bottom of a steep patch of hard snow or ice. Lift your uphill ski and see if you can maintain a carving track. If your ski sideslips, increase your edging or change your leverage to stand more in the ski's center. While traversing, experiment to see how easily any of these positions cause a skid: rising abruptly to an upright stance; rotating your

(1) Practice balancing on an edge. (2) Washing out the lower tail by deangulating and rotating uphill.

Step to maintain a carve on ice.

uphill hand, shoulder, or hip behind the downhill ones; or pressuring the tips too much. When you feel confident in maintaining an edge, begin to ski increasingly steeper arcs on the ice, until you end up by starting in the fall line. Leave rounded, carved tracks.

As you found out, edging is crucial to maintaining a carve on ice. This is no place for lazy, upright banked turns.

For better control on ice, you should try the exercises in "Carving," in "Step Turns," and the absorption exercises in "The Man-Eaters." In brief, you'll need to maintain pressure and edge on the skis. If you lose the flowing S turn line by overpivoting, or by not edging, your skis will skid. This is especially critical at the start of each turn. One way to maintain a smooth transition into each turn is to keep the skis on the snow. Avoid excessive unweighting and rebounding in which both skis lose snow contact.

All up-and-down motions on ice must be gentle rather than jerky. Think of being as powerful but as stealthy as a tiger on the prowl. You won't have to up unweight, although you may want to rise to start a new turn. At higher speed and with shorter turns however, your skis will rebound. Absorb this by extending into the new turn, pressing downward on the skis to keep them on the snow. That way you can feel what they are doing and can subtly steer them into the fall line.

Extension to maintain carve. Flex downward toward the finish of a turn on ice and drive your knees in the new turn direction. As the skis go flat, extend your legs, keeping pressure on the new outside ski and guiding its power edge into the new turn. You will be fully extended by the fall line and should begin flexing to finish the turn.

This extension also puts weight on a ski earlier, so it will bite into the snow and begin carving. It's similar to a down unweighting.

Perhaps the surest way to avoid skids on ice is to prevent both skis from becoming flat on the snow at the same time. If you go immediately from one carving power edge to the other carving power edge, you'll eliminate the flat ski.

Step turn for ice. Finish a turn in a flexed stance, carving on the lower ski. Step your upper ski outward and parallel onto its inside edge. Smoothly step to that edge and ride it around into the fall line, stepping your other ski in to match the power ski. Flex to finish the turn and repeat, always stepping to an edge.

With a step turn you edge early and pressure a ski early, both secrets to maintaining a carve.

Despite all these words of advice, the best skiers in the world skid and chatter on ice. Chatter is simply a skid in which the edges grab and release rapidly, an unsettling experience and one that will loosen the fillings in your teeth. To eliminate chatter, you should reduce its four main causes:

1) Overturning: pivoting a ski too rapidly places it across the direction of travel, forcing a skid. Reduce the tendency to rotate a flat ski.
2) Applying too much edge: overedging before pressure builds up loses a firm edge hold along the whole length of the ski. Apply edge gradually, especially if you step stem a ski somewhat across your direction of travel.
3) Applying weight abruptly to an edge: this forces the edge to suddenly bite in and rebound. Keep the weight transfer smooth.
4) Wrong leverage: standing too far forward on your skis at a turn finish causes the tail to wash out. Use even pressure on your foot sole to make the whole ski length carve.

Once you do get in a skid the best thing to do is simply go with it. Immediately step the upper ski into the skid direction and transfer weight to that ski's inside edge. Now you're carving again. If you're chattering but can't change direction, flatten the lower ski, pivot into the skid, then re-edge it and carve again.

During fall line tight-radius turns you'll probably skid. Just set your edges for a quick, sharp bite and immediately turn again. Strive for a maximum number of edgesets. In the moguls throw in extra turns. You can make two where you'd only make one in packed powder. At all times keep feet apart for balance, but transfer pressure from foot to foot.

Admittedly, ice is demanding. However, it's a great test of your skill refinement. You might even enjoy the extra challenge and take pride in being able to master the ice. It will definitely make you a better skier for all other snow conditions.

18
Competition

One person on a slope is called a skier. Two people on a slope is called a race. Skiers love to compete. Some find a challenge in pitting themselves against the terrain. Others like to challenge friends to see who is fastest. The most common method is on a timed course, set with gates to control speed.

You won't need special techniques in racecourses. When you watch champion skiers, you'll notice they are smooth, fluid, and efficient. Refined skills used every day on the mountain work well in races. A well-laid-out course imposes rhythm and discipline on a skier. Gates force you to turn, there and then, not fifty yards later. Plus it's so satisfying to beat your best friend by half a second!

WHERE TO RACE

Races aren't only for experts. They are fun for everyone. Even when you're wedge turning you can enjoy the challenge. If you belong to a ski club you'll have several races scheduled each season.

Many ski areas have their own fun racecourses complete with electronic timing. For a nominal fee you can run the gates and compare your time

(Photo courtesy Lange, USA)

to that of your friends. The area's ski school or race department may offer special clinics where you'll practice on courses all day. Some resorts set up courses especially for members of visiting ski clubs and host a postrace party on the slope for the competitors.

The National Standard Race, commonly called NASTAR, is available at over 130 areas. The eighteen to twenty-four gates of this timed course are negotiable by most every skier no matter what their age or ability. All you have to do is sign up on a race day, pay a small fee, and show up on time at the starting gate. About a quarter-million skiers run NASTAR each year. It's popular because it offers a way to compare your time with that of any other skier who skis any NASTAR course.

Basically, NASTAR standardization works like this. Each area has a pacesetter, a racer who runs the course each race day. The pacesetter has already competed in preseason race events against other pacesetters. The fastest person in these trials gets a "zero" handicap and becomes the national pacesetter. Let's say the pacesetter for your area's course was 2 percent slower than the national pacesetter. His or her handicap is then a two. When your area pacesetter runs your course, his or her measured time for that day is decreased by 2 percent to establish a standard. Now this particular course on this particular day has a "par" time determined. It's the same time that the country's fastest pacesetter would have set in this course.

Your time in the NASTAR course will come within a certain percentage of the "par" time for that day. This percentage is your handicap, and you can compare this number against any other NASTAR racer. Obviously, the faster racer has the lower handicap. What also makes the race fun is that medals are awarded, depending upon your time for that race, your age, and your sex. For instance, let's say you came within 40 percent of the course standard time (a forty handicap). If you are female, between thirty and thirty-nine, you'd win a silver medal. A male in the same age group would receive a bronze.

Start aggressively.

THE COURSE

You'd like to practice now and then before a real race. Some areas set up special bamboo gates for this. If not, make your own course out of other objects or use imaginary gates. Don't ski someone else's closed course. Miles of free skiing, especially in short turns or through bumps, is good long-term preparation.

Once you've entered a race there are three areas to concentrate on. (1) Be explosive at the start; (2) choose a good line; and (3) stay aggressive through the finish. We'll examine each of them.

The Start

The start area will be flat, with a wand at shin height. When your legs push the wand open the timer starts. If you wait for gravity to get you up to racing speed, you're losing a valuable second or two. You'll need an aggressive start to propel yourself quickly down the course.

Stand with your legs close to the wand—your ski tips will be out in midair. Point your skis toward the first gate, rather than just downhill. Securely plant your poles *in front* of the wand, and flex, sitting back. At the "go" signal rock forward, driving your hands and upper body forward. Push powerfully off your legs and off your poles. Continue the pole push until your hands go behind your legs. (If you've done the cross-country double-pole push, this will come naturally.) Now you have an explosive start. Your head is up and you're heading for the first gate. If it's far enough away, throw in a skate off one ski or double pole again to gain more speed.

The Line

Take a look at the course before you ski it. The gates will be offset to induce rhythmic turning. The object is to go around the gates and not through them. You can see a good curved line running around the gates passing near each one. Visualize yourself in this smooth line.

On the course your most common mistake will be to turn too late. You must turn early. As soon as you're at a gate you should be turning for the next one. If you wait too long, you'll be below your ideal line and will probably skid, and consequently lose time, trying to get around the next gate.

You'll want to keep your skis running at top speed. This means keeping them riding on their edges in a carved arc. Anytime you skid you lose

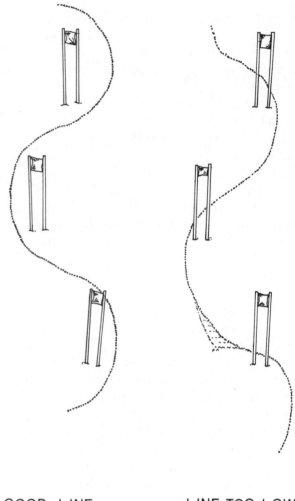

GOOD LINE   LINE TOO LOW

Choose a good line, turning early.

precious time. Step turns will keep you in a good line and reduce skidding. If you get the competitive fever, carefully study "Carving" and "Step Turns" in the chapter on advanced technique.

After a number of skiers run through a course ruts develop. You'll enjoy the course more without them, so sign up for the race early if it affects your starting time. If you do encounter ruts, just regard them as a bobsled run and stay in them. They'll help bank your skis around the turns. Enter each turn where the rut starts. If you try to cut inside the ruts, you may go bouncing into them or run your ski tips across them.

The Finish

The race isn't over when you pass the last gate. Your time is complete when you break the electronic timing light on the finish line. Don't even think of slowing down until you're past that line. In fact, be aggressive enough to gain time between the last gate and the finish. If the course is steep in this section, step or double pole out of the last gate and tuck the remaining distance. If the slope is flat, skate to increase your speed.

Some skiers go through contortions to try to break the timing beam earlier. They'll thrust out a hand, lift a ski tip, or push their feet forward. This won't affect your overall time much. You'll gain as much by staying in your tuck or skating an extra step, and save your balance at the same time.

SKILL LEVEL TESTS

Another form of competition is measuring your level of skiing ability against a national standard, such as the Test International in Canada and Europe. In the United States, the STAR Test (STAndard Rating Test) is given by specially trained instructors at certain Professional Ski Instructors of America—affiliated schools. In this program you pay a fee to be tested in one of three categories, bronze, silver, or gold. The instructor takes you on a specified slope, explains and demonstrates the maneuvers, and then grades how well you do. Each area that sponsors the STAR test uses the same type of slopes, and examines the same maneuvers thus standardizing the results.

If you're an early intermediate, you'll try out for a Bronze Star. You'll show your skill level by demonstrating a stable traverse, linked wedge turns, controlled sideslipping, linked skidded turns, and stepping to a stop. As a high intermediate skier you'll try for a Silver. Here you'll be asked to display a traverse without slippage on varying terrain, ten linked long-radius turns, skating steps, parallel stops (hockey stops) to both sides, and linked short-radius turns. The Gold Star Test is designed for an advanced or expert skier. In this test you'll demonstrate step turns, thousand steps, short-radius turns, medium-radius turns in bumps, and medium-radius turns in varying conditions.

These tests are rigorous, but they also indicate exactly what your skill level is and how to improve. You can proudly wear the pin of each stage you pass.

19
Alpine Glossary

ABSORBING—Reducing the "ski jump effect" of bumps by actively reducing pressure on the skis while riding up a bump.

ANGULATING—Bending one part of the body laterally to form an "angle" with another part, as opposed to a perfectly straight stance. This allows balance on the edges while varying the edge angle.

ANTICIPATING—Twisting the torso in the direction of the upcoming turn. This coiled position "unwinds" the skis toward the fall line upon release of edge pressure.

ATM—The American Teaching Method, a standardized holistic method that teaches functional skiing.

ATHLETIC STANCE—A balanced, alert stance common to many sports. In this ready position a skier has feet apart, ankles and knees flexed, weight on the balls of the feet, hands in front, torso bent forward slightly, and head up.

AVALEMENT—An active folding and unfolding of the body to control pressure of the skis on the snow.

BALANCING—Maintaining equilibrium despite changes in terrain and speed.

BANKING TURNS—Placing the skis on edge by leaning the whole body into a turn without angulating.

BEVELED EDGES—Edges ground at a slight angle upward from the base for easier turning.

BRAKING WEDGE—A wedge in which both inside edges angle against the snow for speed control.

CAMBER—The bowlike arch shape of the ski, which distributes weight throughout its length.

CANT—A mechanical compensation that allows a skier to stand neutrally on a flat ski when his natural lower leg alignment would tend to place him on an edge.

CARVING—Running a ski efficiently on its edge without sideways slippage (skidding). Carved tracks are narrow, showing the edge imprint in a distinct arc.

CENTRIFUGAL FORCE—The inertial force that pulls a skier to the outside of a turn.

CHECKING—Dynamically engaging the edges to slow down.

CHRISTIE (CHRISTY)—A turn that is finished by skidding on both uphill edges.

COUNTERROTATION—A twisting of the upper body while skis are unweighted, causing the skis to twist in the opposite direction.

DIN—A European set of standards that apply to boot shape and binding settings. Each skier has a DIN release setting suitable to his or her weight and ability.

DOUBLE FALL LINE—A route that angles across the terrain's true fall line.

DOWNSTEM—Pushing the lower ski tail outward. This digs in the edge more to slow and provide a support point to launch into a new turn.

DOWN UNWEIGHTING—Flexing to momentarily reduce weight on the skis so they may be turned easier.

EDGESET—An abrupt increase in edge angle or pressure on the edge, causing it to dig into the snow.

EDGING—Controlling the angle of the ski base relative to the snow.

EDGE CHANGE—Tilting a ski from riding on one edge to riding on the other.

EXTENSION—An active straightening of the legs to maintain snow contact or to reduce angulation.

FALL LINE—The path down which a snowball would roll if released from a skier's feet.

FINISHING A TURN—Continuing to ski uphill for speed control before starting a new turn.

FLEX (SKIER)—Bending in the body joints, particularly the knees and the ankles, rather than being straight upright. "To flex" means to contract, bringing the feet and head closer together.

FLEX (SKIS)—The temporary bending of a ski when force is applied against its camber (longitudinal flex). Also the amount a ski will twist in its long direction to a rotary force (torsional flex).

GARLAND—Repeated small direction changes that don't make a turn across the fall line. These leave a garlandlike track across the hill.

GLIDING WEDGE—A wedge in which the ski bases are essentially flat on the snow, without much edging.

GLM—The Graduated Length Method places beginning skiers on short skis and increases ski length with improving ability.

HIP PROJECTION—A sideways motion of the hips to help displace the skis into a new turn.

HOCKEY STOP—A rapid parallel stop accomplished by flexing downward while pivoting the skis across the direction of travel. Skidding on the edges then causes a stop.

INCLINING—Leaning into a turn to balance against centrifugal force.

INDEPENDENT LEG ACTION—Allowing each leg to flex or rotate independently of the other, rather than locking both legs together into one unit.

INSIDE EDGES—The two ski edges on the big toe sides of the feet.

INSIDE SKI—The ski of a turn that follows the inside, shorter path.

JETTING—A sudden leap forward of the skis at the start of higher-speed short turns. It occurs when a skier balances back against deceleration and then releases edge pressure abruptly.

KICK TURN—A standing 180-degree change of direction initiated by kicking the lower ski upward.

LATERAL PROJECTION—A sideways motion of the ski. This usually refers to a step turn in which the uphill ski is stepped outward, followed by the other ski.

LEVERAGE—Applying additional pressure to the shovels or tails of the skis.

MATCHING—Moving one ski to align it in the direction the other is facing.

MOGULS—Bumps formed by skiers turning in the same spot.

NASTAR—The National Standard Race in which amateur skiers compete on a course that is calibrated to a national par.

ORTHOTIC—A custom footbed for support and improved edging capability.

OUTSIDE EDGES—The ski edges on the little toe sides of the feet.

OUTSIDE SKI—The ski that follows the outside, longer path in a turn.

PARALLEL—Where both skis point in the same direction, although not necessarily close together. During a parallel turn both skis rotate simultaneously to maintain a similar alignment.

PIVOTING—Rotating the skis about an axis perpendicular to the bases.

PLATFORM—When "creating a platform" a skier sharply edges, pressuring the ski base into the snow. This sets up a firm point of resistance for a rebound or step.

POLE PLANT—Placing the downhill pole tip in the snow temporarily at the start of a turn. The planting may aid timing, unweighting, balancing for weight transfer, deflecting the skis, accelerating, or stabilizing the upper body.

PRESSURING—Controlling the force the skis exert on the snow. This includes transferring weight from one foot to another, raising or lowering the body to vary weight on the skis, and leveraging weight to the front or back of the ski.

PRETURN—A tightened-radius uphill turn prior to initiating a new turn across the fall line.

QUIET UPPER BODY—A torso that faces somewhat down the fall line while the legs turn the skis back and forth.

REBOUNDING (REBOUND UNWEIGHTING)—A spring upward from the snow upon the release of pressure that has compressed the skier's body and forced his skis into reverse camber.

RETRACTION—Active flexing, primarily in the legs, to compress the body.

REVERSE CAMBER—A flexing opposite a ski's normal arch shape, caused by pressure on the ski.

ROTATION—A turn method in which the upper body or hips are twisted in one direction while the skis are weighted. This impulse transfers to the skis to rotate them in that direction also.

ROUND TURNS—Continuous arcs, in an S shape, without any straight traverse sections.

SCHUSS—Running downhill without turns.

SCISSOR STEP—A stepping movement in which the tip of one ski diverges from the other one.

SHORTSWING—Linked short-radius round turns with a definite edgeset and rebound.

SIDECUT—The hourglass shape of a ski as seen from the top. This allows a ski to go into reverse camber when it is edged.

SIDESLIPPING—A downward slide while the skis point across the fall line. It is started by decreasing edging and stopped by increasing edging.

SIDESTEPPING—Stepping up or down the fall line, staying on the uphill edges to prevent slipping.

SINTERED BASE—An extremely hard polyethylene base material that resists abrasion and holds wax well.

SKID—A sideways slip of a ski at the same time it is sliding forward.

SLALOM—A course in which the skier must turn around each control gate.

SLOPE TRANSITION—A point where the pitch of a run suddenly changes.

SNOWPLOW—A position with the tips close together and the tails far apart, resembling a V-shaped snowplow blade, to control speed.

SQUARE TO THE SKIS—Continually facing the ski tips with the torso.

STAR TEST—A Standard Rating Test, which evaluates a skier's proficiency.

STEMMING—Displacing one ski tail so that the skis converge in a wedge.

STEERING—Guiding the skis with muscular effort in a subtle pivot.

STEP TURN—A change of direction initiated by picking up and laterally moving one ski farther away. The inside ski is stepped closer again during the turn.

TERRAIN WEIGHTING—An increase in ski pressure caused by skiing up a bump.

TERRAIN UNWEIGHTING—A lightening of pressure on the skis when skiing past the crest of a bump or other convex terrain.

TRAVERSING—Skiing on two uphill edges across the slope, at an angle to the fall line.

TUCK—An aerodynamic eggshaped stance for reducing wind resistance.

UNWEIGHTING—Reducing pressure on the skis.

UP UNWEIGHTING—Reducing ski pressure by first extending upward before flexing. This "jumping" type of motion gives a long period of weight reduction.

WEDEL—Continuous skidded turns in the fall line.

WEDGE—A stance with the tips close together and the tails apart. It provides stability and turning ease.

WEIGHTING—Increasing the pressure of the skis to the snow.

WEIGHT TRANSFER—The change of pressure from one ski to the other.

WIDE TRACK—A stance with feet comfortably apart for better lateral balance and a stronger turning force.

Index

Page numbers in *italics* refer to illustrations.